T0362415

A Landmark in Accounting Theory

First published in 1996, this book seeks to establish Gabriel A.D. Preinreich as an important accounting theorist and redress the neglect that his work has suffered despite its foundational importance to prominent areas of modern research. Two criteria were used to select the papers included in this volume — papers related to dividends, yield, valuation, goodwill and depreciation were selected while those that were primarily concerned with mathematical economics were omitted. The collected articles and other items were written between 1931 and 1944 and grouped into three sections: accounting from the investor's viewpoint; valuation and goodwill; and depreciation.

A Landmark in Accounting Theory

The Work of Gabriel A.D. Preinreich

Edited by
Richard P. Brief

Routledge
Taylor & Francis Group

First published in 1996
by Garland Publishing Inc.

This edition first published in 2017 by Routledge
2 Park Square, Milton Park, Abingdon, Oxon, OX14 4RN
and by Routledge
711 Third Avenue, New York, NY 10017

Routledge is an imprint of the Taylor & Francis Group, an informa business

© 1996 Richard P. Brief

The right of Richard P. Brief to be identified as the author of this work has been asserted by them in accordance with sections 77 and 78 of the Copyright, Designs and Patents Act 1988.
All rights reserved. No part of this book may be reprinted or reproduced or utilised in any form or by any electronic, mechanical, or other means, now known or hereafter invented, including photocopying and recording, or in any information storage or retrieval system, without permission in writing from the publishers.

Publisher's Note
The publisher has gone to great lengths to ensure the quality of this reprint but points out that some imperfections in the original copies may be apparent.

Disclaimer
The publisher has made every effort to trace copyright holders and welcomes correspondence from those they have been unable to contact.

A Library of Congress record exists under LC control number: 94123590

ISBN 13: 978-1-138-64488-5 (hbk)
ISBN 13: 978-1-315-62835-6 (ebk)

A LANDMARK IN ACCOUNTING THEORY

The Work of Gabriel A.D. Preinreich

Edited by

Richard P. Brief

Introduction copyright © 1996 by Richard P. Brief

Library of Congress Cataloging-in-Publication Data

Preinreich, Gabriel A.D., 1893–
  A landmark in accounting theory : the work of Gabriel A.D.
Preinreich / edited by Richard P. Brief.
    p. cm. — (New works in accounting history)
  Includes bibliographical references (p.).
  ISBN 0-8153-2250-X (acid-free paper)
    1. Accounting—History. I. Brief, Richard P., 1933–
II. Title. III. Series.
HF5611.P727   1996   95–46235
657—dc20   CIP

All volumes printed on acid-free, 250-year-life paper.
Manufactured in the United States of America.

Design by Marisel Tavarez

CONTENTS

Accounting from the Investor's Viewpoint

Goodwill and Valuation

The Depreciation Problem

EDITOR'S NOTE

A general application for a teaching position, "Record for Teaching Appointment," was prepared by Preinreich in 1938. This document contains biographical data and was on file in the Department of Economics at Columbia University. I am grateful to staff in the department for taking the time to find it.

PREFACE

Getting involved in the work of a writer like Preinreich is very exciting and may lead to certain biases. Nevertheless, I hope that the reader will share my view that Preinreich's contributions are a landmark in accounting theory.

I am indebted to Gary Cramer for helping me to prepare this book for publication. Without his support, I would not have been able to make Preinreich's work more widely available.

Richard P. Brief
New York, N.Y.
October 4, 1995

ACKNOWLEDGMENTS

"Accounting Problems of the Unincorporated Investment Trust," by Gabriel A. D. Preinreich: *Journal of Accountancy*, May 1931, The American Institute of Certified Public Accountants, is reprinted with permission.

"Goodwill in Accountancy," by Gabriel A. D. Preinreich: *Journal of Accountancy*, July 1937, The American Institute of Certified Public Accountants, is reprinted with permission.

"Valuation and Depreciation," by Gabriel A. D. Preinreich: *Journal of Accountancy*, July 1938, The American Institute of Certified Public Accountants, is reprinted with permission.

"Economic Theories of Goodwill," by Gabriel A. D. Preinreich: *Journal of Accountancy*, September 1939, The American Institute of Certified Public Accountants, is reprinted with permission.

"Stock Yields, Stock Dividends and Inflation," by Gabriel A. D. Preinreich: *The Accounting Review*, December 1932, © 1932, The American Accounting Association, is reprinted with permission.

"The Fair Value and Yield of Common Stock," by Gabriel A. D. Preinreich: *The Accounting Review*, January 1936, © 1936, The American Accounting Association, is reprinted with permission.

"The Law of Goodwill," by Gabriel A. D. Preinreich: *The Accounting Review*, December 1936, © 1936, The American Accounting Association, is reprinted with permission.

"Valuation and Amortizaton," by Gabriel A. D. Preinreich: *The Accounting Review*, September 1937, © 1932, The American Accounting Association, is reprinted with permission.

"The Principles of Public Utility Regulation," by Gabriel A. D. Preinreich: *The Accounting Review*, June 1938, © 1938, The American Accounting Association, is reprinted with permission.

"Book review of Robley Winfrey, *Depreciation of Group Properties* (Ames: Iowa State College Bulletin, by Gabriel A. D. Preinreich: *The Accounting Review*, April 1944, © 1944, The American Accounting Association, is reprinted with permission.

"The Practice of Depreciation," by Gabriel A. D. Preinreich: *Econometrica*, July 1939, © 1939, Econometric Society, is reprinted with permission.

"Note on the Theory of Depreciation," by Gabriel A. D. Preinreich: *Econometrica*, January 1941, © 1941, Econometric Society, is reprinted with permission.

INTRODUCTION

While names like Canning, Hatfield, Littleton, Paton, and other early writers are well-known, Preinreich, who should be recognized as an important accounting theorist, has not achieved similar status. His work on goodwill and valuation models is the foundation for an important area of current-day research. He also made significant contributions to depreciation theory. The bibliography at the end of this introduction contains an impressive list of publications on these and other subjects.

Why hasn't Preinreich been given greater recognition? His contemporaries might have viewed him an outsider; he was a sole practitioner and not a member of the academic community. Also, his research was based on mathematical models applied to accounting, economic and financial problems, and this kind of work did not appear in accounting literature until the 1960s and 1970s. And Preinreich often was extremely critical of others and this behavior probably did not increase his popularity. But what about the present? Why isn't Preinreich better known today?

Gabriel A. D. Preinreich was born in Sopron, Hungary, on July 30, 1893. According to the Editor's Note in Preinreich (1951b), he died on April 17, 1951. His academic training included the Austro-Hungarian Naval Academy (1908–1912), where he graduated as an ensign; City College of the City of New York (1922–1928), B.S. and M.B.A.; New York University (1930-1932), and Columbia University (1932–1935), Ph.D. He received the C.P.A certificate from the State of New York in 1930.

Preinreich's personal data in the "Record for Teaching Appointment" on file at Columbia University also shows that he "traveled" in central and western Europe, the Balkans, and Mediterranean basin including North Africa and the Near East from 1908-1922 when, evidently, he was in the Austro-Hungarian navy during World War I and after. He came to the United States in 1922, working as a clerk and bookkeeper (1922–1926), a junior, senior and supervising senior accountant with public accounting firms (1926–1931) and as an accountant under his own name from 1931 until a year or so before he died. A biographical note in Preinreich (1947) stated that "The author, a certified public accountant, is an economist, statistician and tax consultant in

New York City." A note in Preinreich (1948) said that "The author is a certified public accountant, tax consultant and econometrician in New York City." His office address was 17 West 42nd Street.

Preinreich indicated that he was married and had no children, weighed 145 pounds, and was 5' 7" tall. He gave his nationality as Czechoslovakian (second U. S. citizenship papers were filed on October 5, 1938) and race as German. Preinreich said that he read "easily almost any European language" and spoke the "six principal ones and some others." He was a member of the Econometric Society, Royal Economic Society (London), American Institute of Accountants, American Accounting Association, Columbia University Club, Poughkeepsie Yacht Club, and Skate Sailing Association of America.

His education (before Columbia) showed the following (in semester hours): economics, 36; mathematics, 42; accounting, 34; statistics, 6; business and law, 12; physics and engineering, 28. At Columbia, he took public finance (6 hours) with Haig; mathematical economics (6 hours) with Hotelling; economic theory (6 hours) with Mitchell; U.S. economic history (6 hours) with Goodrich; and advanced statistics (6 hours) with Ross. He gave five references: Dean R. C. McCrea and Professors R. B. Kester, W. C. Mitchell, J. C. Bonbright, and F. A. Ross.

The application for a teaching appointment also shows that at this stage in his life, when he was about 45 years old, Preinreich considered devoting most of his time to "economic research along mathematical lines." He sought a teaching position (lowest salary of $4,000 in "neighborhood of New York", $5,000 elsewhere) that would "leave ample time for this purpose." As the list of his publications shows, he had published 18 articles and notes from 1929 to 1940, which is rather remarkable since, in this period, the evidence suggests that he was a full-time practicing accountant.

The preface to his Ph.D. thesis, "The Nature of Dividends" (1935), cited the members of his dissertation committee: James C. Bonbright (economics and law), Harold Hotelling (mathematics, statistics and economics), Benjamin Graham (finance), and Roy B. Kester (accounting). Bonbright was his thesis supervisor. One doesn't need to know too much history to recognize the names in this distinguished group. The preface also indicates that Preinreich must have had greater than usual contact with the American Institute of Accountants, since he thanks A. P. Richardson for editorial assistance. Richardson was the Secretary of the American Association of Public Accountants (later becoming American Institute of Accountants and then America Institute of Certified Public Accountants) as well as editor of the *Journal of Accountancy* from 1911 to 1936 (O'Neill, 1980).

The only other information about Preinreich comes from a letter (February 28, 1995) from Paul A. Samuelson to the editor:

I remember Preinreich at annual meetings of the Econometric Society. He and J. J. Lotka often argued: Lotka liked to solve demographic integral equations $B(t) = f(t) + \int_o m(a)L(a)B(t-a))da$ by infinite exponential series; G.P liked to write $m(a)L(a)$ as special functions that permitted differentiation to convert the integral equation into a solvable differential equation. For my money, one of Preinreich's most interesting ideas was to correct Hotelling's problem of when to optimally replace one machine by considering an infinite chain of such machines. When years later I wrote on when to chop down a tree, I vindicated the 1849 Faustmann rule (as, unknown to me, the young Ohlin had done) by using Preinreich's idea.

Now you know all I know about G. P.

Preinreich (1940, p. 30) refers to Lotka's work on industrial replacement and comments on the origin of the method used by Lotka. He also criticizes Lotka because "his approach consists of substituting a generalized Fourier Series for the real solution and gives very poor results during the early years to which foresight can possibly extend." Preinreich (1939c) wrote a paper on the subject, apparently a critique of Lotka's article, in the same journal in which Lotka originally published his article.

Preinreich seems to have made cutting remarks about other academic work fairly often. (Or was he simply pointing out errors?) In an unsolicited book review (1938b), reprinted in this volume to give the reader a flavor of his barb, he is highly critical of both the reviewer of the book, Earl Saliers, and the book's author, Edwin Kurtz. In another book review (1944), also reprinted, Preinreich is devastating. Elsewhere (1939a), he states that *A Statement of Accounting Principles* (Sanders, Hatfield and Moore 1938) contain the "hoary platitude," that "a balance sheet is a statement which purports to exhibit the financial condition of the business" (p. 55). Then Preinreich goes on to say that "To understand how little this means . . . ."

An article published after his death (1953) further illustrates Preinreich's nature. While mainly concerned with Euler's calculus of variations, the concluding section deals with depreciation.

> There are three main schools on the subject. The first believes that it can define the true method of depreciation and hence is in a position to deduce from it the correct date of replacement; the second would like to find the true method, but admits that the optimum date of replacement must be determined first by an independent approach; and the third is not interested in the true method at all, but merely wants to make sure that the cash needed for replacement is being saved currently in one way or another.

Preinreich then discusses each of the three schools. "The most ambitious school starts from the misconception that the value of a machine can be neither more nor less than cost . . . ." He then discusses Taylor (1923) and Norton and Grant (1942),

> Taylor, although right within his oversimplified example, was unaware that his rule is limited not only to a hypothetical mature line of a homogeneous infinite chain, but also to constant sales. He accordingly failed in his attempts to find the correct date for replacing a machine by an improved model (p. 84).

Norton and Grant are described as "Among more recent searchers for truth by arithmetic" (p. 84).

Preinreich says this about the second school: "The second school has also published millions of words without any real results" (p. 85). The third school, on the other hand, "takes the most practical view" and for them, "depreciation is only a device to prevent the spending of money needed for replacement" (p. 85). Then he mentions Roos's "futile" efforts (1928). (Roos was a Fellow in the Econometric Society.)

> Since any deduction and addition of the same thing in the same breath can change only form and not substance, it is worth mentioning Roos's curiously futile attempts. He set out to determine, from just such a formula, the optimum time-shape of the sinking-fund contribution (which he mistook for depreciation), but even the calculus of variations could not find what was not really there (p. 85).

It is, of course, impossible to determine whether some of these critical remarks reflected a hostile personality or, instead, was simply displaying "that rare and wonderful intellectual honesty that was practiced so generally a century ago" (Stigler, 1995, p. 803). In either case, Preinreich could have been misinterpreted by his contemporaries.

Preinreich's bibliography shows that from 1929-1939, he published almost exclusively in accounting journals in the areas of valuation, goodwill, depreciation and taxation. He also wrote an article on terminology. From 1938 until 1941, his main interests turned to problems in depreciation theory, renewal, replacement and the life of industrial equipment. Most of these articles were published in *Econometrica*. Preinreich then wrote several papers on taxation (one appearing in the *American Economic Review* in 1948) and his last four papers dealt with issues related to the mathematical theory of the firm. There was often some overlap in the subject matter in these articles and sections of one article sometimes were copied verbatim in other articles.

While most of Preinreich's work has historical interest and scholarly value, two criteria were used to select the papers that are reprinted in this volume. First only those papers related to the nature of dividends, yield, valuation, goodwill and depreciation were selected. Second, articles which seemed mainly of interest to mathematical economists were not reprinted. These criteria were not always easy to apply. Some sections of almost every paper Preinreich wrote might be of interest to accountants.

The articles and other items that are reprinted in this book were written between 1931 and 1944 and are grouped into three sections (which are not mutually exclusive): accounting from the investor's viewpoint; valuation and goodwill; and depreciation. The discussion that follows is intended to give a broad overview and some historical perspective.

Accounting from the Investor's Viewpoint

"Accounting Problems of the Unincorporated Investment Trust" (1931) is important because it signals Preinreich's initial interest in the question of how to account from the investor's viewpoint. Littleton (1935, p. 413) notes that this article also was the basic framework of Preinreich's Ph.D. thesis at Columbia: "The kernel of the dissertation, therefore, appears to be the common stock problems of investment trusts and the inequities which the usual rules regarding the determination of income may produce when applied to stock dividends, stock rights, and stock warrants." The 1932 article "Stock Yields, Stock Dividends and Inflation," which must have been written when Preinreich was a student at New York University (where he did not receive a degree), is closely related to his dissertation. Indeed, the mathematical appendix in the thesis has very close similarities to the models developed in this article. Aspects of this work also are related to the more recent interest in shareholder value (Brief and Lawson, 1992, pp. 241–242).

Littleton (1935, p. 414) criticized the framework developed by Preinreich because it "would practically merge the financial identity of the corporation and the investor, and bring about a change in net worth accounting . . . ." In "The Fair Value and Yield of Common Stock" (1936, p. 140), Preinreich explains that the principle of preparing consolidated financial statements for affiliated groups subject to a single control "applies with equal force in the absence of control, from investment trusts on down to the last few shares acquired by a bona-fide operating company for the temporary storage of excess cash." In the 1936 article, Preinreich also presents a graph (p. 131), which is used to show that a firm's present value can be calculated either by discounting future cash dividends or by discounting excess (residual) earnings to obtain goodwill and then adding goodwill to book value to obtain the firm's present value. This relationship is discussed by Preinreich in one form or another in 1937a, 1937b, 1938b, 1939b and 1941a. The last article contains interesting comments about the "capital value formula," i.e., the formula to value goodwill based on discounted residual earnings. Preinreich states (1941a, p. 83) that the verbal equivalent of the formula can be "found in any accounting textbook" and then gives a reference to an article by J. H. Bourne in the September 22, 1888 issue of *The Accountant.* While this article discusses goodwill valuation, it is difficult to infer the capital value formula from Bourne's discussion. In any event, the capital value formula has acquired much greater significance in recent years (Brief and Peasnell, 1996).

The 1936 article also contains a statement about the relevance of dividends in valuation: "*The yield of common stocks is not dependent upon the corporate dividend policy so long as that policy conforms to the principle of good management*" (italics in original). Preinreich was, therefore, one of the first writers to consider the issue of "dividend irrelevance," a subject which students of finance link to the classic paper by Modigliani and Miller (1958).

Goodwill and Valuation

For the next several years, Preinreich focused on goodwill. "The Law of Goodwill" (1936) is an excellent history of the subject and the section on "The Valuation of Goodwill" (pp. 327–329) has special significance in that it links court-approved methods of valuing goodwill to excess profits. The next article, "Goodwill in Accountancy" (1937), is an extensive survey of the accounting literature on the subject. Unfortunately, space limitations prevented the inclusion of about 150 references (p. 50). Of particular relevance today is the section on the valuation of goodwill.

"Valuation and Amortization" (1937) links goodwill and depreciation to the question, "What is a balance sheet?" The answer is that "the task [purpose of the balance sheet] is to connect original cost with liquidation value in a way which will give due consideration to both risk and time" (p. 210). Viewing assets as discounted services, Preinreich goes on to discuss depreciation in the context of one machine and many machines. Preinreich also connects the subject to the amortization of goodwill and then goes on to discuss in more detail the relationship between goodwill valuation and discounted excess profits. He states: "no matter at what value an asset is placed on the books and no matter in what haphazard way it is amortized over is unexpired life, the discounted excess profits plus the recorded value will always give the true fair market value . . ." (p. 220). In the end, Preinreich supports the investment or amount of money advanced concept of the balance sheet and is "strenuously opposed" (p. 224) to the capital-value, property, or true-net worth concept on the ground that appraisal is not a function of accounting.

The next selection, "Economic Theories of Goodwill" (1939), was, with the exception of a book review in 1944, the last paper that Preinreich published in either the *Journal of Accountancy* or *The Accounting Review.* The article models the subject in classical economic terms and then (once again) addresses the question of goodwill valuation. The graphs in Figures 5 and 6 are identical to those appearing in "The Fair Value and Yield of Common Stock" (1936).

The Depreciation Problem

Most of the articles written by Preinreich between 1938 and 1941 dealt with various aspects of the depreciation problem. "Annual Survey of Economic Theory: The Theory of Depreciation" (1938), which was reprinted in Brief (1986), concludes that "The principal error, of which mathematical economists and accountants are equally guilty, is that both groups have so far examined the problem only in terms of a single machine, disregarding the actuarial theory of composite plant, which introduces various new aspects" (p. 240). In this paper, Preinreich also derives the capital value formula, i.e., "Capital value equals the book value, plus the discounted excess profits" (p. 240).

"The Principles of Public-Utility Depreciation" (1938) draws from the *Econometrica* paper and the same four page-sized graphs appear in both papers. The article was motivated by Mason (1937):

> I have read Professor Perry Mason's monograph on the "Principles of Utility Depreciation" with great interest and consider it as valuable a contribution to the literature of accountancy and public utility regulation as can be made by the traditional discursive method of presentation and by what is still essentially a "single machine" approach. Unfortunately, the subject is far too complex for these limitations (p. 149).

Thus, Preinreich shows that contrary to Mason's view, "the replacement rate always enters directly into the depreciation rate, unless the discussion is carried on in terms of a single machine" (p. 159). Preinreich concluded by saying that "All I set out to do was merely to show that purely literary efforts have very little chance of probing beneath the surface" (p. 165).

This issue of composite depreciation also is dealt with in a comment on a review of a book by Edwin Kurtz, "Valuation and Depreciation" (1938). The note is probably one of the most scathing reviews ever to appear in an accounting journal. Preinreich is harshly critical of both Earl Saliers, who reviewed the book, and the author of the book: "The foregoing comments will suffice to show that Professor Kurtz's new book does not measure up either to its sanguine preface and introduction, or to Professor Saliers, benevolently neutral review" (p. 48).

The next paper, "The Practice of Depreciation" (1939) is more technical than the title suggests. Drawing on the 1938 article in *Econometrica*, it assumes a large number of machines are installed initially and that the life expectancy is known. Eleven depreciation methods, including one proposed by Canning, are then evaluated. Preinreich's conclusion is not optimistic: "A study of the question, what method is most suitable for competitive enterprise, must start from the principle already established that the depreciation problem is fundamentally indeterminate" (p. 256). Since there are "innumerable different ways" to depreciate an asset and the choice is "a matter of opinion," some "progress can be made in accomplishing practical objectives." Preinreich then proposes that "The principal objective should be that of facilitating forecasting, i.e., appraisal, by the stock market" (p. 256). To implement this policy, "a method is required that distributes all costs as evenly or proportionately as possible" (p. 256). This basic idea can be traced to earlier work by Canning (1933) and, later, to Brief and Owen (1970, 1973), Demski and Sappington (1990) and the literature on income smoothing.

"Note on the Theory of Depreciation" (1941) was written as a critique of a paper by Hagstroem (1939) which itself is a comment on Preinreich (1938c). Hagstroem argued that if Preinreich had been aware of his (Hagstroem's) principles, he (Preinreich) would not have said what he did say. Then Preinreich responded: "I studied the remainder of his paper with care, hoping to discover, what principles I had overlooked. Having failed to find any, it occurred to me that a further discussion of this important point might be of interest."

This short note also revisits issues relating to the "famous capital value formula" (p. 83) and then elaborates on the idea that the objective of accounting is to facilitate forecasting.

> Before one depreciation method can be proclaimed superior to any other, it is necessary to answer the question, what purpose such apparently irrelevant figures can possible serve. The principal one may well be that of facilitating the appraisal of an enterprise by its past record (p. 88).

Preinreich ends the discussion by stating that "I have been trying for some time to break a path in this general direction, but realize that most of the work still remains undone" (p. 88). He then outlines a "curriculum" for "earnest students" of the depreciation problem.

The final item in this anthology is a book review (1944). As has been suggested, one reason why Preinreich's work has not had the influence it deserves might be related to his bluntness. A comment in this review is a classic:

> The mathematics department, called in for the purpose, rises to the occasion in nine pages of calculus which boil down to a formula given by this reviewer four years ago . . . . The obvious is thus explained in terms of the abstruse in the best tradition of mathematicians (p 208).

Preinreich's contribution to accounting merits greater recognition. Hopefully, this book will make students and academicians more aware of his work.

References

Brief, R. P. , and J. Owen. "The Estimation Problem in Financial Accounting," *Journal of Accounting Research* (Autumn 1970), pp. 167–177.

_____, and J. Owen, "A Reformulation of the Estimation Problem," *Journal of Accounting Research* (Spring 1973), pp. 1–15.

_____. *Depreciation and Capital Maintenance.* New York: Garland Publishing, Inc., 1986.

_____, and R. A. Lawson, "The Role of the Accounting Rate of Return in Financial Statement Analysis," *The Accounting Review* (April 1992), pp. 411–426.

_____ , and K. V. Peasnell. *Clean Surplus: A Link Between Accounting and Finance.* New York: Garland Publishing, Inc. 1996.

Canning, J. B. "A Certain Erratic Tendency in Accounting Income Procedures," *Econometrica* (1933), pp. 52–62.

Demski, J. S., and D. E. M. Sappington. "Fully Revealing Income Measurement," *The Accounting Review* (April 1990), pp. 363–383.

Hagstroem, K.-G. "Remarks on the Theory of Depreciation," *Econometrica* (October 1939), pp. 289–303.

Littleton, A. C. Book review of G. A. D. Preinreich, *The Nature of Dividends* (Lancaster, Pa.: Lancaster Press 1935), in *The Accounting Review* (December 1935), pp. 412–414.

Mason, P. *The Principles of Public Utility Regulation.* Chicago: American Accounting Association 1937.

Modigliani, F., and M. Miller. "The Cost of Capital, Corporation Finance, and the Theory of Investment," *American Economic Review* (March 1958), pp. 261–297.

Norton, P. T. and E. L. Grant. "Depreciation Estimates in Appraisals of Manufacturing Equipment," *Transactions of the American Society of Mechanical Engineers* (1942).

O'Neill, M. T., ed. *A. P. Richardson: The Ethics of a Humanist.* New York: Arno Press, 1980.

Roos, C. F. "The Problem of Depreciation in the Calculus of Variations," *American Journal of Mathematics* (1928), pp. 218–228.

Sanders, T. H., H. R. Hatfield, and U. Moore. *A Statement of Accounting Principles* (Institute of Accountants 1938).

Stigler, S. M. Book review of P. Mirowski, ed., *Edgeworth on Chance, Economic Hazard & Statistics* (Lanham, Md.: Rowman & Littlefield, 1994), *Journal of the American Statistical Association* (June 1995), p. 803.

Taylor, J. S. "A Statistical Theory of Depreciation," *Journal of the American Statistical Association* (December 1923), pp. 1010–1023.

Bibliography: Gabriel A. D. Preinreich

"Profit-sharing Problems and Their Solution," *Journal of Accountancy* (November 1929), pp. 341-353.

"Accounts of the Fruit and Produce Commission merchant," *Journal of Accountancy* (September 1929), pp. 173–186.

"Accounting Problems of the Unincorporated Investment Trust," *Journal of Accountancy* (May 1931), pp. 361–380.

"Stock Yields, Stock Dividends and Inflation," *The Accounting Review* (December 1932), pp. 273–289.

"Accounting Terminology," *The Accounting Review* (June 1933), pp. 113–116. Originally given as Address to the American Association of University Instructors in Accounting, Cincinnati, Ohio, December 28 and 29, 1932.

"Taxation and the Natural Business Year," *The Accounting Review* (December 1933), pp. 317–322.

The Nature of Dividends. Lancaster, Pa.: Lancaster Press 1935. Reprinted by Arno Press (New York, 1978).

"The Fair Value and Yield of Common Stock," *The Accounting Review* (June 1936), pp. 130–140.

"The Law of Goodwill," *The Accounting Review* (December 1936), pp. 317–329.

"Goodwill in Accountancy," *Journal of Accountancy* (July 1937), pp. 28–50.

"Valuation and Amortization," *The Accounting Review* (September 1937), pp. 209–226.

"The Principles of Public Utility valuation," *The Accounting Review* (June 1938), pp. 149–165.

"Valuation and Depreciation," *Journal of Accountancy* (July 1938), pp. 46–48.

"Annual Survey of Economic Theory: The Theory of Depreciation," *Econometrica* (July 1938), pp. 219–241.

"The Practice of Depreciation," *Econometrica* (July 1939), pp. 235-265.

"Economic Theories of Goodwill," *Journal of Accountancy* (September 1939), pp. 169–180.

"The Theory of Industrial Replacement," *Skandinavisk Aktuarietidskrift* (1939), pp. 1–9.

"The Economic Life of Industrial Equipment," *Econometrica* (January 1940), pp. 12–44.

The Present Status of Renewal Theory. Baltimore: Waverly Press, 1940.

"Note on the Theory of Depreciation," Econometrica (January 1941), pp. 80–88.

"Theory and General Principles of Depreciation," in American Society of Civil Engineers, *Fundamental Aspects of the Depreciation Problem: A Symposium* (New York 1941), pp. 3–18.

Theory and General Principles of Depreciation (Baltimore: Waverly Press 1941)

Book review of R. Winfrey, *Depreciation of Group Properties* (Ames: Iowa State College Bulletin), in *The Accounting Review* (April 1944), pp. 207–209.

"The Theory of Progressive Taxation," *Taxes—The Tax Magazine* (August 1947), pp. 742–745.

"Progressive Taxation and Proportionate Sacrifice," *The American Economic Review* (March 1948), pp. 103–117.

"The Mathematical Theory of the Firm," *Economia Internazionale* (March 1949), pp. 322–340 and 492–508.

The Mathematical Theory of the Firm. Baltimore: Waverly Press, 1950.

"Models of Taxation in the Theory of the Firm," *Economia Internazionale* (May 1951), pp. 372–397.

"Discontinuities in the Theory of the Firm," *Metroeconomica* (August 1951), pp. 55–69.

"Replacement in the Theory of the Firm," *Metroeconomica* (August 1953), pp. 288–295.

ACCOUNTING FROM THE INVESTOR'S VIEWPOINT

"Accounting Problems of the Unincorporated Investment Trust"

Journal of Accountancy (May 1931),
pp. 361–380

Accounting Problems of the Unincorporated Investment Trust

By Gabriel A. D. Preinreich

That this article was written at all is due largely to accident. In the course of a regular audit, I was requested by a client to explain the contents of a printed report on the affairs of a certain trust described as an accumulative fund. In the opinion of the client, the report contained several contradictions and utterly failed to satisfy his very natural curiosity on two points:

1. How was it possible for the fund to close its operations with a huge profit notwithstanding the fact that he had just been notified of a reduction in the value of his certificate and of the amount of his losses deductible for income-tax purposes?
2. How could he determine from the audited income account presented in the report whether the notification received was correct or not?

The trust in question is of the management type and consists merely of a fund contributed by holders of non-negotiable certificates. Control and custody is vested in a manager and a trustee respectively, the certificate holders' rights being limited to the privilege of calling for the redemption of their certificates at the end of any calendar week.

Since I was inclined to agree with the client, at least in part, it has occurred to me that a brief study of the problems confronting such trusts and an independent attempt to solve them, might be timely and lead not only to fruitful discussion but to a gradual standardization of the still somewhat untried accounting procedure used by a form of financial enterprise which is steadily gaining in public favor.

The main advantages of the unincorporated investment trust over its corporate kin consist of greater ease and flexibility in organization and management and the fact that it is not subject to federal or state income taxes in any form whatever, each certificate holder being taxed exactly in the same manner as though he had been personally engaged in buying, holding and selling securities to the extent of his participation in the total fund.

361

This, undoubtedly, is an advantage, which, however, is offset by certain disadvantages springing from the same source.

Corporations are not burdened with the redemption of their stock, nor do stockholders have to report income unless the corporation pays dividends. The unincorporated trust must be able to determine the exact redemption value of its certificates on each redemption date and must advise the certificate holders of their shares in as many as seven or eight different kinds of income, not only annually, but whenever they elect to retire from the trust. Certificates issued during the year must be sold at their exact value as of the date of issue and income accumulated thereon for the remainder of the year must be determined correctly to safeguard each holder's individual interests. If we add that good accounting procedure requires that the lower of cost or market be used as the basis of investment valuation, whereas admissions and redemptions are closed at market values, and if we further remember that cost for tax purposes is not always equal to cost, we have a fair picture of the difficulties besetting the bookkeeper of the unincorporated trust, from all of which his more fortunate confrère working for a corporation is happily exempt.

The principal accounting problems of the unincorporated trust may therefore be summarized as follows:

1. The exact financial condition of the trust must be known as of each date of admission or redemption.
2. Such financial condition must be stated on three different bases, namely:
    (a) Cost as defined by income-tax regulations.
    (b) The lower of cost or market, as defined by correct accounting procedure.
    (c) Market.
3. Income must be segregated into the following classes:
    (a) Profit on sale of securities.
    (b) Capital gain on sale of securities.
    (c) Dividends of domestic corporations.
    (d) Dividends of foreign corporations.
    (e) Interest on tax-exempt bonds.
    (f) Interest on bonds (tax paid at source).
    (g) Interest (fully taxable).
    (h) Non-taxable income arising from differences between income-tax regulations and accounting procedure.

362

4. The proportionate amounts of each class of income due each shareholder must be readily available on each balance-sheet date, with due consideration for fractional periods reducing the shares of holders who:

   (a) Joined after the beginning of the year.
   (b) Retired before the end of the year.
   (c) Joined after the beginning and retired before the end of the year.

5. Compensation due the management and the proportionate amounts thereof chargeable against each certificate holder must be ascertainable to the same extent as income.

At first sight, this appears to be a large order, but it may be noted that, after all, the number of general-ledger accounts required is not large. The balance-sheet will, in all probability, list the following items:

   I. Assets:
      1. Cash on deposit.
      2. Call loans.
      3. Securities long (at cost).
      4. Unrealized market appreciation of securities long.
      5. Accrued interest receivable.
      6. Accrued preferred dividends receivable.
      7. Common dividends declared.

  II. Liabilities:
      1. Brokers' balances.
      2. Securities short at selling price.
      3. Market appreciation of securities short.
      4. Management compensation payable.
      5. Subscriptions to certificates not issued.

 III. Capital:
      1. Certificates outstanding.
      2. Surplus.
      3–10. Income of current year.
      11. Unrealized profits.

The foregoing list makes allowance for a broader scope of operations than will be conducted by the average investment trust. Accounts used for trading on margin may probably be dispensed with, as well as several of the income accounts, since investments may well be limited to common stocks of domestic corporations. The list was made comprehensive to show the flexibility of the system outlined in the following paragraphs, which makes it adaptable to the needs of different classes of investors.

Since the number of accounts is small and accountings must be rendered frequently, it becomes apparent that the record best suited for the purpose is a columnar book combining the functions of cashbook, journal, general ledger and trial balance, the size of which will be reduced to the limit by avoiding the cumbersome distinction between debit and credit columns through the use of red ink for credits or some similar arrangement. For the sake of clarity the record proposed is reproduced in exhibit A in its simplest form. Examples of transactions occurring in the course of regular operations are entered and will be discussed in the order recorded.

Opening entry Sept. 1, 19...

Cash.....................	$1,000,000.00	
To certificates outstanding		$1,000,000.00
Details are posted to a subsidiary certificate ledger in the usual way.		

Purchase of securities Sept. 1:

Securities owned...........	977,750.00	
To cash................		977,750.00
Details are posted to the subsidiary investment ledger.		

Interest received Sept. 30:

Cash.....................	55.62	
To interest on bank balance		55.62

Sale of securities, Oct. 3:

Cash.....................	153,250.00	
To securities owned (cost of 1,000 U. S. Steel).......		147,750.00
Profit on sale..........		5,500.00

The capital gain column will be used in all cases where securities were held over two years. In the final or annual accounting to

364

certificate holders the capital gain is transferred to profit on sale for all holders whose certificates were issued less than two years before sale of the investment.

Money lent on Call, Oct. 3:

Call loans.................	$150,000.00	
To cash...............		$150,000.00

Interest received, Oct. 31:

Cash.....................	59.80	
Call loans................	1,050.00	
To interest..............		1,109.80

Accruals to close books, Nov. 3:

Accrued interest on bank balance.................	6.40	
Accrued interest on call loans	112.50	
Dividend receivable.........	10,500.00	
To interest..............		118.90
Dividends..............		10,500.00

Management compensation, Nov. 3:

The fee payable to the management is the only expense of the trust. It may be computed in various ways, such as:

1. Fixed amount per month.
2. Percentage of income.
3. Percentage of market appreciation of securities.
4. Percentage of net worth.

In exhibit A the fee equals $\frac{1}{101}$ of the face value of certificates issued and $\frac{1}{101}$ of income and unrealized market appreciation. The former is not returnable upon redemption of the certificates; the latter, however, is charged back to the management if losses are subsequently suffered. The results of the computation may best be observed in exhibit B. Since the illustration is that of a trust in its first period of operation, the fee includes the original levy on capital. The correctness of the amount charged may be proved as follows:

365

9

A. White—December 31, 19...

Certificates outstanding........	$500,000.00	
Profit on sale and interest......	11,472.79	
Dividends..................	5,250.00	
Non-taxable income..........	2,128.32	
Unrealized appreciation........	21,052.63	
		$539,903.74
Management expense 1%......		5,345.58
Equity 100%...............		$534,558.16

Unrealized market appreciation, Nov. 3:

Only a memorandum entry is made, supported by a list of securities priced at both cost and market as of the close of the day.

Issue of additional certificates, Nov. 4:

The price at which new certificates must be issued is determined by dividing the total equity, including unrealized market appreciation on securities, by the number of old certificates outstanding. The total to be paid by the new entrant is then computed in the following manner:

n_o = Number of old certificates outstanding.

E_o = Net worth including unrealized market appreciation at the close of the day as of which new shares are to be issued.

$$\frac{E_o}{n_o} + \frac{100}{101} = \text{Cash price of 1 new certificate.}$$

Using this formula for the computation of the entry shown in exhibit A, we have

$$\frac{1.106.222.10}{10.000} + \frac{100}{101} = 111.61231$$

The issue of 500 shares is therefore recorded in detail as follows:

Cash......................	$55,806.15	
Management compensation.....	58.06	
To certificates outstanding...		$50,000.00
Surplus................		....
Profit on sale and interest		339.21
Capital gain............		......
Dividends..............		525.00
Non-taxable income......		5,000.00

366

10

Postings are made to the income accounts of the general ledger and to the certificate ledger as shown in exhibit B. The posting of new contributions to income distorts the actual earnings of the trust, but it simplifies the computation of individual incomes.

For the benefit of the reader inclined to be skeptical about such an innovation it may be well to recall the case of the cadi of *Arabian Nights* who had to execute the will of a man who died leaving three sons and nineteen camels. The will provided that one half of the camels was to go to his eldest son, whereas the two others were to receive one fourth and one fifth respectively. As may be remembered, the cadi solved the baffling problem by directing his attendant to lead his own camel alongside the others. The division was then effected smoothly by allotting 10, 5 and 4 camels respectively, to the three heirs, and the cadi's camel, left over, was returned to its grazing place.

That is about what is proposed here. Further explanation and algebraic proof of the correctness of this procedure is furnished in a later paragraph. The payment made for the new entrant's proportion of the unrealized market appreciation was included in non-taxable income for reasons discussed under that caption. Just what such a contribution really represents may be determined as follows:

M = Unrealized market appreciation.

n_o = Number of old certificates outstanding.

n_e = Number of new certificates to be issued.

$\dfrac{M}{n_o}$ = Unrealized appreciation owned per old certificate and therefore to be contributed by each new certificate.

$\dfrac{n_e M}{n_o}$ = Total payment of new entrants for unrealized market appreciation.

$\dfrac{M}{n_o+n_e}$ = Unrealized appreciation owned per certificate after admission of new entrants.

$\dfrac{\dfrac{n_e M}{n_o}}{n_o+n_e} = \dfrac{n_e M}{n_o(n_o+n_e)}$ = Market appreciation realized by each old certificate.

The admission of a new entrant, therefore, amounts to the sale of the security holdings to the extent of the expression $\dfrac{1}{n_o} - \dfrac{1}{n_o+n_e}$

367

11

for cash, and to the realization of that proportion of the market appreciation.

If, therefore, the amount of $\dfrac{n_e M}{n_o}$ is paid in, that amount may be properly posted to profit on sale or capital gain, since it represents appreciation converted into cash to the extent of $\dfrac{n_e M}{n_o + n_e}$ and a contribution of new entrants to match that gain in the amount of $\dfrac{n_e^2 M}{n_o(n_o + n_e)}$.

$$\frac{n_e M}{n_o} = \frac{n_e M}{n_o + n_e} + \frac{n_e^2 M}{n_o(n_o + n_e)}$$

Redemption of certificates, Dec. 9:

The amount to be paid to certificate holders wishing to retire from the trust is similarly determined by first recording all accruals and dividing the sum of book equity and unrealized market appreciation by the number of certificates outstanding. Conversely to the issue of certificates, a redemption may be considered the purchase by the remaining certificate holders of the retiring holders' interest in securities owned. The price paid for that interest in excess of the book value is therefore an addition to cost rather than a distribution of income, since the income so distributed has not been realized as yet.

$\dfrac{M}{n_o}$ = Portion of market appreciation owned by each certificate.

n_r = Number of certificates to be redeemed.

$\dfrac{n_r M}{n_o}$ = Portion of market appreciation due to retiring members.

$\dfrac{M}{n_o - n_r}$ = Portion of market appreciation per remaining certificate.

The amount of unrealized market appreciation purchased for cash or the additional cost of securities owned will, therefore, be

$$\frac{M}{n_o - n_r} - \frac{M}{n_o} = \frac{n_r M}{n_o(n_o - n_r)}$$

Apart from this addition to cost, each remaining certificate holder will also own a larger portion of the portfolio than before; this increase, however, is reflected by the increased number of

368

shares held per certificate, not by an increase in the cost price, and is offset by a corresponding decrease in cash.

The solution appears to be correct from the strictly mathematical and theoretical point of view, but it gives rise to doubt as to the conservativeness of the procedure. Suppose for instance, that equal numbers of certificates are issued and retired on the same day. The result would be to charge cost and credit profit on sale by

$$\frac{n_e M}{n_o} = \frac{n_r M}{n_o}$$

although none of the old holders is actually affected. By placing

$$n_o = n_r = n_e$$

it would be possible to imagine that all the certificates were constructively retired and immediately reissued, whereupon the unrealized market appreciation would suddenly be realized.

It may therefore be better practice to charge the portion of unrealized market appreciation to profit on sale as a distribution of profits which, it must be hoped, will ultimately be credited to that account. This procedure will meet no opposition, when the trust is of the accumulative type, paying no distributions whatever, except upon redemption of its certificates. If, however, income is regularly distributed, zealous protagonists of the propriety of increasing cost will no doubt arise. Their best argument is that the trust has no separate entity distinct from its members and that, therefore, changes in the value of individual equities are actually realized at each bona-fide issue or redemption of certificates.

NON-TAXABLE INCOME ARISING FROM DIFFERENCES BETWEEN INCOME TAX REGULATIONS AND ACCOUNTING PROCEDURE

The first item to be considered under this heading is the realization of market appreciation which takes place upon the issuance of additional certificates. It may be said that the case is similar to that of admitting a new partner. In accordance with established precedent, the old partners are not liable for income taxes on their proportion of the excess paid in until the assets to which the increased value attaches have been sold. The question at issue is merely: When does realization really take place? The tentative inclusion of the item in non-taxable income for the purpose of this essay should not be interpreted as a definite

369

13

answer to this question, which is really outside the scope of this discussion. Its inclusion in surplus might be just as proper, but it would complicate the technique of the annual closing. The creation of a special capital-surplus account should not be considered, since all income accounts are already distorted by the inclusion of capital items.

The excess over book value paid for redeemed shares is the second item tentatively recorded in this account, although, for purposes of the retiring member it must, of course, be transferred to taxable income (see F. Brown's account in exhibit B). So far as the remaining holders are concerned, the amounts so disbursed might be described as the exchange of realized profits for unrealized ones, and the continuous writing up of cost may well result in inflation beyond the market price prevailing at a later date.

Another discrepancy between income-tax regulations and accounting procedure will be found in the treatment of stock dividends. Without wishing to pass upon the merits of other opinions held upon this subject, the writer believes that, *Eisner* v. *Macomber* to the contrary notwithstanding, a stock dividend declared from surplus earned after the acquisition of the stock represents realized income at least to the extent of the recipient's proportion of the amount transferred from surplus to capital stock by the issuing company. The exception applying to the case of parent companies which record the stock of subsidiaries at their respective book values must, of course, be recognized.

The entry shown in exhibit A uses the well known illustration of the North American Company, which transfers $10.00 a share from surplus to capital stock upon issuance of its quarterly 2.5% stock dividends. If a considerable part of the equity were invested in the stock of this company, the trust would be unable to pay distributions commensurate with earnings, unless the correctness of the income theory were recognized. That some of the dividend stock may have to be sold in order to make cash distributions possible is readily admitted, but whether such a course of action is in the best interests of the trust or not is a question of investment management rather than accounting theory.

The journal entries will be as follows:

Upon declaration:

Dividends declared.....................	$250.00	
To non-taxable income...............		$250.00

Upon receipt:

Securities owned	$250.00	
To dividends declared		$250.00

Upon sale:

Cash	2,325.00	
To securities owned		250.00
Profit on sale		99.39
Non-taxable income		1,975.61

The last entry is computed in accordance with income-tax regulations:

1,000 shares cost	$91,250.00	
25 " "	. . . .	
1,025 " "	91,250.00	
1 " "	89.02439	
25 " "	$2,225.61	
25 " sold for	2,325.00	
Taxable profit	$99.39	

The entries seem theoretically correct, whenever the common stock is diluted at a lower rate than the rate of earnings upon the entire equity of common stockholders and so long as the long-term trend of market values remains a constant multiple of annual earnings. All these factors have been present so far in the case of the North American Company. Strictly speaking, a further qualification must be made to the effect that if the stock was purchased at a higher cost than the constant multiple referred to, the excess purchase price must be amortized out of the proceeds of stock dividends sold.

If the procedure outlined is followed, careful memorandum records must be kept with respect to the difference in cost according to the books and cost for income-tax purposes. The proper proportion of this difference must be transferred from non-taxable income to profit or capital gain on sale, when part of the original stock is sold.

Closing, Dec. 31:

When a certificate is issued, the consideration received is entered in detail in the subsidiary certificate ledger (exhibit B). Upon redemption, the price is posted in a similar manner. The

371

15

difference between the two entries is the amount to be reported as income. At the annual closing, the balance of each income account in the general ledger is divided by the number of shares outstanding and multiplied by the individual holdings. The results so obtained are again posted to the certificate ledger, whereupon the accounts are balanced to obtain the income to be reported by those who were members of the trust at the end of the year.

Attention has already been called to the fact that the closing balances of the income accounts do not reflect the income of the trust, but, since additions and deductions arising from changes in the number of certificates outstanding were always in proportion to the respective equities, those balances divided by the number of certificates outstanding at the end of the year will equal the amount earned by a certificate for the entire year. Algebraic proof of this may be furnished as follows:

Let us assume that at some time after the beginning of the year, new certificates were issued and then, after a second period had elapsed, other certificates were redeemed. This divides the year into three periods symbolized as follows:

	Number of cert. outstanding	Income for period
First period..................	n_o	i_o
Second period................	n_o+n_e	i_e
Third period.................	$n_o+n_e-n_r$	i_r

The income of a certificate held throughout the year is:

$$\frac{i_o}{n_o} + \frac{i_e}{n_o+n_e} + \frac{i_r}{n_o+n_e-n_r}$$

In actual practice, this expression would attain considerable length, since admissions and redemptions occur weekly or even daily. Let us now add the proportionate share of each entrant to the income already earned. The balance of the income account will then be:

$$i_o + \frac{n_e}{n_o}i_o + i_e - \frac{n_r}{n_o+n_e}\left(i_o + \frac{n_e}{n_o}i_o + i_e\right) + i_r$$

or simplified:

$$\left(i_o\left(1 + \frac{n_e}{n_o}\right) + i_e\right)\left(1 - \frac{n_r}{n_o+n_a}\right) + i_r$$

372

This expression, divided by $n_o+n_e-n_r$ yields the original formula for the income of one certificate held throughout the year, thereby furnishing the proof required:

$$\frac{\left(i_o\left(1+\frac{n_e}{n_o}\right)+i_e\right)\left(1-\frac{n_r}{n_o+n_e}\right)+i_r}{n_o+n_e-n_r}=\frac{i_o}{n_o}+\frac{i_e}{n_o+n_e}+\frac{i_r}{n_o+n_e-n_r}$$

It may, therefore, be seen that by surrendering the largely imaginary advantage of having the books reflect the total income of the trust, a convenient base is derived for the quick computation of each certificate holder's individual income, without the cumbersome procedure of posting profits to every account, whenever there is a change in one or the not much less cumbersome alternative of keeping separate income accounts for each succeeding partnership, of which there may be 52 or even 300 a year.

At the end of the year, when the certificate ledger is closed, the total of the individual incomes to be reported will give the total income of the trust. The proof of this total may be obtained as follows:

Certificates outstanding at end.................	$950,000.00
Surplus after closing.........................	25,660.50
	$975,660.50
Less: Certificates outstanding at beginning...............................	
Surplus at beginning...................	
Transactions in certificates for period................... $950,249.36	
	950,249.36
Income of trust.............	$25,411.14

The trial balance of the certificate ledger showing this reconciliation is reproduced in exhibit B. In order to facilitate the procedure, it is advisable to use a separate column in the general ledger for cash transactions affecting certificates. This column will act as a controlling account for the certificate ledger throughout the year. The bank balance must, obviously, reconcile with the algebraic sum of the two cash columns.

373

17

STATEMENTS FOR CERTIFICATE HOLDERS

With the routine of bookkeeping disposed of, we may now return to the question: What information is most interesting to the certificate holder? In general, the data may be grouped under three headings:

1. Balance-sheet and supporting schedules;
2. Income account;
3. Comparative statistical data.

The information conveyed by the balance-sheet is especially needed when certificates are issued or redeemed. When we buy or sell something, we are more interested in values than at any other time during the period of ownership and it is only natural that we should like to see a bill of sale itemizing the details of the transaction. If the client mentioned earlier in this article had received a balance-sheet as of the date he acquired his certificate (on or about September 1, 1929), a comparison of the figures with the closing balance-sheet as of December 31, 1929, would have answered his query, even though the unpleasant subject was avoided in the report, which stressed the success of operations for the year 1929. We may say therefore, that no trust of the kind described is organized with due regard to the wishes of its certificate holders, if its accounting system cannot produce a balance-sheet correct to the last detail upon the shortest notice, or if it fails to furnish that information to every certificate holder at least:

1. As of the day of purchase;
2. Quarterly;
3. As of the day of redemption.

The form of record shown in exhibit A is a perpetual balance-sheet, ready to furnish the exact figures at the close of any business day. For example, a balance-sheet for the use of H. Greene, Esq., may be prepared as follows:

THE UNINCORPORATED INVESTMENT TRUST
Comparative balance-sheet for H. Greene, Esq.

	November 3	December 8	Increase *Decrease*
Cash......................	$ 25,615.42	$ 38,638.80	$13,023.38
Call loans..................	150,000.00	400,000.00	250,000.00
Accrued interest receivable....	1,168.90	3,656.64	2,487.74
Dividends receivable..........	10,500.00	10,500.00	....

374

Securities owned (at cost).....	$830,000.00	$682,250.00	*$147,750.00*
Unrealized appreciation on securities....................	100,000.00	50,000.00	*50,000.00*
	$1,117,284.32	$1,185,045.44	$ 67,761.12
Less: Management fees payable	11,062.22	1,717.16	*9,345.06*
	$1,106,222.10	$1,183,328.28	$ 77,106.18
Certificates outstanding (par 100).....................	$1,000,000.00	$1,100,000.00	$100,000.00
Surplus: Realized...........	6,222.10	33,328.28	27,106.18
Unrealized..........	100,000.00	50,000.00	*50,000.00*
	$1,106,222.10	$1,183,328.28	$ 77,106.18
Value of 500 Certificates......	$ 55,311.10	$ 53,787.65	
Management fee paid........	495.05		
Total....................	$ 55,806.15	$ 53,787.65	*$ 2,018.50*

It will probably be unnecessary to furnish a detailed schedule of securities owned, except upon special request.

The income account of the report referred to is fairly representative of several others. It is a copy of the old-fashioned profit-and-loss account, with all the emphasis upon the earnings of the trust and scant regard for the individual owner. In the comments upon income figures there occurs this statement:

"As subscriptions to the accumulative fund were received continuously throughout the year ended December 31, 1929, the income and unrealized profits on securities held as reported in statement 2 are not properly applicable to the face value of certificates outstanding at the end of the year. The following tabulation is therefore designed to disclose the rate per cent. per annum on the average face value of certificates outstanding during the year."

(Table omitted)

"It should, however, be borne in mind that the rates per cent. per annum upon face value in the above tabulation relate only to a theoretical average certificate."

That describes the matter very well. In other words, no certificate holder, even though he may have been a member of the

375

trust for the entire year, is in a position to find out from the audited income account how much his holdings earned, in order to verify the accuracy of the statement received from the trust to attach to his income-tax return. (N.B. The earnings of the theoretical average certificate as described would be equal to those of a certificate held throughout the year only if the income had never varied from a constant percentage of the changing equity. This, however, was obviously not the case in 1929, when huge profits were made in the first three quarters, only to be lost during the fourth.)

The income account, therefore, is of little practical value, except as a bookkeeping device for the reconciliation of surplus at the beginning and end of the year. What the certificate holder looks for in an annual report is the appreciation of a certificate held throughout the year, with at least quarterly if not monthly subdivisions, so as to permit a rough approximation of the increase in the value of his investment for the period the certificate was actually held. The next question of interest would be: What part of that appreciation is realized and how much of it represents paper profits?

As already pointed out, the amount earned by a certificate held throughout the year is obtained by dividing the footings of each income account in the general ledger by the number of certificates outstanding at the end of the year and summarizing the result. Unrealized market appreciation was recorded as a memorandum and may be similarly treated for statement purposes. The income account of 1,000 certificates held throughout the year may then be prepared in the following form:

Value of 1,000 certificates at beginning	$100,000.00	100.00%
Income per 1,000 certificates:		
Profit on sale and interest........	$2,294.56	2.29%
Less: Management expense........	1,069.11	1.07%
Income subject to normal tax.....	$1,225.45	1.22%
Capital gain.....................	....	......
Dividends......................	1,050.00	1.05%
Non-taxable income..............	425.66	.43%
Total realized income...........	$2,701.11	2.70%

376

Unrealized market appreciation....	$4,210.53	$4.21%
Gross increase in value of 1,000 certificates.................	$6,911.64	6.91%
Less: Distributions...............	....	......
Net increase in value of 1,000 certificates.....................	$6,911.64	6.91%
Value of 1,000 certificates at end of period........................	$106,911.64	106.91%

For the first year, percentages may be omitted, since the amounts give the same information in greater detail. In subsequent years, percentages will show appreciation during the year, whereas the amounts will continue to express the rate of increase on the par value of the certificates. The subdivision of this income account into quarterly or even monthly figures is essential, whenever the annual rate of earnings per certificate during the several months varied substantially from its average for the year.

The simplest form of the report furnished to the certificate holder for filing with his income-tax return is undoubtedly a carbon copy of his page in the certificate ledger. The total income or loss reported must agree with the net increase or decrease as shown by the comparative balance-sheet furnished at the same time. The certificate ledger best adapted for this purpose will consist of an alphabetical tray containing the individual accounts in original and duplicate. At the annual closing or upon redemption, the duplicate is detached and mailed, whereas the original is filed in an inactive binder.

377

21

Exhibit A

THE UNINCORPORATED

Combined cash book,

| Cash | | Call loans | Accrued interest | Dividends declared | Securities owned | Folio | Description |
Certificates	General						
							Sept. 1
							A. White
							F. Brown
$1,000,000.00							J. Black
					$886,500.00	1	6,000 U. S. Steel
	$977,750.00				91,250.00	2	1,000 North American
	55.62						Sept. 30
							Oct. 3
	153,250.00				*147,750.00*	1	1,000 U. S. Steel
	150,000.00	$150,000.00					New York Trust Co.
	59.80	1,050.00					Oct. 31
							Nov. 3
			$ 6.40				Interest bank balance
			112.50				Interest call loan
				$10,500.00			6,000 U. S. Steel
							Market apprec. $100,000
							Management fee
$1,000,000.00	*$ 974,384.58*	$151,050.00	$ 118.90	$10,500.00	$830,000.00		
							Nov. 4
							H. Greene 500 sh.
111,612.31							F. Greene 500 "
	161,300.00				*147,750.00*	1	1,000 U. S. Steel
	250,000.00	250,000.00					New York Trust Co.
	111.07	1,775.00	118.90				Nov. 30
							Dec. 8
			31.64				Interest on bank balance
			800.00				Interest on call loan
							Market apprec. $50,000
							Management fee
	10,000.00						Management fee paid
$1,111,612.31	*$1,072,975.51*	$402,825.00	$831.64	$10,500.00	$682,250.00		
							Dec. 9
107,575.30							F. Brown 1,000 sh.
53,787.65							H. Greene 500 "
	152,825.00	*152,825.00*					New York Trust Co.
	11,331.64		831.64	$10,500.00			Dec. 31
					250.00	2	25 Stock Div. North Am.
	2,325.00				*250.00*	2	" " " "
			57.11				Interest bank balance
			1,250.00				Interest call loan
							Market apprec. $40,000
							Management fee
$ 950,249.36	$ 906,491.87	$250,000.00	$1,307.11		$682,250.00		
950,249.36	950,249.36						Closing entry
	$ 43,757.49	$250,000.00	$1,307.11		$682,250.00		

INVESTMENT TRUST

journal and general ledger

Folio	Certificates outstanding	Surplus	Profit on sale Interest	Capital gain on sale	Dividends	Non-taxable income	Management compensation Expense	Liability
1	$ 500,000.00							
2	100,000.00							
3	400,000.00							
			$ 55.62					
			5,500.00					
			1,109.80					
			6.40					
			112.50					
					$10,500.00			
							$11,062.22	$11,062.22
	$1,000,000.00		$ 6,784.32		$10,500.00		$11,062.22	$11,062.22
4	50,000.00		339.21		525.00	$ 5,000.00	58.06	
5	50,000.00		339.22		525.00	5,000.00	58.06	
			13,550.00					
			1,767.17					
			31.64					
			800.00					
							654.94	654.94
								10,000.00
	$1,100,000.00		$23,611.56		$11,550.00	$10,000.00	$11,833.28	$ 1,717.16
2	100,000.00		2,146.51		1,050.00	5,454.54	1,075.75	
4	50,000.00		1,073.25		525.00	2,727.27	537.87	
						250.00		
			99.39			1,975.61		
			57.11					
			1,250.00					
							63.06	63.06
	$ 950,000.00	$25,660.50	$21,798.30		$ 9,975.00	$ 4,043.80	$10,156.60	$ 1,654.10
1-5			21,798.30		9,975.00	4,043.80	10,156.60	
	$ 950,000.00	$25,660.50						$ 1,654.10

Exhibit B

The Unincorporated Investment Trust

Certificate Ledger

Date	Description	Folio	Certificates outstanding	Surplus	Profit on sale / Interest	Capital gain on sale	Dividends	Non-taxable income	Management expense
				A. White					
Sept. 1	Original issue 5,000	1	$500,000.00	$13,505.53					
Dec. 31	Closing entry	1			$11,472.79		$5,250.00	$2,128.32	$5,345.58
Dec. 31	Income (*Loss*) reported				$11,472.79		$5,250.00	$2,128.32	$5,345.58
				F. Brown					
Sept. 1	Original issue 1,000	1	$100,000.00						
Dec. 9	Redeemed 1,000	1	100,000.00		$ 2,146.51		$ 1,050.00	$5,454.54	$ 1,075.75
	Transfer				5,454.54			5,454.54	
Dec. 31	Income (*Loss*) reported				$ 7,601.05		$ 1,050.00		$ 1,075.75
				D. Black					
Sept. 1	Original issue 4,000	1	$400,000.00	$10,804.42					
Dec. 31	Closing entry	1			$ 9,178.23		$ 4,200.00	$1,702.65	$ 4,276.46
Dec. 31	Income (*Loss*) reported				$ 9,178.23		$ 4,200.00	$1,702.65	$ 4,276.46
				H. Greene					
Nov. 4	Issued 500	1	$ 50,000.00		$ 339.21		$ 525.00	$5,000.00	$ 58.06
Dec. 9	Redeemed 500	1	50,000.00		1,073.25		525.00	2,727.27	537.87
Dec. 31	Transfer				2,272.73			2,272.73	
Dec. 31	Income (*Loss*) reported				$ 1,538.69				$ 479.81
				F. Greene					
Nov. 4	Issued 500	1	$ 50,000.00	$ 1,350.55	$ 339.22		$ 525.00	$5,000.00	$ 58.06
Dec. 31	Closing entry				1,147.28		525.00	212.83	534.56
Dec. 31	Income (*Loss*) reported				808.06			$4,787.17	$ 476.50
				Trial Balance					
Dec. 31	A. White 5,000	1	$500,000.00	$13,505.53	$11,472.79		$ 5,250.00	$2,128.32	$ 5,345.58
	F. Brown	2	400,000.00	10,804.42	7,601.05		1,050.00	1,702.65	1,075.75
	D. Black 4,000	3	50,000.00	1,350.55	9,178.23		4,200.00		4,276.46
	H. Greene	4			1,538.69			4,787.17	479.81
	F. Greene 500	5			808.06				476.50
			$950,000.00	$25,660.50	$27,521.44		$10,500.00	$ 956.20	$11,654.10
			950,249.36	25,411.14					
			$ 249.36	$ 249.36					

"Stock Yields, Stock Dividends and Inflation"

The Accounting Review (December 1932), pp. 273–289

STOCK YIELDS, STOCK DIVIDENDS AND INFLATION

GABRIEL A. D. PREINREICH

I

THE yield of bonds has long been recognized as capable of mathematical determination; bond tables have long been in general use. In the case of stocks variations of income and differences of opinion as to what constitutes income make the computation of the yield more difficult. The methods in use are less scientific and the meaning of the word "yield" is subject to various interpretations.

The simplest ratio often called "yield" is obtained by dividing the annual dividend payments per share by the market value of a share. This ratio disregards corporate earnings, which may amount to more or less than the dividends paid. A second conception of the yield has accordingly developed, commonly represented by the quotient of corporate earnings and market value per share. Theoretically, the yield of an investment is the ratio which the difference between two consecutive measurements of the capital level bears to the average capital level of the period elapsed. Practically a host of disturbing influences makes it difficult to measure the capital level with the desired degree of accuracy. In the present essay an attempt is made to separate secondary disturbances from the basic phenomenon and to develop the laws of the yield to serve as a trend-line or axis marking the theoretical position of the equilibrium around which the actual oscillations of market values must, in the long run, be evenly distributed.

In the case of a bond it is well known that its present value is obtained by discounting each of the future payments promised on its face at the money rate prevailing at any given moment. The money rate, in this sense, is individual rather than general, that is, it includes a charge for risk dependent upon the merits of the bond. Disregarding all legal and even some economic differences between common stocks and bonds and considering only their income-yielding possibilities, it may be said that a common stock is a bond which promises future payments indefinite in number and amount.

The value of a perpetual bond depends upon two main factors: the effective coupon rate and the money rate. The former divided by the latter gives the market price of each dollar of face value. In the case of common stock, the rate corresponding to the effective coupon rate is the earning rate, e.g., the ratio which the annual earnings of a share bear to its average book value for the year. In emulation of the procedure followed for the valuation of a perpetual bond, the market price of a share of common stock is often considered to depend upon the quotient of the earning rate over the individual money rate reflecting the merits of the stock.

At this point attention must be called to an essential difference between a bond and a share of common stock. A bondholder earns a constant return on a constant capital, whereas a stockholder frequently obtains a more or less constant rate of return on an increasing capital, because a portion of the corporate earnings has been reinvested by the company. There are various kinds of corporations: some are unable to reinvest their earnings, others can do so only in part, still others can use every cent they earn and there are exceptional cases where the retention of the entire earnings is insufficient to provide for expansion. It is an important duty of the corporate management to formulate dividend policies which conform to these conditions. Thus a company which can not reinvest its earnings must distribute them; slowly expanding companies will distribute the difference

27

between the total earnings and that fraction which can be reinvested, while rapidly expanding companies will not only endeavor to retain all earnings but will in addition distribute subscription rights to attract new capital. A seemingly contradictory procedure, which is nevertheless quite common, is to distribute cash dividends and then get back more than the amount distributed by issuing rights. Stock dividends are well adapted for the purpose of giving the stockholder a tangible evidence of an increase in his wealth without reducing the resources available for expansion.

It is not generally realized that one of the principal considerations affecting the market value of common stock is this capacity of a corporation to expand, that is to compound its own earnings. The rate at which the company can increase its capital from year to year without decreasing the earning rate per dollar invested may be called the expansion rate. If a company can earn a constant return on each unit of capital and if the number of units increases through reinvestment of earnings, it follows that, instead of a constant principal plus an annuity of equal payments, the stockholder owns a principal sum and an annuity, both of which grow at the expansion rate. It further follows that if the expansion rate is equal to or higher than the money rate at which future payments are discounted to obtain their present value, the theoretical market price of the investment is infinite.

This is the first important conclusion which must be reached by the explorer of the laws of the yield. It emphasizes the tremendous difference in value between a constant and an expanding investment and shows that the time-honored method of appraising a security through the simple process of dividing the annual earnings by the desired rate of return leads to an acceptable result only in the case of a bond or a share of stock in a corporation which has reached the limit of its expansion.

To obtain a formula which will do justice to the often neglected factor of expansion,

it is necessary to reason further. If the theoretical value of an investment expanding at a rate higher than the money rate is infinite, why can it be bought at a price which, although higher than that of a stationary investment, is still moderate? Because it is impossible to imagine that a company will go on expanding forever. The investor appraising the stock is willing to concede only that the company will continue to expand for a small number of years representing the limit of visibility into the future. For what lies beyond, he is not willing to pay more than the present value of a perpetuity of equal payments (N.B. The difference between the present value of a perpetuity and that of a bond maturing in a hundred years or more is negligible for ordinary purposes). Whenever the limit of visibility is shorter than the actual period during which the company will continue to expand, an undervaluation of the stock must result.

To illustrate, let us assume that a corporation has in the past demonstrated not only its power to earn an average of $1 per annum on every $10 of book value, but also its ability to reinvest those earnings from year to year without bringing about a decrease in the return stated. As far as expansion is concerned, the investor refuses to look more than—let us say—ten years ahead, but he believes that the company will be able to earn 10% on its capital for several generations after it has lost the ability to reinvest those earnings. What is the fair present value of this investment to yield 5%?

The present value of a perpetuity of $1 a year would evidently be $20, but this stock is expected to yield considerably more than $1 a year. First of all, a present capital investment of $10 will increase to 10×1.1^{10} in ten years. At that time, according to the assumption, the company will cease to expand further, but will continue to earn 10% on the accumulated capital. In the absence of an opportunity for reinvestment these earnings will have to be distributed, yielding to the present purchaser of a $10 equity a perpetuity of 1.1^{10} or $2.59 per annum, the first payment to be made eleven years from now. The present value of this perpetuity one year before the date of the first payment is $51.87. Dividing by 1.05^{10}, the value of a present corporate equity of $10 is found to be $31.844 instead of $20.00, as estimated on the basis of mere earning power, without due regard to the capacity for expansion.

Let us see now, what happens a year after the acquisition of the $10 equity for $31.844. If the investor's original estimate, that the company will expand for 10 years and no more is borne out by the consensus of opinion a year later, the value of the stock will have risen to $51.87 : 1.05^9 = $33.436; an increase of $1.592 yielding a 5% return as expected. As a matter of fact, however, the investor did not really estimate that the company would stop expanding at the end of ten years; he merely refused to look farther ahead. If prospects remained unchanged during the year elapsed, he will again be willing to look ten years ahead and, seeing no signs of an approaching saturation point, will be inclined to repeat last year's bargain of buying a $10 equity for $31.844. By doing so, he will pay $31.844 for ten-elevenths of the equity which cost the same amount a year ago, that is, the market price of last year's $10 equity, which has become this year's $11 equity, has risen from $31.844 to $35.028; a yield of 10%. Through disinclination to look far enough into the future, the investment has been undervalued last year and will remain undervalued from year to year until the end of the expansion period is actually in sight. In the meantime the investor's wealth, originally equalling the purchase price of $31.844, will be compounded at the rate of 10% per annum, notwithstanding the fact that the company is compounding only the original book value of $10 at the same rate. For every $1 earned by the company, the investor's wealth increases by $3.18!

From the foregoing it may be seen that an investment in an expanding company legitimately enjoys a much higher average annual advance in its market value than an equal initial investment in a stationary company. In other words, the half-truth, which has become almost axiomatic, namely that no investor can in the long run earn more on an investment in common stock than his share of corporate earnings, is valid only with respect to stationary companies. The stockholder of an expanding company, strange as it may seem, earns much more on his stock than the company earns on the same stock. In the long run his wealth increases, not by the amount of corporate earnings, but by the present value of all future services which those corporate earnings are capable of rendering in their capacity of new capital.

When the earning and expansion rates are not equal, the situation is not so simple as in the example given. In general, the market value of the book equity consists of three separate items:

A. The present value of the principal sum invested in the company which is to be returned on the unknown date of liquidation.

B. The present value of all dividend payments made during the period of expansion. To avoid an accumulation of sterile capital, all earnings in excess of the expansion rate are distributed.

C. The present value of all dividend payments after the end of the expansion period. The entire earnings are distributed during this period.

These three elements of the market value may be computed by recourse to algebra.

Let
e = earning rate
x = expansion rate
i = money rate
n = number of years during which the earning rate will be maintained
k = number of years during which the expansion rate will be maintained
v = book value of a share
m = market premium above book value
$v + m$ = market value of a share
$\dfrac{v + m}{v}$ = market value of each dollar of book equity
$(1 + x)^k$ = compound amount of one dollar of present book equity increasing at the expansion rate for k years.

$(1 + i)^n$ = compound amount of one dollar increasing at the money rate for n years.

$\dfrac{(1 + x)^k}{(1 + i)^n}$ = present value of one dollar of book equity compounded for k years at the expansion rate and remaining constant thereafter, to become payable at the end of n years from now. (Item A.)

$e - x$ = excess of earning rate over expansion rate (annual cash dividends per \$1 book equity during the expansion period).

$(e - x)\dfrac{1 - \left(\dfrac{1+x}{1+i}\right)^k}{i - x}$ = present value of an annuity of k payments consisting of a first payment of $e - x$ and subsequent payments growing at the rate x (Item B.).

$e(1 + x)^k$ = the amount which a book equity of $(1 + x)^k$ will earn in the year $k + 1$ and subsequent years.

$e\left(\dfrac{1+x}{1+i}\right)^k \dfrac{1 - \dfrac{1}{(1+i)^{n-k}}}{i}$ = present value of a deferred annuity of $n - k$ payments of $e(1 + x)^k$ each; the first payment to be made at the end of $k + 1$ years from now (Item C.).

Adding items A, B and C together, the following formula is obtained:

$$\frac{v+m}{v} = \underbrace{\frac{(1+x)^k}{(1+i)^n}}_{A} + \underbrace{(e-x)\frac{1-\left(\frac{1+x}{1+i}\right)^k}{i-x}}_{B} + \underbrace{e\left(\frac{1+x}{1+i}\right)^k\frac{1-\frac{1}{(1+i)^{n-k}}}{i}}_{C}$$

If the company is expected to maintain its earning rate indefinitely, the formula can be simplified by placing n equal to infinity. (N.B. When earning and money rates are normal, a period of 100 years or more may be considered infinite, without causing a substantial error).

For $n = \infty$

I. $\dfrac{v+m}{v} = \dfrac{e-x}{i-x}\left[1 - \left(\dfrac{1+x}{1+i}\right)^k\right] + \dfrac{e}{i}\left(\dfrac{1+x}{1+i}\right)^k = \left(\dfrac{1+x}{1+i}\right)^k\left(\dfrac{e}{i} - \dfrac{e-x}{i-x}\right) + \dfrac{e-x}{i-x}$

Or expressed in words:

$$\begin{bmatrix}\text{market value} \\ \text{of \$1 book} \\ \text{equity}\end{bmatrix} = \begin{bmatrix}\text{\$1 compounded at} \\ \text{the expansion rate} \\ \text{and discounted at} \\ \text{the money rate for} \\ \text{the expansion period}\end{bmatrix} \times \left[\dfrac{\left(\substack{\text{earning} \\ \text{rate}}\right)}{\left(\substack{\text{money} \\ \text{rate}}\right)} - \dfrac{\left(\substack{\text{earn.} \\ \text{rate}}\right) - \left(\substack{\text{exp.} \\ \text{rate}}\right)}{\left(\substack{\text{money} \\ \text{rate}}\right) - \left(\substack{\text{exp.} \\ \text{rate}}\right)}\right] + \left[\dfrac{\left(\substack{\text{earn.} \\ \text{rate}}\right) - \left(\substack{\text{exp.} \\ \text{rate}}\right)}{\left(\substack{\text{money} \\ \text{rate}}\right) - \left(\substack{\text{exp.} \\ \text{rate}}\right)}\right]$$

This is the formula from which the conservative market price of an expanding investment should be computed. An appraisal on the simple basis of e/i (earning rate over money rate) disregards the fundamental factor of expansion. An examination of the formula for special values shows that for

1. $e = i$ .... $\dfrac{v+m}{v} = 1$

2. $x = 0$ .... " $= \dfrac{e}{i}$

3. $x = i$ .... " $= \dfrac{e}{i} + k\dfrac{e-i}{1+i}$

4. $x = e$ .... $\dfrac{v+m}{v} = \dfrac{e}{i}\left(\dfrac{1+e}{1+i}\right)^k$

5. $\begin{cases} k = 0 \text{ ....} & \text{"} = \dfrac{e}{i} \\ k = \infty \text{ and } x \geqq i \text{ ....} & \text{"} = \infty \\ k = \infty \text{ and } x < i \text{ ....} & \text{"} = \dfrac{e-x}{i-x} \end{cases}$

6. $i = \infty$ .... " $= 0$

7. $i = 0$ .... " $= \infty$

8. $i > e$ .... $\begin{cases} x = 0 \\ k = 0 \\ \dfrac{v+m}{v} = \dfrac{e}{i} \end{cases}$

These results may be restated in the form of rules:

(1) When the earning rate equals the money rate, the book value will equal the market value.

(2) When an investment does not expand, its market value is based upon the quotient of earning rate over money rate.

(3) When the expansion rate equals the money rate, the investment is worth more than if it did not expand at all, depending upon the excess of the earning rate over the money rate and the number of years of future expansion.

(4) When the expansion rate equals the earning rate, the basic market value of an investment can be obtained by multiplying that value which it would have in the absence of expansion, with the present value of the final corporate equity.

(5a) When the investor does not pay a premium for expanding power, even though it be present, the market prices of stationary and expanding investments will not differ.

(5b) The value of an investment expanding indefinitely at a rate higher than the money rate is infinite.

(5c) The value of an investment expanding indefinitely at a rate lower than the money rate can be obtained by diminishing both the earning rate and the money rate by the expansion rate and dividing the result of the first subtraction by that of the second.

(6) If money rates are very high, the market prices of investments are very low.

(7) If money rates are very low, the market prices of investments are very high.

(8) A corporation earning less than the money rate on the equity invested in it can not compound those earnings profitably and therefore capacity for expansion will pass unrecognized, giving the investment a stationary status (See 2 and 5a).

If the market price of a share of stock is given, and the earning and expansion rates have been computed or estimated on the basis of past performance, it is interesting to ascertain for how many years the company would have to continue expanding to make the present price attractive. For this purpose the formula can be transformed into:

$$\text{II.} \quad k = \frac{\log i - \log x + \log \left(1 + \dfrac{m}{v} \cdot \dfrac{i - x}{i - e}\right)}{\log (1 + x) - \log (1 + i)}$$

$$\begin{pmatrix} \text{expansion} \\ \text{period} \end{pmatrix} = \frac{\begin{pmatrix} \text{logarithm} \\ \text{of money} \\ \text{rate} \end{pmatrix} - \begin{pmatrix} \text{logarithm} \\ \text{of expansion} \\ \text{rate} \end{pmatrix} + \text{logarithm of} \left[1 + \dfrac{\begin{pmatrix} \text{market} \\ \text{premium} \end{pmatrix}}{\begin{pmatrix} \text{book} \\ \text{value} \end{pmatrix}} \times \dfrac{\begin{pmatrix} \text{money} \\ \text{rate} \end{pmatrix} - \begin{pmatrix} \text{exp.} \\ \text{rate} \end{pmatrix}}{\begin{pmatrix} \text{money} \\ \text{rate} \end{pmatrix} - \begin{pmatrix} \text{earn.} \\ \text{rate} \end{pmatrix}} \right]}{\text{logarithm of} \left[1 + \begin{pmatrix} \text{exp.} \\ \text{rate} \end{pmatrix} \right] - \text{logarithm of} \left[1 + \begin{pmatrix} \text{money} \\ \text{rate} \end{pmatrix} \right]}$$

The value of the investment derived from formula I. may be called the "trend value" because it is based upon a study of graphs which compare the long-term trend constructed from daily market quotations over a period of years with book values and distributions. The formula, of course, is valid only in cases where earning and expanding power are the principal price-building factors. It gives goodwill valuations and can not apply to investments which derive a portion of their value from other sources such as the appreciation of real estate, etc. Furthermore, the trend value computed will not be more trustworthy than the elements entering into the computation and therefore the scope of the formula is limited to the stocks of large companies engaged in the production of essential commodities or services which command a sufficiently wide and stable market. These conditions are apparently met by many public utility or quasi-utility stocks listed on the New York Stock Exchange.

Within these limitations the general law of the yield can be developed without difficulty. To simplify matters, the annual increase in wealth will be divided by the wealth at the beginning rather than by the average wealth for the year to obtain the rate of yield. That is an approximation which is commonly accepted.

It was found that as long as earning rate and money rate remain constant, the market (trend) value of a dollar of book equity invested in the productive unit remains constant. If the number of dollars invested increases at the expansion rate, the market price of the investor's holdings will tend to increase in proportion. The total increase in the investor's wealth will therefore consist of the difference between the market prices (trend values) of the stock at the beginning and end of the year, plus any earnings distributed in cash or property. Assigning the symbol "ϵ" to the yield:

$$\epsilon = \frac{(v+m)(1+x) - (v+m) + v(e-x)}{v+m}$$

$$\left(\begin{array}{c}\text{yield per \$1}\\\text{of trend value}\end{array}\right) = \frac{\left(\begin{array}{c}\text{trend value}\\\text{at end}\end{array}\right) - \left(\begin{array}{c}\text{trend value}\\\text{at beginning}\end{array}\right) + \left(\begin{array}{c}\text{cash}\\\text{dividends}\end{array}\right)}{\left(\begin{array}{c}\text{trend value}\\\text{at beginning}\end{array}\right)}$$

Performing the operations indicated and reducing:

III.

$$\epsilon = \frac{ve + mx}{v+m}$$

$$\left(\begin{array}{c}\text{yield per \$1}\\\text{of trend value}\end{array}\right) = \frac{\left(\begin{array}{c}\text{book}\\\text{value}\end{array}\right) \times \left(\begin{array}{c}\text{earning}\\\text{rate}\end{array}\right) + \left(\begin{array}{c}\text{trend}\\\text{premium}\end{array}\right) \times \left(\begin{array}{c}\text{expansion}\\\text{rate}\end{array}\right)}{\left(\begin{array}{c}\text{trend}\\\text{value}\end{array}\right)}$$

The annual return yielded by an investment equals in the long run the earning rate on the book equity plus the expansion rate on the market (trend) premium.

When the entire corporate earnings can be reinvested, that is when the expansion rate equals the earning rate, this statement means that an investment in the trend value will, in the long run, increase at the same rate at which the corporate book equity is increasing through the retention of earnings. For an expansion rate lower than the earning rate the situation may be illustrated as follows:

Let $e = $ 10%   = earning rate
         $x = $ 6%   = expansion rate
         $i = $ 5%   = money rate
         $k = $ 10 years = limit of visibility ahead (e.g. forecast of expansion period)
         $v = $ \$10   = unit of book equity

With these data, formula I. gives a trend value of \$25.97, of which \$10 is the book equity and \$15.97 the market premium. A year later, the company will have increased the book value to \$11, of which \$10.60 is

the productive capital of the second year and 40¢ is the dividend awaiting distribution in cash or property. The market price of the productive capital increased in proportion to its book value by \$1.5582 to \$27.5282, to which must be added the cash value of the dividend (unproductive capital) to obtain \$27.9282 as the market (trend) price of the stock before the dividend. The investor has experienced an increase in his wealth totalling \$1.9582. The same result is obtained from formula III.

10% of book equity (\$10)..................\$1.00
6% of market premium (\$15.97)............ .9582

     Amount of yield......................\$1.9582

The rate of yield is accordingly

$$\epsilon = 1.9582 : 25.97 = 7.54\%$$

Let us now assume that the expansion rate is 14%, all other data remaining unchanged. The trend value from formula I. will be \$39.843. At the end of a year the company will have earned $1 as before, but the capital needed for next year's operations is now $11.40, so that a shortage of 40¢ must be raised outside. If this amount is readily obtainable, the market value of the $11 equity will not be 1.1 × $39.843 = $43.8273, but $45.021 in anticipation of the fact that a payment of 40¢ into the corporate treasury will make it worth 1.14 × $39.843 = $45.421. Rights entitling to the subscription, at book value, of one share for every 27½ shares held are thus worth $1.1937 on holdings purchased for $39.843 a year ago. The new wealth of the investor is therefore composed of:

Trend value of stock ex rights	$43.8273
Trend value of rights received	1.1937
Total investment	$45.0210

Or computed from formula III:

10% of book equity ($10)	$ 1.00
14% of trend premium ($29.843)	4.178
Amount of yield	$ 5.178
Purchase price	39.843
Total investment	$45.021
Rate of yield	13.0%

In this case then, the company earned 10% on $10, while the stockholder earned 13% on $39.843 invested in the same stock. If the rights are sold, the new stockholder is admitted upon the same basis as his predecessor. Paying $1.5937 for a book equity of 40¢ is the same as paying $39.843 for $10.

By substituting the trend value of an investment per formula I. into formula III. and examining the result for special values of e, x_s, k, and i, various subsidiary laws of the yield can be obtained.

$$\text{III. } \epsilon = \frac{ve + mx}{v + m} = \frac{e + \left(\dfrac{v+m}{v} - 1\right)x}{\dfrac{v+m}{v}} = x + \frac{e - x}{\dfrac{v+m}{v}}$$

$$\text{I. } \frac{v+m}{v} = \left(\frac{1+x}{1+i}\right)^k \left(\frac{e}{i} - \frac{e-x}{i-x}\right) + \frac{e-x}{i-x}$$

$$\text{IV. } \epsilon = x + \frac{e - x}{\left(\dfrac{1+x}{1+i}\right)^k \left(\dfrac{e}{i} - \dfrac{e-x}{i-x}\right) + \dfrac{e-x}{i-x}}$$

$$\begin{pmatrix} \text{yield per \$1} \\ \text{of trend value} \end{pmatrix} = \begin{pmatrix} \text{expansion} \\ \text{rate} \end{pmatrix} + \dfrac{\begin{pmatrix} \text{cash} \\ \text{dividend} \end{pmatrix}}{\begin{pmatrix} \text{trend} \\ \text{value} \end{pmatrix}}$$

For

1.	$e = i$	....	$\epsilon = i$
2.	$x = 0$	....	$\epsilon = i$
3.	$x = i$	....	$\epsilon < 2i$

$$4.\ \begin{cases} x < e & \dots\dots\dots \quad \epsilon < e \\ x = e & \dots\dots\dots \quad \epsilon = e \\ x > e & \dots\dots\dots \quad \epsilon > e \end{cases}$$

(1) If the corporate earning rate equals the money rate, the investment will not yield more than that rate, irrespective of whether the company is capable of expansion or not.

(2) If the company is not expanding, the investment will not yield more than the money rate, irrespective of how high the earning rate may be. The amount yielded cannot be greater than the amount of corporate earnings.

(3) If the expansion rate equals the money rate, the investment will yield more than that rate only if the earning rate is higher, but even if earnings were infinitely high, the yield could not be higher than double the money rate.

(4a) If the expansion rate is lower than the earning rate, the rate of the yield will also be lower but, since it is computed on the market (trend) value, the amount yielded may well be higher than the amount of corporate earnings.

(4b) If the expansion rate equals the earning rate, the investment will yield that rate on its market (trend) value which the company earns on its book value.

(4c) If the expansion rate is higher than the earning rate, the investor will earn a higher rate on the market (trend) value of the stock than the company earns on its book value.

The influence of the exponent k (number of years of expansion for which the purchaser is willing to pay a premium) may next be examined.

$$5. \begin{cases} k = 0 \dots \dots \dots & \epsilon = i + x\left(1 - \dfrac{i}{e}\right) \\ k = \infty \text{ and } x > i \dots \dots & \epsilon = x \\ k = \infty \text{ and } x < i \dots \dots & \epsilon = i \end{cases}$$

(5a) The longer the period of future expansion for which the purchaser is willing to pay, the closer the yield corresponds to the expansion rate, but it cannot be lower than the money rate. (N.B. Formula III. defines the yield as the weighted average of the earning rate on the book equity and the expansion rate on the market premium. The higher k, the higher the market premium in comparison to the book value and therefore the greater the weight of the expansion rate.)

(5b) An investment with an earning rate higher than the expansion rate will yield the highest return when the market's estimate of the future expansion period is conservative. Conversely an investment with an expansion rate in excess of the earning rate will be favored by a liberal estimate.

The effect of the money rate is expressed by the following limits:

$$6. \quad i = \infty \dots \dots \dots \dots \quad \epsilon = \infty$$
$$7. \quad i = 0 \dots \dots \dots \dots \quad \epsilon = x$$
$$8. \quad i > e \dots \dots \dots \dots \begin{cases} x = 0 \\ k = 0 \\ \epsilon = i \end{cases}$$

(6) When the money rate at which future payments are discounted is very high, the market value of securities is very low and their yield therefore very high.

(7a) When the money rate is very low the market value of securities is very high and the yield is therefore determined entirely by the capacity for expansion. (See rule 5a.)

(7b) An investment with an earning rate higher than the expansion rate will yield the highest return when the money rate is high. Conversely an investment with an expansion rate in excess of the earning rate will be favored by low money rates.

(8) When the earning rate of an investment is lower than the money rate, expansion would involve a loss to the investor and therefore no premium will be paid for future capacity to expand. In such circumstances then, no investment can earn more than the money rate.

The subsidiary rules of the yield here enumerated refer to static rather than dynamic conditions. The elements e, x, k and i entering into the computations of the market (trend) value and the yield were assumed to have remained constant for the periods examined. Fluctuations in the market value of securities arise because these elements are really variable. The greater the number of variables entering into the appraisal of a security, the greater are the fluctuations in its value. In the case of a safe bond, the only variable is the money rate; the market value of common equity in a stationary (non-expanding) company depends upon the money rate and the earning rate; the market value of an investment in expanding corporate equities, finally, depends not only upon these two factors but upon the rate and period of expansion as well.

Changes in the market value of securities are generally classified into the long-term trend, the cyclical movement and various short-term fluctuations. An investor engaged in holding securities rather than in buying and reselling them, is interested primarily in the long-term trend. Other fluctuations enter into his calculations only upon acquisition and final disposal. A long period comprising a number of business cycles will normally elapse between the two transactions.

The probable future yield of an investment as modified by the individual trends of e, x, k and i can be computed from formula III. by using separate symbols for the opening and closing values of all variables. The index "z" will distinguish values at the end of the period from those at the beginning.

$$\epsilon = \frac{(v + m_z)(1 + x_z) - (v + m) + v(e_z - x_z)}{v + m}$$

$$\epsilon = \frac{e_z - x_z + \dfrac{v + m_z}{v}(1 + x_z)}{\dfrac{v + m}{v}} - 1$$

Formula I. furnishes both the original and the corrected trend values of the market premium at the beginning of the year for insertion into this modified form of formula III.:

$$\text{V.} \qquad \epsilon = \frac{e_z - x_z + (1 + x_z)\left[\left(\dfrac{1 + x_z}{1 + i_z}\right)^{k_z}\left(\dfrac{e_z}{i_z} - \dfrac{e_z - x_z}{i_z - x_z}\right) - \dfrac{e_z - x_z}{i_z - x_z}\right]}{\left(\dfrac{1 + x}{1 + i}\right)^k\left(\dfrac{e}{i} - \dfrac{e - x}{i - x}\right) + \dfrac{e - x}{i - x}} - 1$$

$$\left[\begin{array}{c}\text{yield per \$1}\\ \text{of trend value}\end{array}\right] = \frac{\left[\begin{array}{c}\text{earning}\\\text{trend}\\\text{at end}\\\text{of year}\end{array}\right] - \left[\begin{array}{c}\text{expansion}\\\text{trend}\\\text{at end}\\\text{of year}\end{array}\right] + \left[1 + \left(\begin{array}{c}\text{expansion}\\\text{trend}\\\text{at end}\\\text{of year}\end{array}\right)\right] \times \left[\begin{array}{c}\text{Trend value of \$1 book}\\\text{equity at beginning of}\\\text{year recomputed by us-}\\\text{ing new trends of vari-}\\\text{ables as ascertained at}\\\text{end of year.}\end{array}\right]}{\left[\begin{array}{c}\text{Trend value of \$1 book}\\\text{equity at beginning of}\\\text{year obtained by using}\\\text{original trends of all}\\\text{variables.}\end{array}\right]} - 1$$

An examination of this expression shows that the yield will increase if:

a. the earning rate increases....................$(e < e_z)$
b. the expansion rate increases...............$(x < x_z)$
c. the willingness to rely upon future expansion increases.........................$(k < k_z)$
d. the money rate decreases................$(i > i_z)$

Movements in the opposite direction will correspondingly decrease the yield.

A situation deserving special attention is introduced by the exponent k. It was already stated that after the end of the expansion period is definitely in sight, no expanding investment can earn more than the money rate, because k, instead of remaining constant, begins to decrease by a unit for each year elapsed to become zero when expansion stops on the date foreseen. Solving formula V. for

$$\left.\begin{array}{l}k_z = k - 1\\ e_z = e\\ x_z = x\\ i_z = i\end{array}\right\} \text{accordingly gives the result}\ldots\ldots\underline{\underline{\epsilon = i}}$$

In practice the date when expansion will stop can hardly be guessed correctly the first time. In all probability the expansion rate will begin to decrease first and disinclination to look as far ahead as before will grow gradually. In such circumstances the yield will no longer conform to the general law (formula III.) but will slowly decrease toward the money rate, without suddenly dropping to its level as assumed above. On the other hand, disappointments arising from too optimistic forecasts may also occur and result in unexpected drastic cuts of investment values. This uncertainty as to the actual length of the expansion period, subject as it is to psychological reactions is probably the most powerful influence opposed to stability. A survey of stock quotations appears to prove that rapidly expanding corporate equities are especially volatile.

Whether formula V. is of any value to the short-term investor watching the business cycle is open to question, but it is barely possible that four separate estimates as to the probable cyclical changes in e, x, k and i would give a more accurate answer than a single guess endeavoring to estimate the net result of their complex interplay, even though such a guess be made by an investor fully conversant with the static laws of the yield.

II

The problem of stock dividends is closely connected with the problems of the yield. With the introduction of the Federal income tax almost twenty years ago, the question of whether stock dividends are income to the investor or not has become a favorite topic of debate in financial circles. The U. S. Supreme Court in its famous five-to-four decision of *Eisner v. Macomber* (252

U. S. 189) endeavored to settle the matter once and for all by decreeing that stock dividends were not income within the meaning of the Sixteenth Amendment, but it must be admitted now, more than a decade after the decision, that it has merely added fuel to the flames instead of extinguishing them.

To a considerable extent the difficulties are created by differences of opinion as to what is meant by "income" and "income realization." It is, indeed, impossible to draw conclusions as to whether stock dividends or any other dividends and distributions are income or not, without stating clearly, upon what interpretation of the two ambiguous terms those conclusions are based.

According to a standard definition, income is that flow of wealth which capital can yield without alteration of value. The ultimate form of income is cash in the hands of the investor, but the same income may be identified at much earlier stages as gravitating toward him in intermediate forms. An investor unwilling to recognize income in any other form than cash will say that realization takes place only upon final conversion into that medium. Another may, with equal justification, measure his income immediately at the source or in any one of the subsequent stages and forms assumed in the course of its flow toward him. Realization then, is a relative term implying conversion of income from an unrecognized form into a recognized, that is a measured form. How close to the final stage measurement shall take place depends upon the investor's needs. The greater the distance from the source, the simpler the measuring process, but the less even the flow measured by it.

Let us take the simplest case, that of a long-term investor who must receive cash before he concedes that he has received income. To him, evidently, stock dividends are just scraps of paper. What he wants to know is whether the proceeds from the sale of stock are income or not.

At first sight, the answer appears to be easy. If the original cost of the corporate equity was less than the present value of the equity not disposed of, the entire proceeds of the shares sold are income, otherwise the impairment of capital must be made good from the proceeds and only the remainder, if any, is income. In other words, the number of shares which may be sold without encroachment upon the original capital bears that proportion to the number of shares owned immediately before the sale, which the increase in the value of the investment since acquisition bears to its present trend value.

In circumstances conforming to the example introduced on page 274, this rule of proportion would work perfectly. As long as the end of the expansion period is not in sight, earning and expansion rates of 10% result in an annual increase of 10% in the trend value of the stock. If the company distributes a 10% stock dividend at the end of each year, the proceeds from its sale can be considered income, because such action reduces the investment to the exact original value. The investor will start each succeeding year with an initial investment of $31.844 per share, consisting of $10 of book equity and $21.844 of market premium. This investment will increase to $35.028 by the end of the year, whereupon one-tenth of a share will be received free of charge, reducing both the book equity and the trend value of a share to what they were at the beginning.

The trend value and the book value of the investment can also be maintained constant irrespective of whether and at what rate the company chooses to distribute stock dividends. For instance if it distributed 21 shares for each 100 held, 11 shares could be sold; if it distributed 3200 shares for each 100 held, 300 would represent the increment of wealth accrued since the beginning of the year. In the absence of any distribution whatever, the sale of $9\frac{1}{11}$ original shares would accomplish the same purpose.

Conditions are slightly different whenever the earning and expansion rates differ. Let us take the case of a company which has an earning rate of 10% and an expansion rate of 6% (see page 278). At the end of a year a book equity of $10 has increased to $11 as in the first example and this would apparently enable the company to claim that a 10% stock dividend was paid entirely out of earnings for the year because, after such a distribution, the book value of a share would be $10 as at the outset. Actually, the $10 represent productive capital only to the extent of $10.60 : 1.1 = $9.63. The rest, e.g. 40¢ : 1.1 = 36¢ is sterile, because earnings in excess of the expansion rate cannot be reinvested and should have been distributed in cash. This explains why a 10% stock dividend, said to be entirely out of corporate earnings, reduces the trend value of a $10 book equity from $25.97 at the beginning of the year to $27.9282 : 1.1 = $25.39 at the end. The same amount invested in the company is worth less, because its earning power has decreased from 10% to 9.64%.

To maintain the earning power of a $10 share at 10% the company should have issued a 40¢ cash dividend and a 6% stock dividend. Failure on its part to do so will make it necessary for the stockholder to safeguard his productive equity. For every share of stock he owned at the beginning of the year, he should retain 1.1 : 1.06 = $1\frac{2}{53}$ shares, at the end, and sell only $\frac{33}{530}$ of a share instead of the entire one-tenth received. The total trend value of the investment at the end of the year will then be $1\frac{2}{53} \times $25.39 = 26.347, as against $25.97 at the beginning. The difference of .40 : 1.06 = .377 represents the undistributed sterile equity of 36¢ per new share. It is noteworthy that this difference cannot be cashed by selling stock without impairing the productive equity owned. All that can be done is to borrow 36¢ a share in anticipation of cash dividend. Such a step, in turn, would demonstrate conclusively that the retention of sterile wealth by the company entails a loss of interest to the stockholder.

The third example given (page 278) may now be examined. The earning and expansion rates are 10% and 14% respectively and a 10% stock dividend is again declared, reducing the book value of the holdings from $11 to $10 and their trend value from $45.021 to $40.928. While the book value thus returns to the starting point, the market considers the stock more valuable than at the beginning of the year. The difference of $1.085 is the value of the privilege of contributing 36¢ to the corporate treasury for every $10 of equity already outstanding. As in the case of the sterile cash dividend of the second example, there is no way in which the stockholder can cash the additional yield of $1.085 per new share, equal to $1.1937 per old share, without impairing his productive equity, unless the company distributes subscription rights. And if such rights are not distributed, the stock will be reduced to the level of an investment expanding at the rate of 10%, that is to $31.844 for a $10 book equity.

If the company chooses to distribute stock dividends at a rate other than 10%, the stockholder can again compensate the effects of such a step. A stock dividend of 13% would, for instance, reduce the book equity from $11 to $9.734 and the trend value from $45.021 to $39.841. Thus the trend value would return to its approximate level at the beginning of the year, but the book value would drop lower, indicating a loss of productive equity. As in the second example, the number of shares to be retained at the end of the year for every share held at the beginning is found by performing the division 1.13 : 1.1 = $1\frac{3}{110}$. After selling $\frac{113}{1100}$ of a share the total trend value of the investment will be $1\frac{3}{110} \times 39.841 = 40.928$, exactly as if a 10% stock dividend had been sold in its entirety.

From the foregoing, the following conclusions may be drawn with respect to income realization through the sale of stock:

1. It does not matter in essence whether or at what rate the company distributes stock dividends since the number of shares representing the increment of wealth to be cashed can be determined in any event.

2. The company can, however, simplify the investor's problems by declaring stock dividends at that rate which will give the

dividend stock a value equal to the increment of wealth to be cashed.

3. The rate of distribution which will give stock dividends a value equal to the increment of wealth to be cashed is the rate at which corporate earnings are reinvested, e.g. the lower of the earning or expansion rate.

4. Corporate earnings in excess of the expansion rate should not be cashed through the sale of stock. The proper procedure is to await the declaration of a cash dividend.

5. The increment of wealth arising from the company's ability to expand at a rate higher than the earning rate should not be cashed through the sale of stock. The proper procedure is to await the distribution of subscription rights and sell them.

6. The value of the subscription privilege equals the value of the rights issued only if the subscription price equals the book value. If the price is lower, the rights are worth more, the difference being in effect a stock dividend. If the price is higher, the rights are worth less, and stock is, in effect, returned.

In general it may be said that from the stockholder's point of view the ideal corporate dividend policy would be one which would distribute his entire increase of wealth at regular intervals by :

a. declaring stock dividends at the rate at which corporate earnings are reinvested.
b. paying cash dividends with that portion of corporate earnings which can not be reinvested.
c. issuing subscription rights which equal in value the premium payable for the privilege of contributing new capital.

If such a policy were followed, the book value of a share would be maintained constant. As for the trend value, changes would be limited to the trends of the money rate, the earning and expansion rates and the forecast of the expansion period.

The fact that corporations make no attempt to maintain the book value of a share constant makes it much harder for the lay-investor to grasp the significance of corporate actions, because the value of dis-

tributions is seldom equal to the increment of wealth which he may cash without impairing his capital. To safeguard investors against the dangers which might arise from considering all distributions as income to the full extent of their market value, various rules have been formulated at one time or another. The oldest and best-known of these rules limits income-realization to the receipt of dividends in cash, property and evidences of indebtedness and to profits on sale. Stock dividends or rights are said to effect only a change in the number of paper certificates evidencing corporate equities and therefore their sale can result in income only to the extent that the selling price exceeds the pro-rata cost. This is the rule upheld in *Eisner v. Macomber* and prescribed by income tax regulations. As a protective measure, it is ineffective in some respects and too stringent in others. Thus it does not guard against impairment of capital through the distribution of corporate earnings accumulated during the period preceding the purchase of the stock by the investor nor against the dilution of equities through the issuance of bonus shares or other distributions and subscriptions not made pro-rata. On the other hand it prevents the investor from realizing the greater part of the increase in the value of his investment from year to year, because expansion makes corporations reluctant to part with a substantial portion of the wealth derived from their earnings. Upon final sale of the stock, the increments of many years are realized in one lump sum. Apart from the injustice resulting from progressive rates of taxation, such a method makes it impossible for the investor to live in a style commensurate with his wealth.

The second rule is sponsored by the New York Stock Exchange. It proposes to measure the value of any distribution by the amount charged to surplus by the issuing company. Immediately upon receipt, stock dividends are recognized to result in income to that arbitrary extent, which is usually the par or stated value of a share. This amount is accordingly added to cost and credited to the income account. Upon sale, further income may arise in the form of a profit on sale to the extent that the selling price exceeds the pro-rata cost so adjusted. If the corporate surplus is small, e.g. when the book value of the stock consists mostly of its par value, the rule provides a limited relief from the income tax rule. Unfortunately, the modern tendency toward stocks without par value or with only a nominal par value has, in many cases, reduced the amounts charged to surplus to negligible pittances, because par or stated values are merely insignificant fractions of the total book value. In such circumstances, the relief is likewise negligible.

The Stock Exchange rule would become far more equitable, if it also compelled the issuing company to charge the entire book value of all distributions to earned surplus. No matter what corporations choose to call their distributions the amount of the corporate equity which the investor liquidates when selling any distribution is its book value, which remains unaffected by transfers from surplus to capital stock made for the sake of record. Melons, split-ups, stock dividends said to be out of current earnings and subscription rights alike represent corporate equity to the extent of the difference between the book value of a share immediately before and after the distribution (subscription). And this is really the crux of the problem. Justified as it would seem to compel a corporation to record all its distributions at their book value instead of at arbitrary figures dependent upon irrelevant or misleading descriptions, considerations or intentions, there is no real need for placing either the investor or the corporation under tutelage. The general rule for the guidance of the investor can be summed up in four words: "Watch the book value!"

The rule that the stockholder's investment has been impaired whenever its total book value becomes less than it was at the time of acquisition provides effective protection against impairment of capital through the distribution of corporate earnings accumulated prior to purchase and against the dilution of equities through the

issuance of bonus shares or other distributions and subscriptions not made pro-rata. In other respects the rule can be used exactly as the Stock Exchange rule. The only difference is that whereas, under the Stock Exchange rule the phrase "earnings distributed" is subject to arbitrary interpretation by the company, the book value rule gives it a uniform meaning. Distributions are defined as that portion of the total book equity, which is transferred from the original symbol of investment to the newly distributed symbol, whether that be a cheque, a right or an additional stock certificate. "Earnings distributed" in turn, equal that fraction of the entire book value of a distribution which will not reduce the book value of the old stock certificate below what it was at the date of acquisition. By using these definitions, it will be possible to realize a greater portion of the total annual increment of wealth without departing from the fundamental principle of the Stock Exchange rule, designed to prevent inflation (see part III.).

The next step forward will be to recognize that profits on sale arise not only from secondary market fluctuations which offer an equal chance for losses, but also from a disregard of the laws of the yield described in part I. It was shown that the income yielded by an expanding investment is not limited to corporate earnings, but must in the long run be higher at least in amount, if not also in rate. What repercussions a change in book value has upon the trend value of various stocks was also illustrated. Generalizing, it may be said that the trend value of each dollar of book equity will remain constant as long as the elements entering into the computation of the trend remain constant and as long as the common equity is managed properly. Proper management, in this sense, means that excess earnings or excess expansion are currently distributed: the former in cash or property and the latter in the form of subscription rights. The issuance of stock dividends is not necessary, but desirable. (N.B. The fact that cash dividends and subscription rights often occur together should not be taken as a sign of improper management. In such cases subscription rights are issued not at the excess of the expansion rate over the earning rate, but at that differential plus the cash dividend rate per dollar of book equity.)

The rule that each dollar of book value commands a constant premium, may be called the "proportionate premium" rule. Its application to the problem of the investor who considers cash as the only realized form of income is simple:

The entire cash proceeds of any distribution irrespective of form and even the selling price of original shares may be consumed without encroachment upon the original capital, provided the book value of the shares retained does not drop below that of the original investment at the time of purchase.

All that need be done upon receipt of any distribution, whether in the form of a cheque, a right or a stock certificate, is to compute the book value of the investment "ex" the distribution. If it is more than it originally was, all is well; if it is less, enough stock must be retained from distributions or reacquired from their proceeds to restore the shortage in book value. Normally, the information furnished by quarterly balance sheets permits the computation of book values at intermediate dates with sufficient accuracy. Familiarity with the corporate dividend policy will enable the investor to formulate a simple routine for cashing as much of his annual increase in wealth as he likes without being forced into a position which makes reinvestment necessary. (See examples on pages 282-283.)

If no investor owned stock in more than one corporation, insistence upon the annual cashing of the entire yield of a stock would probably be more widespread. A diversified portfolio introduces a somewhat different problem: How to cash the yield of a good investment by selling one not so desirable. That can be done only if it is permissible to write up the cost of the good investment by crediting income. Cash capital realized from the sale of the less desirable invest-

ment can then be withdrawn and spent by charging income. Naturally enough, investors confronted with such a situation are inclined to deny that the receipt of cash or property from the company is a prerequisite of income-realization. The problem is particularly acute in the case of trusts which must distribute cash to their beneficiaries while receiving little or no cash from the very stocks which have the highest yields. The Stock Exchange rule was originated to remedy this evident defect of the income tax rule but, as already stated, the relief is never adequate and often negligible. The inimical pressure forcing the sale of good stocks when it would be better to hold them, accordingly persists, because profit on sale is the only substantial form of income realization permitted.

The proportionate premium rule as applied to income-realization from distributions not cashed will read as follows:

The entire trend value of any distribution may be charged to cost and credited to the income account provided the resulting cost bears no higher ratio to the total book value of the entire holdings after the distribution than the original cost of the investment bore to its original book value.

Further examination will show that income-realization need have no connection whatever with distributions, but may be achieved by the simple expedient of comparing the opening and closing balance sheets of the company.

The increase in the book value of the holdings multiplied by the quotient of the recorded cost over the opening book value will give the number of dollars to be added to cost and credited to the income account.

Under this method of accruing income, distributions are entirely divested of their function as income-carriers and are considered mere changes in the form of the investment.

The limitations of the proportionate premium rule as applied to the problems of the private investor may be restated once more:

1. The recorded cost of the investment must not be greater than its trend value.

2. The long-term outlook must warrant the conclusion that the elements entering into the computation of the trend value have remained constant.

3. The corporate management must neither retain sterile wealth, nor overlook possibilities for expansion.

An additional responsibility is placed upon the corporate management, when the total capitalization includes not only common stock, but senior securities as well. In such cases the earning and expansion rates of the corporation should not be confused with the earning and expansion rates of the common stock. The latter are no longer independent variables reflecting business conditions alone, but are also subject to change whenever the proportionate volume of senior capital is changed. The problems of financing through senior securities have not been injected into the deductions concerning the yield of common stocks because they are worthy of separate consideration. Without entering into details beyond the scope of this essay, it may be said that established corporations usually maintain an approximately constant ratio between the common equity and the senior capital outstanding. As long as this ratio remains constant, the changes in the earning and expansion rates of the common stock will be proportionate to the changes in the earning and expansion rates of the entire corporate capital.

An examination of a number of the leading common stocks for a period of years shows that adherence to the proportionate premium rule would have resulted in a more even income-realization than actually obtained through the use of other rules. That, however, does not mean that periodic investment analyses have become unnecessary. After all, a rule is merely a more or less successful attempt to translate a complicated theory into simple terms. It can never be superior to the detailed application of the theory itself. When all is said and done, it will be difficult to improve upon a method of income realization which consists of measuring and comparing capital levels annually by giving due consideration to all factors affecting security prices.

The truth that present facilities for the measurement of the capital level are inadequate need not lead to the conclusion that no improvement is possible. The first step forward ought to be the definite establishment of the economic principles involved and the elimination of the legal concept of income from the discussion of stock values and yields. Income arises when money or money's worth passes, not from one legal person to another, but from one economic unit to another. A corporation and its stockholders are different entities only in contemplation of law. Corporate distributions accordingly do not create income, but merely carry it from one pocket to another and their receipt may or may not be considered to result in realization, depending upon where the flow is measured. In the last analysis, income is created by corporate operations.

A second obstacle, e.g. the halo of mystery and prestidigitation surrounding corporate finance could be lessened greatly by standardizing the tools used, so as to make their nature and purpose clear even to the uninitiated. All legitimate aims of management can be reached by means of a few very simple devices; the infinite variety available at present merely obscures the facts. If those facts could be readily understood, gullibility would decrease and market fluctuations would be subject to greater restraint. Elimination of unethical speculative practices would further compress the daily quotation curve toward the long-term trend, thereby greatly enhancing its practical value.

III

An outline of the investment theories advanced would not be complete without a brief reference to the dangers of inflation which may arise from their indiscriminate application. This danger may be illustrated as follows:

The stock of an operating company having earning and expansion rates of 10%

is valued on the books of a corporate investor at \$3.18 for a \$1 book equity in accordance with the example given on page 274. It was demonstrated that, *as long as the end of the expansion period is not in sight*, the investor's wealth of \$3.18 is compounded at the rate of 10%, although the company itself compounds only \$1 at that rate. If the stock of the holding company is offered for sale, it can apparently be urged that it also has an earning and expanding power of 10% and is therefore likewise worth \$3.18 per \$1 of its book equity. Any number of additional holding companies organized in a chain and owning no assets other than the stock of their respective predecessors in the chain could advance the same pretension. The result is that a book equity of \$1 invested in the operating company, which costs only \$3.18 if acquired at first hand, will cost 3.18^2, 3.18^3, 3.18^4 and so on up to 3.18^n, depending upon whether it is represented by the stock of the second, third, fourth or n-th link of the chain.

That is manifestly absurd, but it would be premature to conclude that the whole theory must needs be fallacious. Mathematically, the solution is indicated by the phrase italicized above: ". . . as long as the end of the expansion period is not in sight. . . ." In the circumstances assumed, a price of \$3.18 for a \$1 book equity means that the purchaser is willing to pay for only the first ten years of expansion. The first holding company, however, can expand for ten years only if the operating company will expand for thirty-five years. The stock of the third link of the chain, in turn, can be worth the same selling price per unit of its book value only if the second link expands for thirty-five years, which it can do only if the first link expands for sixty years. The price of the n-th company's stock, finally, implies the continuous expansion of the operating company for $10 + 25(n - 1)$ years. (N.B. These results are obtained from formula II. on page 277. The pyramid was built by neglecting to investigate the expansion periods of the holding companies.

If the operating company will expand for only ten years, the first holding company cannot expand at all. Its earnings will be limited to the money rate on the book value (See pages 274 and 281, which gives its stock a market (trend) value equalling the book value (See page 276, item 1). All other holding companies will be in the same position and no inflation can arise, except by misrepresentation.

From the economic point of view the error consists of overlooking that there is a difference between legal entities and economic entities, and that economic theories can be applied only to the latter and not to the former. The chain may well consist of n legal units, but it is obvious that it represents only a single economic unit; the operating company. The holding companies are scraps of paper and nothing more. Pursuing this thought to its logical conclusion, it will be found that ownership, by a company, of another company's stock is meaningless. Economic theory recognizes only the instrument of production and its ultimate owner; intervening symbols of legal ownership have no substance. Any attempt to consider such empty symbols as original instruments of production will lead to inflation whenever the element of expansion is present.

In final analysis, then, no negotiable symbol of productive and reproductive wealth should be appraised on the basis of its yield, if it is issued in whole or in part against similar symbols already so appraised. This principle requires that consolidated balance sheets and income accounts be prepared in accordance with standard accounting procedure for the entire group whose ownership is evidenced by the stock to be appraised. The proportionate premium rule, therefore, can be used only by private investors or by organizations which do not issue publicly marketable evidences of equity. Public corporations can take up income from corporate stock only within the limits of the book value rule (see page 285) or by the process of consolidation, depending upon whether distributions are considered necessary to income realization or not. Accruing increases in book value would be a substitute for consolidation in the case of minority interests.

The apparent restrictions which are thus placed upon the practical application of the yield-theory may, in the eyes of many, detract a great deal from its value. It should be remembered, however, that ultimately all wealth is owned and enjoyed by natural persons, not by legal or artificial persons. The scope of the theory is, therefore, universal; at any rate in so far as the universe itself is natural and not artificial.

"THE FAIR VALUE AND YIELD OF COMMON STOCK"

The Accounting Review (June 1936), pp. 130–140

THE FAIR VALUE AND YIELD OF COMMON STOCK

Gabriel A. D. Preinreich

ONE OF THE most important problems of corporate finance is the valuation of proprietary equities. A good deal has been said and written upon the subject, chiefly from the viewpoints of buyer and seller bargaining for a going concern, and the fundamental principle governing valuation for such purposes is, generally speaking, well understood. The same principle, however, has a much wider scope; it not only explains the basic phenomena of the stock markets, but also furnishes the essential clue to a unified theory of corporate distributions.

Any number of contradictory and often absurd notions are still current on the ways and means of determining the investor's income from common stock, those incorporated into laws or handed down by courts being by no means always the most reasonable. No progress can be made in this field, which is of the utmost practical importance to investors, until a solid foundation of theory is laid. Only after the general principles underlying the value and yield of common stocks are thoroughly understood, will it be possible to formulate subsidiary principles concerning the nature and meaning of the often highly complex economic services, which an investor derives from common stock.

The general law governing the value of capital goods has been known for some time. It may be stated briefly by saying that any capital good may be bought or sold for the present value of all future services expected from it. This rule is continuously being applied in practice by bond-traders and all bond tables are based upon it. Nevertheless, apparently no one has made systematic use of it to explain the formation of common-stock values. Discussions upon the subject are frequent, but they seldom clear the hurdle of terminological difficulties. Indeed they are often adjourned, before the participants realize that they have not been speaking the same language.

To review this preliminary difficulty,

Fig. 1 may be examined. The bar C at the extreme left represents the corporate capital paid in upon organization. It is connected to the right with a shorter bar representing corporate earnings for the first year. These earnings are shown divided into two parts: The lower black area equals one year's interest on the capital and the unshaded area atop it indicates corporate earnings in excess of the normal interest rate. The diagonally shaded bar connecting the top of the first year's earnings with the bottom of those of the second is the cash dividend paid at the end of the first year. For subsequent years, earnings and dividends alternate in the same manner, until the entire capital is returned by a final liquidating dividend at the end of the tenth year.

In accounting terminology the black bars are called "interest on investment," the unshaded bars "excess (corporate) earnings" and the sum of both "(corporate) earnings." The terms "income" and "profits" are synonymous with "earnings" for all purposes germane to the present discussion. The diagonally shaded bars are "dividends," except that the last one, or at least that portion of it which returns the original investment is known as a "liquidating dividend."

A number of economists, Irving Fisher among them, use a different terminology. To them "income" means the diagonally shaded bars ("dividends" to the accountant). "Earnings" are used in the accountant's sense; "capital gain" is the difference between "earnings" and "income." Finally the phrase "services actually rendered by capital" is synonymous with "income," while "capital gain" is further defined as "services which capital might have rendered in addition without suffering reduction below its original level."

Apparently discussion will be facilitated by avoiding the use of the term "income." "Earnings," from the investor's point of view, are that portion of the entire corporate earnings, which are applicable to his hold-

46

ings. The investor's return from his investment is usually called the "yield." "Services" may be used interchangeably with "distributions" as generic terms including "dividends" as well as all other valuable things received from the company, e.g., rights, warrants, etc.

"Capital value," "fair value," "fair market value" or "present value" is the theoretical level around which the continuous oscillations of actual market quotations are, in

the same data have been redrawn in Fig. 2, giving recognition to the fact that earnings accrue gradually, while dividends are distributed suddenly. Fig. 2 accordingly shows book values prevailing at various dates in a form suggestive of the edge of a saw. Above this curve of book values, the corresponding capital values have been plotted. The descending steps are the cash dividends and are therefore equal for both curves but, whereas book values between dividend dates

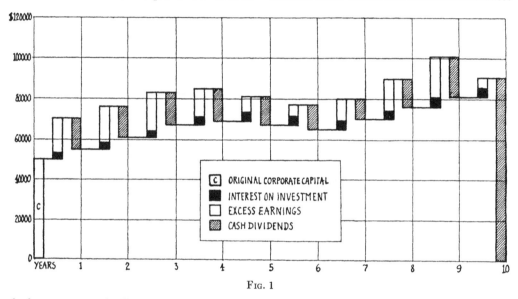

FIG. 1

the long run, evenly distributed. Prof. Fisher devotes considerable space in his works to the proof that capital value can be obtained only by discounting "services" (which he calls "income") and not by discounting "earnings." That is true, although accountants have long been using an alternative method of computation, which is equally correct. Goodwill is commonly obtained by discounting "excess earnings." If the original investment (C) is added to the goodwill, the same capital value results as from the discounting of "services." In other words, the discounted value of the unshaded areas in Fig. 1 equals the discounted value of those shaded diagonally. The black areas are mere payments for time and must be disregarded.

To show clearly the connection between the (corporate) book values presented in Fig. 1 and the corresponding capital values,

increase irregularly by greater or smaller earnings, capital value increases instead at a constant rate, the rate of interest. From this comparison a fundamental rule of investment can immediately be derived:

No investment can yield either more or less than the money rate, if all data upon which its value depends are known.

This is the case of a safe bond. The complications surrounding the computation of the fair value of common stock arise chiefly from uncertainty regarding the extent of the future services which may be expected. In the absence of definite information, it is necessary to fall back upon estimates based upon past performance, analysis of the future market in the corporation's product and forecasts of general economic conditions. For comparative purposes, information so obtained is most useful when expressed in terms of a common unit, i.e., when converted into rates. To accomplish this task, a fundamental difference between loan-funds and business-equities must be borne in mind.

In the money-market it is always assumed that the earning power of capital is matched by an equal power to compound its own earnings. This assumption is justified, whenever earning power is derived from a contract enforceable at law and backed by the borrow-

tal good and is therefore at work under special conditions which enable it to produce earnings at one individual rate and opportunities for new investment at another. The market-dollar, on the other hand, merely has an expectation of earning the money rate and expanding at the same rate. The problem of finding the fair market value of equities accordingly consists of finding that number of market-dollars, which equal

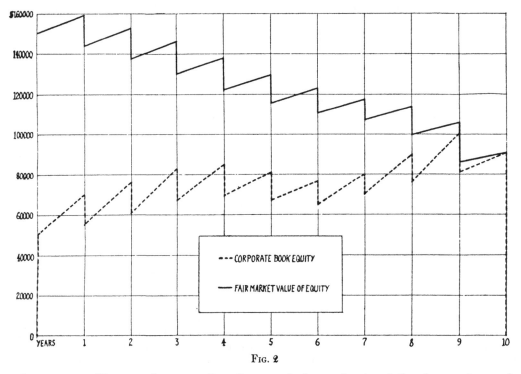

FIG. 2

er's resources. The proprietary equity of a business, however, is in a different position; its earning power is derived, not from a contract, but from successful business operations. It will depend entirely upon the degree of success, how much, if any new investment is needed from year to year in that particular business. In such circumstances, it must be recognized that earning power and ability to expand are two distinct concepts, neither of which is necessarily governed by the other.

In effect then, there are two kinds of dollars, which may be called the production-dollar and the market-dollar, respectively. The former is invested in a productive capi-

a single production-dollar in earning and expanding power.

So far the analysis has called attention to the existence of three different rates, which may be defined as follows:

1. The *earning rate* is the quotient of earnings by that portion of the corporate net worth which represents productive assets. This excludes idle assets which may have been hoarded.
2. The *expansion rate* is the rate of increase of the productive corporate net worth owned by the investor.
3. The *money rate* is the rate at which the future services of capital are discounted.

The derivation of these fundamental rates from primary business data often requires extensive mathematical and statistical analysis, the various steps of which cannot be described in an outline of theory. The mere mention of these rates, however, is sufficient to call attention to another fundamental principle of investment:

The fair market value of any investment capable of the perpetual compounding of its own earnings at a rate higher than the money rate must be infinite.

the problem of appraising common stocks is shown in Fig. 3 on the usual semi-logarithmic or ratio chart.

The straight line *I* represents the sum of $1 compounded at the prevailing money rate. Line *II*, having a slope twice as steep, accordingly represents an investment, the earning and expansion rates of which equal twice the money rate. If it is guaranteed to retain its productivity for say *n* years, its present value (capital value) P_n can be ascertained graphically by drawing the cor-

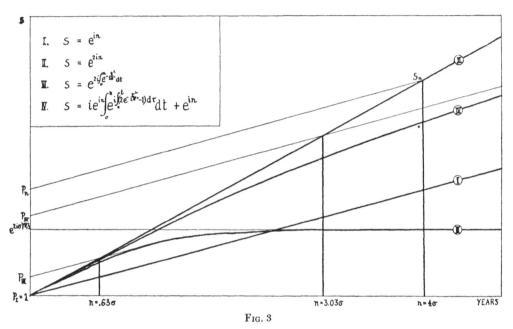

FIG. 3

This proposition is self-evident because, in such circumstances, the shrinkage through discounting is less than the growth through compounding. There are many listed stocks which have in the past demonstrated earning and expanding capacities in excess of the money rate. That their market quotations have not reached infinity even at the height of the 1929 boom is due to the fact that future services are discounted not only at the money rate, but also at the *rate of risk*, which rises to practically infinity even for comparatively short finite periods. The mathematical expression of risk is the probability curve or curve of error described in textbooks on statistics. Its application to

responding ordinate to obtain the sum S_n and then tracing a discount line parallel to *I*, until it intersects the axis of ordinate at the point P_n.

Curve *III* represents an investment, the the earning and expansion rates of which, although estimated to equal those of *II*, have both been discounted for their probability over a period of *n* years by using a curve of error with a standard deviation of $n/4$. The present value P_{iii} of this investment is obtained by drawing a tangent discount line, which intersects the axis of ordinate at the point P_{iii}.

Curve *IV*, finally, was plotted on the supposition that an earning rate equalling twice the money rate can be expected indefinitely,[1] but that a similar expansion rate must be discounted for its probability over a period of n years. The present value P_{iv} of this investment is indicated by the asymptote having the slope of the money rate, which must be retraced from infinity to the intersection P_{iv}.

Curves *III* and *IV* were chosen at random from many other possibilities to illustrate the two extremes in the application of the theory of probability to future earnings and expansion. In the natural order of development, when the market of the corporate product becomes more and more saturated, the expansion rate will decline first, while satisfactory earnings may be maintained for a long period thereafter. The expansion rate, therefore, must usually be discounted for its probable duration over a shorter period than the earning rate. Thus, most actual situations could be covered by applying some compromise method less extreme than either of those used in computing *III* and *IV*.

All these compromises, using curves of error with different standard deviations for the earning and expansion rates respectively are too difficult to compute for practical purposes, but fortunately their relationship to simpler curves not involving the probability-integral is easily established. All that need be noted is the approximate location of the points where the discount lines determining the present values of the complicated curves intersect the simple curves, of which *II* is an illustration. Thus, for instance, the present value of *III* for $.19n$ years (i.e., up to the point where its earning and expansion rates have been discounted for risk to the level of the money rate) is the same as that of *II* for $.15n$ years approximately. Similarly, the present value of *IV* for an infinite period is the same as that of *II* for about $.75n$ years.

For practical purposes, therefore, all the intricacies connected with the curve of error can be avoided by substituting shorter periods not discounted for risk for the longer discounted ones. Whether consciously or not, this principle has long been observed in practical computations of goodwill, which generally estimate the period of future excess earnings at a very conservative number of years, varying somewhat according to the type of business. In effect then, a *horizon* or sudden limit to perfect visibility is set up as a substitute for a greater distance of gradually declining visibility into the fog of the future. This *horizon* has the same function as the date of maturity in the case of a bond and is the fourth element determining the value of common stock, the other three being the earning, expansion and money rates already introduced.[2]

Now it may be objected that, just as the price of a bond is computed from the coupons, it seems easiest to appraise common stock by estimating the future stream of dividends, without paying any attention to such mathematical intricacies as earning and expansion rates. That is indeed often done in practice, but since common stocks have no coupons, such guesses can have but little value, unless it is clear to the person making the guess that it is the interplay of earning and expansion rates which determines both the form and the size of the distributions which it is reasonable to expect.

Even cursory observation shows that there are various kinds of corporations. In certain cases the retention of the entire earnings is insufficient to provide for necessary expansion. Other corporations can reinvest only a portion of their earnings, while some are unable to do so at all. These apparent differences in kind often represent merely successive stages of development reached by different corporations. It is an important duty of the corporate management to formulate dividend policies which conform to these conditions. A company which cannot reinvest its earnings, must distribute them; slowly expanding companies will distribute the difference between the total earnings and

---

[1] At normal money rates the difference between the respective values of a perpetuity and a hundred-year bond is negligible. Any period exceeding a hundred years may therefore be considered infinite for practical purposes.

[2] The computation of the horizon for a given common stock involves the mathematical fitting of a trend line to the time series of actual market quotations per dollar of book equity.

that portion which can be reinvested. Rapidly expanding companies, in turn, will not only endeavor to retain all earnings, but must in addition attract new capital. This fundamental connection between earnings, expansion and distributions may be called *the principle of good management* which *requires that corporate directors shall neither retain sterile earnings, nor overlook opportunities for expansion.*

Upon this foundation it is possible to build a unified theory of corporate distributions which will clear up all the apparent contradictions and misconceptions so prevalent in this important field.[3]

The interplay of the four elements determining the value of common stock may be illustrated by four purposely simplified examples, all of which assume an earning rate of 10% p.a., a money rate of 6% p.a. and a horizon of five years.[4]

Example A

If the expansion rate is nil, $100 of book equity will be worth $116.85, obtained by discounting an annuity of five payments of $10 each and a final payment of $100 due five years hence.

Example B

If the expansion rate is 5% p.a., one-half of each year's earnings will be reinvested and the other half distributed. A book equity of $100 is therefore worth $118.52, computed by discounting an annuity of five payments growing gradually from $5 to $5 × 1.05⁴ and adding thereto (105/1.06)⁵.

Example C

If the expansion rate is 10% p.a., no cash dividends will be available and the value of a $100 book equity is (110/1.06)⁵ = $120.35.

Example D

If the expansion rate is 15% p.a., contributions amounting to one-half of each year's earnings must be obtained outside. A book equity of $100 having this expanding capacity must be worth $122.35, because only an annuity growing from $5 to $5 × 1.15⁴ is lacking to make it worth (115/1.06)⁵.

Let us see now what happens a year after these investments were made. If the appraisal of a year ago is confirmed, investors will now estimate that the horizon is only four years ahead. Accordingly, each of the four investments will increase in value at the money rate; *A* from $116.85 to $123.86 (of which $10 is the cash dividend awaiting distribution), *B* from $118.52 to $125.63 (of which $5 is the cash dividend awaiting distribution), *C* from $120.35 to $127.27 and *D* from $122.35 to $129.69 (because only $5 is needed to make it worth (115/1.06)⁴ = $134.69).

As a matter of fact, however, investors did not really know that the companies would liquidate at the end of five years. They merely refused to look farther ahead. If prospects remained unchanged during the year elapsed, they will again be willing to look five years ahead and, seeing no signs of an approaching end, will be inclined to repeat last year's bargains of buying $100 book equities for $116.85, $118.52, $120.35 and $122.35 respectively. By doing so, they will pay these prices for 100/100, 100/105, 100/110 and 100/115 of the original productive equities which cost the same amounts a year ago, but have expanded in the meantime. In other words, the market values of the four investments have risen as follows:

Example A

From $116.85 to $126.85, accounted for by $10 of sterile earnings awaiting distribution.

Example B

From $118.52 to $129.45. The earnings are again $10, but one-half of them can be invested productively and therefore creates additional goodwill to the amount of $18.52 × .05 = $.93.

Example C

From $120.35 to $132.39. The earnings of $10 can be reinvested, thereby creating $20.35 × .10 = $2.04 of additional goodwill.

---

[3] See the author's *The Nature of Dividends*, New York, 1935.

[4] The fair values stated in the four examples may be obtained either be discounting each payment separately or from the general formula

$$P = \frac{r-i}{x-i}\left[\left(\frac{1+x}{1+i}\right)^h - 1\right] + 1.$$

In this formula P = fair market value of $1 of book equity; r = earning rate; x = expansion rate; i = money rate and h = horizon.

Example D

From $122.35 to $135.70. The expectation that a contribution of $5 will be invested in addition to $10 of earnings, creates new goodwill amounting to $22.35×.15 = $3.35.

It may therefore be said that:

Until the end of operations emerges upon the horizon, the fair market value of a given proportion of the total corporate equity increases at its expansion rate as adjusted for accrued, but unpaid distributions or contributions.[5]

book equity at the time zero. With the passage of time, they separate, each following its own expansion rate through the interaction of successive earnings and distributions. The slope of the lines representing the earnings corresponds to the earning rate of 10% p.a. for all book-value curves.

The market-value curves start at the respective initial fair values computed for examples A to D on page 135. For the first five years, while the end of corporate opera-

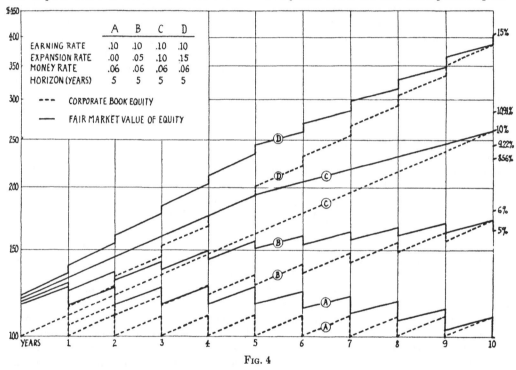

FIG. 4

Fig. 4 presents the four examples graphically on a semi-logarithmic chart covering a period of ten years, at the end of which it is assumed, for the sake of illustration, that the four companies will actually liquidate. Of these ten years of corporate operations, however, the investor's vision extends only to the five years next ahead at any given date.

The book-value curves drawn as dotted lines start from the common origin of $100

---

[5] This definition of the long-term trend is the starting point for investigations into cyclical problems arising from the more or less regular fluctuation or change of the elements here considered constant.

tions is below the horizon, the trend of market values runs parallel to book values (i.e., if the bottoms of successive dividends were connected, the slopes of the resultant lines would equal the respective expansion rates). The yield lines, however, do not run parallel to the earning lines of the book-value curves. Each market-value curve has its own yield-slope, which means that each investment has a different yield (see below, page 138).

For the second five-year period all the different yields are reduced to the money rate, corresponding to the principle stated on page 131. This causes a convergence toward the respective book-value curves, until each pair meets at the end of the tenth year, when liquidation takes place.

It should not be assumed from the foregoing that the dividends (positive or negative) used in the examples are the only ones in the respective circumstances which conform to the principle of good management. There is an unlimited range of equally correct ways, of which only the simplest was illustrated. Distributions may be classified with respect to their effect into three main groups:

1. Dividends in cash, property and evidences of indebtedness decrease corporate net worth;
2. Stock dividends leave corporate net worth unchanged;
3. Rights increase corporate net worth, if they are exercised.

The dividend policies assumed in examples A to D may therefore be supplemented by the declaration of stock dividends at any rate desired and also by any combination of cash dividends and subscription rights so calculated that their offsetting effects will reduce to the assumptions made in the examples. Furthermore, the value of a right equals the value of the subscription privilege only if the subscription price of a share equals its corporate book value. Rights entitling to subscription at lower or higher prices combine the effects of positive or negative stock dividends with those of pure rights.

If the investor exercises all rights and refrains from selling any of the stock dividends received under such an alternative distributive policy, Fig. 4 remains unchanged, since it shows the evolution of the total investment, irrespective of the number of shares which may represent it at different times. If, on the contrary, he sells such distributions, he will reduce the expansion rate of his investment and receive compensation therefor in the form of a higher stream of "actual services." A profit or loss will in addition result from such transactions, whenever the daily market quotations are above or below the long-term trend (capital value) of the investment.

Distributions not conforming to the preëmptive right of stockholders fall into the same three groups as those conforming thereto. They accordingly affect the corporate book value curve in the same manner. As for the investor, the difference is that he receives no compensation for the reduction in the expansion rate of his investment. To the extent that the intention of making such distributions is known in advance, market values will be lower. Unless distributions contrary to the preëmptive right save at least their equivalent in operating expenses (for instance when bonus shares are given away to reduce the interest rates on a bond issue), they violate the principle of good management from the investor's point of view.

Just as there is an infinite variety in dividend policies conforming to the principle of good management, it is possible to imagine any number of policies offending against it in one of two ways: They will either dissipate the productive corporate capital, or they will accumulate more capital than can be used productively. In the first event, the investor will lose the difference between the yield and the money rate on the productive equity improperly distributed and in the second event he will lose interest on the funds unproductively hoarded in the corporate treasury. If the dividend policy is properly chosen, no such losses can result. Another important rule, therefore, is the following:

The yield of common stocks is not dependent upon the corporate dividend policy so long as that policy conforms to the principle of good management.

In the long run, this rule is subject only to secondary qualifications in so far as one kind of distribution may have a form-utility superior to another because it may be easier to dispose of, because it may create a smaller income tax liability, etc. Those, however, are individual considerations differing with each investor.

The concept of the *yield*, as used here, must, of course, be clearly understood. The term is frequently employed in a number of different senses. Sometimes it means the quotient of annual cash dividends over the market price of the stock, sometimes that of corporate earnings over market values and sometimes even less significant ratios. In the sense of the mathematical analysis, upon which this essay is based, *yield* is the first derivative or instantaneous rate of change of capital value, divided by capital value. Shorn of technicalities, it is the annual rate of return of an investment, computed by adding the increase in its fair market value to the fair market value of the distributions received during the year and dividing that sum by the fair market value at the beginning of the year.[6] Thus the yield is for:

Example A $.00 + \dfrac{.10 - .00}{1.1685} = 8.56\%$

B $.05 + \dfrac{.10 - .05}{1.1852} = 9.22\%$

C $.10 + \dfrac{.10 - .10}{1.2035} = 10.00\%$

D $.15 + \dfrac{.10 - .15}{1.2235} = 10.91\%$

In Fig. 4 these yields may be determined graphically by drawing lines from the lower left hand corner parallel to the slopes of the yield-lines of each investment. The results are shown on the scale at the right of the chart. It should be clear from Fig. 4 that the yield formula is valid only so long as the end of corporate operations is below the horizon. To emphasize this limitation, it may be said that yields differing from the money rate can occur merely because errors are continuously made in the appraisal of investments. High-grade common stocks are, on the average, undervalued from year to year for fear that the unforeseen may happen, as it occasionally does. As soon as the information available is so accurate as to preclude error in the appraisal, the yield must fall to the level of the money rate. In

---

[6] This reduces to the general formula

$$\epsilon = x + \frac{r - x}{P}$$

where ϵ stands for the yield. The other symbols are explained in note 4.

the case of most well-known stocks, this contingency is still very remote.

If the dividend policy is not restricted to distributions or contributions of cash, the same yields can be derived from alternative computations indicated in the circumstances. Be it assumed, for instance, that for the first five years in Fig. 4 dividend policies are selected, which will keep both the corporate book value and the fair market value of a share of stock constant by increasing, at the respective expansion rates, the number of shares representing the original investment. This will mean for:

Example A

No change. Cash dividends of $10 each year yield $10/116.85 = 8.56\%$.

Example B

Cash dividends of $5 p.a. as before, followed each year by a 5% stock dividend, yielding $(5 + 124.45/21)/118.52 = 9.22\%$.

Example C

Stock dividends at the rate of 10% per annum, yielding $(132.39/11)/120.35 = 10\%$.

Example D

Either annual rights of 1:22 @ $110 followed by a 10% stock dividend or annual rights of 1:6⅔ @ $33.33. The yield in either event is

$$10.91\% = \frac{(135.70 - 110)/23 + \left(135.70 - \dfrac{25.70}{23}\right)\Big/11}{122.35}$$

$$= \frac{(135.70 - 33.\overset{..}{3}\overset{.}{3})/7.6\overset{.}{6}}{122.35}.$$

It may be worth mentioning that a dividend policy maintaining the book value of a share (ex current earnings) constant would have enormous practical advantages for the stockholder without interfering in the least with legitimate aims and purposes of management. It would make the mystery of corporate earnings and distributions intelligible even to the most unsophisticated investor, because his original purchase would always be represented by the same number of shares. Anything else on hand, whether cash, rights or shares, would have to be the surplus accumulated since acquisition. This situation would prevail until the end of corporate productivity emerges upon the horizon, at which time he had best change to another investment.[7]

Additional light can be thrown upon the behavior of fair market values and yields by considering special cases. Some of the principal rules obtainable in this manner[8] are the following:

1. When the earning rate equals the money rate, the expansion rate and the horizon lose their significance. The fair market value of the investment will equal the book value and the yield will equal the money rate.

2. If the company is not expanding, the fair market value of $1 of corporate equity will be somewhere between $1 and the quotient of the earning rate over the money rate, depending upon the distance of the horizon. The yield will correspondingly be somewhere between those two rates. (The quotient of earning rate over the money rate is the value of a perpetuity, which can yield only the money rate.)

3. If the expansion rate equals the money rate, the goodwill or market premium commanded by the book equity equals the product of the excess earnings by the horizon. This is the rule of thumb often used for computing goodwill.

4. If the expansion rate equals the earning rate, the fair market value of $1 of book equity can be computed by compounding it at that rate up to the horizon and discounting it at the money rate back to the present. The yield will always equal the earning rate and is independent of changes in the money rate or the horizon.

5. Whether the expansion rate is higher or lower than the earning rate, the yield will always be between the two. But a decrease in the money rate or an increase of the horizon will enhance the yield when the expansion rate is higher and reduce it when the earning rate is higher (and vice versa).

6. When the money rate is very high, the fair market value of investments is very low. Whenever the money rate exceeds the

earning rate, any horizon short of infinity will result in a yield lower than the money rate.

7. When the money rate is very low, the fair market value of investments is very high, and their yields correspond closely to their expansion rates.

8. When the visibility into the future is zero, market values will equal liquidating values, regardless of earning, expansion and money rates.

9. If the visibility into the future is unlimited and if the earning rate is higher than the money rate, an expansion rate equal to to or higher than the money rate results in an infinite fair market value. On the other hand, if the expansion rate is lower than the money rate, the fair market value equals the excess of the earning rate over the expansion rate, divided by the excess of the money rate over the expansion rate. The yield will equal the expansion rate or the money rate, whichever is higher.

In using these rules, it is essential to bear in mind that the base of the earning and expansion rates is $1 of corporate book equity, whereas the base of the yield is $1 of fair market value. This means that whenever an earning rate in excess of the money rate occurs in conjunction with an expansion rate, no matter how small, the stockholder's wealth increases by a greater amount than the amount earned by the company on the same block of stock. Thus in examples A to D all four companies make $10 on $100 while the four investors' wealth increases by $10, $10.93, $12.04 and $13.35 respectively.

This conclusion has often been denounced as a fallacy, although it merely states the evident fact that the privilege of converting market-dollars at par into production-dollars is valuable. Outsiders excluded from such a transaction are therefore bidding up the price of stocks entitling to the privilege. Fallacious conclusions are reached, however, if the yield is mistaken for earnings. Earning power is the principal cause of capital value, whereas the yield is merely its effect. If the corporate book equity be compared to a tree, capital value is its shadow. Reinvested earnings correspond to the growth of the

---

[7] For an exposition of this idea cf. note 3, pp. 60 and 64, *The Nature of Dividends*.

[8] By solving for special values the formulae given in notes 4 and 6.

tree, sterile earnings to the fruit and the yield to the lengthening of the shadow. To complete the simile, the horizon and the earning, expansion and money rates correspond to the sun and its rays. The slope of the rays determines the shadow without affecting the tree.

Whereas, in nature, no one can stand a shadow upright and make it cast another shadow, this feat has been made possible in corporate finance by permitting a company to hold stock in another. That is what a company does, when it claims that the yield of the stocks in its portfolio constitutes its own earnings.

In example D it was found that, in the circumstances assumed for illustrative purposes, $100 of corporate book equity had a fair market value of $122.35 and that the investor derived a yield of 10.91% or $13.35 therefrom. By organizing a chain of holding companies, each of which owns no property other than the stock of its predecessor in the chain and by keeping each company's stock recorded at its market value on the books of its parent, it is temporarily possible to inflate the market value of the nth company's stock to the nth power of $122.35, at which level it will apparently yield $13.35 to the nth power.

The structural flaw in this pyramid is, of course that separate legal units are masquerading as separate economic units, although the whole chain taken together represents no more than the operating company alone. The holding companies are scraps of paper, nothing more. Pursuing this thought to its logical conclusion, it will be found that ownership by a company, of another company's stock is meaningless; symbols of legal ownership interpolated between a productive capital good and its ultimate natural owner can have no substance. Any attempt to consider such empty symbols as original instruments of production will lead to inflation whenever the yield is higher than the money rate.

This principle is recognized in the preparation of consolidated financial statements, but the recognition has only a limited effect, because such statements are prepared only for affiliated groups subject to a single control. The principle applies with equal force in the absence of control, from investment trusts on down to the last few shares acquired by a bona-fide operating company for the temporary storage of excess cash. An element of inflation is therefore included in the market quotations of many common stocks, but is most pernicious in the case of investment trusts, where the so-called "leverage effect" is sometimes enormous. The market value of such a stock accordingly rises or falls by a multiple of the rise or fall in the market value of the securities held in the portfolio.

The investor would do well to remember that buying stocks in the market amounts to buying shadows, the length of which depends upon the sun as much as upon the tree. It is all the more important for him to ascertain whether he is buying the shadow of a tree or merely the imaginary shadow of a shadow.

GOODWILL AND VALUATION

"THE LAW OF GOODWILL"

The Accounting Review
(December 1936), pp. 317–329

The Accounting Review

| VOL. XI | DECEMBER, 1936 | No. 4 |

THE LAW OF GOODWILL

GABRIEL A. D. PREINREICH

THE BASIC LEVELS of thought which have guided jurists in their formulation of the legal concept of goodwill are the same as those along which economic analysis has developed. According to the exigencies of the cases before them, the courts have paid attention in turn to consumer-psychology, to the factors which produce goodwill, and to the value which may be placed upon it in terms of money, as well as to the safeguarding of the benefits conferred by goodwill in order to permit its peaceful possession and transfer.

Attempts to define goodwill and list its principal characteristics disclosed, first of all, that it has no independent existence of its own. Early opinions, therefore, are concerned more with what goodwill attaches to than with what it consists of. It originally appeared in the form of the rental value of land and its earliest known mention occurs in conjunction with land in 1571 (Wills & Ind. N.C. Surtees 1835, p. 352): "I gyve to John Stephen . . . my whole interest and good will of my Quarrel" (i.e. quarry).[1]

LOCAL GOODWILL

The oldest known decision on goodwill is said to be *Broad v. Jollyfe*, 1620 (Cro. Jac. 596; Noy 98). It concerns the validity of a promise by a mercer not to keep shop in Newport, in the Isle of Wight, in consideration of the plaintiff's purchasing his stock at prime cost. The court held the promise to be good, remarking that "it is but the selling of his custom and leaving another to gain it."

Far better known is the case of *Crutwell v. Lye*, 1810 (17 Ves. Jr. 335), in which the sale of the goodwill of a country waggoner was in litigation, causing Lord Chancellor Eldon to formulate his famous definition that goodwill "is nothing more than the probability that the old customers will return to the old place." Lord Langdale expressed the same view, when he said in *England v. Downs*, 1842 (6 Beav. 269): "It is the chance or probability that custom will be had at a certain place of business, in consequence of the way in which that business has been carried on." And in *Austen v. Boys*, 1858 (27 L.J.Ch. 714), it was held that, "When a trade is established in a particular place, the goodwill of that trade means nothing more than the sum of money any person would be willing to give for the chance of being able to keep the trade connected with the place where it has been carried on."

The basic idea was put forward even more bluntly in *Comm. of Inland Rev. v. Glasgow, etc. Railway*, 1867 (L.R. 12 A.C. 315): " . . . in strictness, the thing which is to be ascertained is the price of the land." However, "if by reason of the rise in the value of property in the neighbourhood the saleable value of the business has increased, that is a favorable chance which has befallen the tenant" of a public house who was entitled by agreement to receive, upon termination of his lease, a sum equalling the value of the goodwill (*Lewellyn v. Rutherford*, L.R. 10. C.P. 456–7). In *Musselman and Clarkson's Appeal*, 1869 (62 Pa.St. 81) the court held that goodwill "attaches to and enhances the value of reality and the value

---

[1] *Cf.* P. D. Leake: *Commercial Goodwill*, Sir Isaac Pitman & Sons, Ltd., London, 1921.

of it is realized in renting or selling that." And it is affirmed in *Elliott's Appeal* (62 Pa. St. 161) that goodwill is purely local in character and tends to pass with the land to the purchaser or lessee. Among other cases may be mentioned *Rawson v. Pratt*, 1883 (91 Ind. 9), which practically repeats the statements made in *Austen v. Boys* above, and *Cottrell v. Babcock Printing Press Mfg. Co.*, 1886 (54 Conn. 122), where goodwill was found confined to a particular stand. The case of *George v. Coal Co.* (83 Tenn. 458) refers to a monopoly of location through exclusive contracts for the establishment of company stores in lumbering and mining camps.

Attempts at more formal definitions of goodwill are made in *Metropolitan Bank v. St. Louis Dispatch Co.* (36 Fed. 722): "It is intangible property which, in the nature of things, can have no existence apart from a business of some sort that has been established and carried on at a particular place." Also in *Vonderbank v. Smith* (44 La. Ann. 276): "Goodwill is the favor which the management of a business wins from the public and the probability that all customers will continue their patronage. It is the general public patronage and encouragement which a business receives from its customers on account of its local position; that is the subject of value and price and of bargain and sale, though intangible." In this definition the patronage concept is dominant, although its dependence upon location is still mentioned.

PATRONAGE AND TRADE CONNECTION

In general it may be said that the emphasis upon the local aspect of goodwill has declined gradually, although there has been considerable overlapping of views in point of time. It appears that a decision rendered as early as 1743 uses the land concept only by way of analogy. The children of a deceased newspaper printer and publisher demanded their share of the business from his widow and executrix and the claim was allowed by Lord Hardwicke, who said: "Suppose the house were a house of great trade, she must account for the goodwill of

it" (*Giblett v. Reade*, 9 Mod. 459). It is not clear whether the premises were owned by the estate or not. In 1817 it was likewise decided that "the very circumstance of sole ownership gives . . . an advantage beyond the actual value of the property and which may be pointed out as a distinct benefit essentially connected with sole ownership", rather than with location alone (*Kenney v. Lee*, 3 Mer. 441).

Almost sixty years later, Sir John Romilly, Master of the Rolls, cautiously decided that goodwill "seems to be that species of connection in trade, which induces customers to deal with a particular firm" (*Wedderburn v. Wedderburn*, 1855. 22 Beav. 84). The case of *Crawshay v. Collins* (15 Ves. Jr. 224) affirms that this connection consists of the disposition, confidence and faith of customers. And "it is the formation of the connection which has made the value of the thing which the late firm sold and they really had nothing else to sell in the shape of goodwill. Is it to be supposed that they did not sell that personal connection when they sold the trade or business and the goodwill thereof?" (*Ginesi v. Cooper*, 1880. L.R. 14. Ch. Div. 600). In the leading case of *Trego v. Hunt*, 1886 (A.C. 7; 12 T.L. 80) Lord Macnaghten defined goodwill as "the whole advantage, whatever it may be, of the reputation and connection of the firm, which may have been built up by years of honest work, or gained by the lavish expenditure of money." The facts upon which this definition is based were that Trego took Hunt into partnership with the understanding that the latter would not thereby obtain any interest in the goodwill of the firm. Upon Trego's death, his widow commissioned Hunt to carry on for seven years. When this term drew to a close, Hunt employed a clerk to copy the names and addresses of all customers. Held, that Hunt may properly be restrained from "either personally or through his partners, servants or agents, applying privately, by letter or personally or by a traveller, to any person who was prior to the date of the sale a customer of the old firm, asking such customer to continue after the sale to deal with him and not to deal with the purchaser" who he l acquired the goodwill from the widow.

A number of comparatively recent American decisions contain definitions of goodwill much in the same vein. For example in *Rowell v. Rowell*, 1904 (122 Wis. 1) it is called "a beaten pathway from the seller to the buyer" and in *Dodge Stationery Co. v. Dodge*, 1904 (101 Wash. 383) "a well-founded expectation of public patronage." In *Chittenden v. Whitbeck* (50 Mich. 401) the point is emphasized that "the favor which the management has won from the public and the probability that the old customers will continue their patronage" is not transferred by a mere sale of the premises, because trust, confidence and esteem may be attached to some other material object.

GOODWILL ATTACHED TO
STOCK-IN-TRADE

The goodwill of a vendor of victuals was held to be an incident of the stock and license, but not of the premises in *Geo. Fox Co. v. Glynn*, 1906 (191 Mass. 349) and in the two earlier cases of *Cruess v. Fessler*, 1870 (39 Cal. 336) and *Herford v. Cramer*, 1884 (7 Col. 485). The last two decisions overruled the defendants' claims that they had not sold the goodwill because the stock alone was worth the full amount paid by the purchasers.

COMPREHENSIVE DEFINITIONS
OF GOODWILL

The firm name as an element of goodwill is first mentioned in *Churton v. Douglas*, 1859 (1 Johnson 174), when Vice Chancellor Wood gave the following definition:

Goodwill must mean every advantage that has been acquired by the old firm, whether connected with the premises in which the business was previously carried on, or with the name of the firm, or with any other matter carrying with it the benefit of the business.

Lord Lindley in *Comm. of Inland Rev. v. Muller & Co.'s Margarine*, 1901 (A.C. 217) was still more explicit:

Goodwill regarded as property has no meaning, except in connection with some trade, business or calling. In that connection I understand the word to include whatever adds value to a business by reason of situation, name, reputation, connection, introduction to old customers and agreed absence from competition or any of these things, and there may be others which do not occur to me.

Judge Story's definition is also frequently quoted:

The advantage or benefit which is acquired by an establishment beyond the mere value of the capital, stock, funds or property employed therein in consequence of the general public patronage and encouragement which it receives from constant or habitual customers on account of its local position, or common celebrity, or reputation for skill, or affluence, or punctuality, or from other accidental circumstances or necessities, or even from partialities or prejudices.[2]

The foregoing definitions show that there are many forms of goodwill besides that which is attributable to a definite location. Nevertheless, all these forms originally arose from personal efforts or qualities and now differ only to the extent to which it is possible to separate them from persons and attach them to a tangible object or visible sign which may be transferred. The study of goodwill, in this sense, is a study of the ways and means of making it transferable.

PERSONAL GOODWILL

Purely personal goodwill has often been denied recognition merely because it was thought to be entirely untransferable. Thus it was held in *Austen v. Boys*[3] that "the term goodwill seems wholly inapplicable to the business of a solicitor." Similarly in *Bain v. Munro* (5 Rettie 422): "... in a business of a professional nature the goodwill is of so intangible a nature as to be impossible of transference and not of appreciable value." And in an American case: "The practice of a physician is a thing so purely personal, depending so absolutely on his personal skill and ability, that when he ceases to exist it necessarily ceases also, and after his death can have neither an intrinsic nor a market value" (*Mandeville v. Harman*, 1886. 42 N.J. Eq. 185).

---

[2] *Story on Partnerships*, §99.
[3] *Supra*, p. 317.

That portion of professional goodwill which is transferable has been defined by Sir George Jessel in *May v. Thompson*, 1882 (L.R. 20. Ch.D. 705): "What is the meaning of selling a medical practice? It is the selling of the introduction of the patients of the doctor who sells to the doctor who buys. He has nothing to sell except the introduction." In an earlier case such an introduction was mentioned as constituting goodwill when accompanied by a vendor's covenant not to compete with the vendee: ". . . very frequently the goodwill of a business or profession, without any interest in land connected with it is made the subject of the sale, though there is nothing tangible in it; it is merely advantage of the recommendation of the vendor to his connections and his agreeing to abstain from all competition with the vendee" (*Potter v. Commissioner*, 1854. 10 Exch. Rep. 146). That even a posthumous introduction may be valuable was held in *Thomson v. Winnebago County*, 1878 (48 Iowa 155), where a list of names and addresses found among the records of a deceased land agent was ordered sold as an asset of his estate. Similarly the goodwill of a deceased dentist became a part of his estate in *Morgan v. Schuyler* (79 N.Y. 490).

"The goodwill of a commission merchant, originating with himself and carried on without capital for fifteen or twenty years, would seem rather to resemble that of a doctor or lawyer than that of a retail merchant" (*Kremelberg v. Thompson*, 87 N.J. Eq. 659). But in *Davie v. Hodgson* (25 Beav. 181) the goodwill of a commission merchant was declared valuable only if the vendor agreed not to carry on the same business.

Even before the limited transferability of personal goodwill was generally recognized, some attention was given to its special characteristics in English and Scottish land tax cases. For instance, in *Assessor for Lanark v. Selkirk* (14 Rettie 579) the court ruled that to the extent to which goodwill was of a personal nature, it could not be included in the rates assessed. Another English decision concerning personal goodwill is *Cooper v. Metropolitan Board of Works*, 1883 (25 Ch.D. 472), which held that if goodwill depends on the skill of the seller, it is not transferred merely through the sale of the premises. An American case to the same effect is *Smith v. Gibbs*, 1862 (44 N.H. 335), holding that the sale of a business with its goodwill "does not include the popularity and personal qualities of the seller, which are not transferable."

VENDORS' COVENANTS

A promise by the seller that he will not compete with the purchaser derives its importance from the fact that most forms of goodwill are to a certain extent both local and personal. A number of cases already cited refer to vendors' covenants, among them characteristically enough the oldest case on record, i.e. *Broad v. Jollyfe*.[4] Another early decision holding such a promise valid is *Mitchell v. Reynolds*, 1711 (1 P. Williams 181; I.S.L.C., 9th Ed., p. 430). In this case the plaintiff had taken over the defendant's lease for five years of a bake house in the parish of St. Andrews, Holborn, the defendant binding himself not to exercise the trade of baker within that parish during that term.

Where it is evident that goodwill is nothing but a personal connection established in a local area, it has been held that the vendor's covenant is the only valuable consideration involved in the sale, regardless of whether or not it has been expressly mentioned. A Massachusetts case in point is *Angier v. Webber*, 1867 (14 Allen 211), forbidding the seller of a teamster's route to solicit custom along it, even though it was not claimed that the defendant had agreed to refrain from competition. Other decisions which protect the purchasers of newspaper or milk routes against the sellers are *Senter v. Davis*, 1869 (38 Cal. 450), *Tuttle v. Hannegan*, 1874 (54 N.Y. 686), *Munsey v. Butterfield*, 1882 (133 Mass. 492) and *Wenzel v. Barbin*, 1899 (189 Pa. St. 502).

On the other hand, there are cases on record which permit competition by the seller. In *Cottrell v. Babcock Printing Press*

---

[4] *Supra*, p. 317.

Mfg. Co.[5] the decision that goodwill was confined to a particular news stand resulted in judgment for the defendant, who was allowed to compete and did in fact maintain his stand in the immediate vicinity. With respect to the trade of a Boston department store it was held in *Basset v. Percival*, 1862 (5 Allen 345) that the custom or trade appertained strictly to the place of business, which was surrounded by an area containing further inchoate patronage and potential goodwill separate from that already adhering to the store. The seller was, therefore, restrained from soliciting his old customers, but permitted to set up another establishment near the first to compete for the potential custom which might still be attracted.

Crutwell v. Lye,[6] made famous by Lord Eldon's definition of goodwill, also belongs in this category except for the fact that the goodwill was sold, not by the owner, but by his trustees in bankruptcy. It was therefore held that a bankrupt has no obligation to refrain from reengaging in the same business subsequent to his discharge. This privilege of a bankrupt is still recognized.

The case of *Myott v. Greer* (90 N.E. Rep. 895) is of interest because it concerns the assignment of the rights enjoyed under a vendor's covenant, which provided that the seller may not compete for ten years within a radius of twenty miles. The plaintiff organized a corporation, then dissolved it, and resumed the business individually under the original name of the defendant, who had in the meantime likewise reengaged in business in the same town. The complaint was rejected on the ground that a resolution of the company's board of directors reassigning the goodwill and covenant to the plaintiff was not binding upon the defendant and insufficient to give the plaintiff the right to maintain suit.

The general principles governing restraint of trade by voluntary agreement were laid down as early as 1711 in *Mitchell v. Reynolds*.[7] Freedom of contract demands that such agreements be set aside as rarely as possible because the owner of a business possesses the legal right to his custom and goodwill and may part with it under certain conditions. Contracts in partial restraint of trade are, therefore, beneficial to the community, so long as the terms are reasonable, but limitations as to time and place are generally held essential. Unlimited restraint is contrary to public policy, not only because it tends to deprive the seller of his livelihood and the state of the services of a useful citizen, but also because it tends to centralize control over industry and to create monopolies.[8]

FIRM AND TRADE NAMES

The name is a means of identifying the business to which goodwill attaches, and as such it is entitled to protection against unauthorized use. This principle is outlined in *Levy v. Walker*, 1879 (10 Ch.D. 436):

A man has the right to say: "You must not use a name, whether fictitious or real; you must not use a description, whether true or not, which is intended to represent, or calculated to represent to the world that your business is my business, and so by fraudulent misstatement deprive me of the profits of the business which would otherwise have come to me." That is the principle, and the sole principle, on which this court interferes.

The firm name was first included in a definition of goodwill by Vice Chancellor Wood.[9] In the United States, federal court decisions consider it an important element:

"The goodwill of a business comprises those advantages which may inure to the purchaser from holding himself out to the public as succeeding to an enterprise, which has been identified in the name and repute of his predecessor" (*Knoedler v. Boussod*, 45 Fed. 465). " . . . all that good disposition which customers entertain toward the house of business identified by the particular name of the firm, and which induces them to continue giving their custom to it" (*Washburn v. National Wall Paper Co.*, 1897 (81 Fed. 17).

In *Cooper v. Hood*, 1858 (26 Beav. 293) it was held that the use of the name, the vendor's covenant and the trade mark were all

[5] *Supra*, p. 318.
[6] *Supra*, p. 317.
[7] *Supra*, p. 320.

[8] *Cf.* C. J. Foreman: *Efficiency and Scarcity Profits*, University of Chicago Press, 1930, pp. 124–26.
[9] *Supra*, p. 319.

included in the goodwill of the enterprise. The sale of a periodical includes the sale of the right to use the old name or title (*Bradbury v. Dickens*, 1859. 27 Beav. 53). But the name of a theatre attaches to and is transferred with the premises (*Booth v. Jarrett*, 1876. 52 How. Pr. 169). In the case of a deceased dentist the court mentioned separately his goodwill and the name of his firm as assets of his estate,[10] while in *Slater v. Slater*, 1903 (175 N.Y. 143) the name was said to be included in goodwill.

With reference to trade names the decision in *Brock v. Paine*, 1912 (28 R.P.C. 697) deserves mention: "The plaintiffs having for nearly fifty years applied the words 'Crystal Palace' to their goods, it was irrelevant to consider whether they had still got the right to give displays at the Crystal Palace. The words did not imply that they had and therefore the plaintiffs are entitled to a perpetual injunction" restraining the defendants from using the same name, even though they had succeeded to the privilege of displaying fireworks there.

In principle, a person can not be prevented from using his own name in business, even though another person having the same name is already established in the same field. Thus in *Brinsmead v. Brinsmead* (29 T.L.R. 706 C.A.) it was held that "there being no evidence of dishonesty, the defendant could not be restrained." The courts will, however, carefully scrutinize the evidence to detect fraudulent intentions. For instance, when the brother of the original manufacturer of preparations known as "Holloway's Pills and Ointments" opened an establishment only a few doors away and not only called his products by the same name, but also used similar pill boxes, pots, labels and wrappers, the petition for an injunction was granted (*Holloway v. Holloway*, 1850. 13 Beav. 209).[11]

The legal protection accorded to firm or trade names is a step toward increasing the transferability of goodwill by attaching it, not to the person who originated it, but to the organization with which he was originally connected.

The rule is also firmly established that a trade name may not be sold apart from the business which has built up the goodwill adhering to it. *Thorniloe v. Hill,* 1894 (1 Ch. 569) illustrates this rule, the court having held that even if anything was assigned, it was merely the right to use the name John Forrest, London, unconnected with any business. This being a mere assignment in gross, was void.

In the case of *Geo. Fox Co. v. Glynn*[12] the name, as well as certain distinct characteristics of the merchandise, was involved. The decision mentions that "it is important to everyone who has built up a valuable goodwill in that way" (*i.e.* through advertising its name and through square and honest dealing) "to have it protected as his other property is protected." The plaintiff was a well-known bakery and obtained protection against infringement for the particular kind of bread it produced, the loaves of which were of a definite shape, size and quality.

TITLES AND AWARDS

The privilege of displaying coats of arms of the ruler or the princes of royal blood, accompanied by the title: "Purveyor to H. M. the King," etc., is seldom mentioned nowadays as an element of goodwill, although in many countries it is still a distinction in great demand, obtainable only with great difficulty or at great expense. The endorsement of other important personages in the public eye is also valuable on the the theory that their goodwill attracts the custom of the rank and file.

Medals and certificates of merit awarded at expositions are often reproduced on labels, and more recently there has been a tendency to obtain the approval of professional associations or bureaus of standards, such as the American Medical Association, the Good Housekeeping Institute, etc. All these forms of goodwill are protected by the courts against unfair practices.

---

[10] *Morgan v. Schuyler, supra,* p. 320.
[11] *Cf.* also *McLean v. Fleming,* 1877 (96 U. S. Rep. 245), listing over a dozen specific points involved in the protection of trade names and trade marks.

[12] *Supra,* p. 319.

TRADE MARKS

Interesting excerpts from the history of trade names and trade marks have been assembled by Rogers.[13] The identification of traders and their wares by means of symbols is a practice as old as trade itself. Regulation soon followed, capital punishment being inflicted upon many occasions both for failing to mark goods and for marking them improperly or with fraudulent intent.

The modern law of trade marks has developed from these ancient statutes and thus has an independent origin, since goodwill as a legal concept has not arisen until much later. For this reason trade marks are often considered a separate subject, although they are nothing more than one of the many forms in which personal goodwill manifests itself. The tendency to draw a distinction is apparent in *Peltz v. Eichele*, (62 Mo. 177):

The goodwill of a business, as embodied in the firm name or in the labels used will be protected on principles analogous to those applied in cases of infringements of trade marks. It is true that a trade mark is held by some textbook writers and perhaps in some adjudicated cases, to be a part of the goodwill and necessarily included in the sale thereof.

The principles of protection are outlined in *Ransome v. Graham*, 1882 (51 L.J.Ch. 897):

A manufacturer who produces an article of merchandise which he announces as one of public utility, and who places upon it a mark by which it is distinguished from all other articles of a similar kind, with the intention that it may be known to be of his manufacture, becomes the exclusive owner of that which is henceforth known as his trade mark. The property thus acquired by the manufacturer, like all other property is under the protection of the laws and for the invasion of the right of the owner of such property the law affords a remedy similar in all respects to that by which the possession and enjoyment of all property is secured to the owner.

A shorter summary is given in *Cash v. Cash*, 1902 (19 R.P.C. 181):

An honest man will wish to take all reasonable precautions to prevent his goods being confounded with those of other traders. If man is not an honest man, then the law will step in and make him behave like one.

The assignment of a "naked" trade mark is just as invalid as that of a trade name apart from the business to which it used to belong. A case in point is *Pinto v. Badman*. 1891 (18 R.P.C. 181), in which it was held that "a trade mark, when registered, shall be assigned and transmitted only in connection with the goodwill of the business concerned in the particular goods or classes of goods for which it has been registered and shall be determinable with that goodwill." And where an outgoing partner claimed the right to use the trade mark, judgment was rendered in favor of the partners remaining with the business because "if a business were sold without any word being said about the trade mark, the trade mark would be understood and held to pass to the purchaser" (*Shipwright v. Clements*, 1871. 19 W.R. 599).

If the surname of one person is the same as the trade mark of another, the question arises, as in the case of a trade name, concerning the extent to which deception is intended or possible. *In re Cadbury*, 1914 (59 S.J. 161) it was decided that "where the name in everybody's mind refers to the goods of one firm, such name is distinctive," which any valid trade mark must be. To avoid such difficulties, trade-mark statutes generally stipulate that descriptive, personal or geographical names may not be registered, except in the form of, or as parts of, fanciful and distinctive devices. Examples are signatures of misspelled descriptive words, etc.[14]

Modern advertising campaigns tend to concentrate increasingly upon trade marks at the expense of firm names. Certain brands have thus become household words, although not many consumers know the names of the respective manufacturers. This tendency further increases the transferability of goodwill by attaching it altogether to the product.

TRADE SECRETS, PATENTS AND COPYRIGHTS

A trade secret consists of confidential information pertaining to trade, manufacture

---

[13] E. S. Rogers: *Trade Marks and Unfair Trading*, A. W. Shaw Co., Chicago, 1914.

[14] *Cf.* note 11, *supra*.

or invention, the exclusive possession of which entails certain advantages of a differential or monopolistic nature. In order to receive protection as valuable goodwill, trade secrets must actually be secret (*Macbeth Evans Glass Co. v. Schnelbach*, 239 Pa. St. 76). An employee is "in equity and good conscience obliged to preserve them as sacredly as his own, and this as well without a contract as with it" (*Simmons Med. Co. v. Simmons*, 81 Fed. Rep. 163), because "the law will imply a promise to keep the employer's secret" (*Westervelt v. National Paper Co.*, 154 Ind. 673).

Such secrets may range all the way from simple lists of customers (*Stevens & Co. v. Stiles*, 29 R.I. 399; A.R. 802), a code key of prices in a sales catalogue (*Simmons Hardware Co. v. Waible*, 1. S.D. 486) or information in the possession of a counting-house clerk (*Tipping v. Clarke*, 2 Hare 393), to a manufacturing process (*Solomon v. Hertz*, 40 N.J. Eq. 400) or to engine drawings (*Merryweather v. Moore*, 61 L.J. Ch. 506). All these cases referred to employees, but the principle of protection operates in other cases as well. Thus in *National Gum & Mica Co. v. Braendly* (51 N.Y. Supp. 93) and in *Bryson v. Whitehead*, 1822 (1 Sim. & Stu. 74) the defendants were enjoined from using secrets sold by them and from thereby depriving the plaintiffs of valuable goodwill which they had purchased.

The law of patents has developed from a desire to give more adequate protection to certain forms of trade secrets and to reserve for a limited time to their originators the benefits derived from them. The foundations of modern patent law were laid when the Statute of Monopolies was promulgated in England in 1623. This statute granted the privilege "of the sole working or making of any manner of new manufactures within this realm, to the true and first inventors of such manufactures, which others at the time of making such letters patent and grants shall not use, so also as they be not contrary to the law or mischievous to the State."

It is universally conceded that a secret or discovery is patentable only if it involves an exercise of the inventive faculties. As to what is covered by this phrase, the U.S. Supreme Court declared in *McClain v. Ortmayer* (141 U.S. 427) that the word invention "can not be defined in such a manner as to afford any substantial aid" in this respect. "Courts, adopting fixed principles as a guide, have by a process of exclusion determined that certain variations in old devices do or do not involve invention, but whether the variation relied upon in a particular case is anything more than ordinary mechanical skill is a question which cannot be answered by applying the test of any general definition."

There are innumerable decisions in which this negative method of definition by exclusion has been followed in order to narrow down gradually the concept of a patentable invention. Thus it has been held that an application for a patent must be based upon something more than that which any efficient mechanic could easily produce (*Vinton v. Hamilton*, 104 U.S. 491). Nor is it enough that an improvement is new and has great economic advantages (*Hild v. Wooster*, 132 U.S. 700). Duplicating the parts of a machine is no invention, unless it causes a new mode of operation (*Dunbar v. Meyers*, 94 U.S. 197), nor can a mere assembly (*Reckendorfer v. Faber*, 92 U.S. 357) or a combination of old devices (*Hall v. MacNeale*, 107 U.S. 90) be so classified. It is often reiterated that the patent law applies only to subjects which contribute definitely to the useful arts (*Atlantic Works v. Brady*, 107 U.S. 199) and which are a product of the inventive powers (*Magin v. Karle*, 150 U.S. 391).

With respect to the ownership of a patentable invention, it has been said that mere suggestions or assistance from others will not give them a right to share in the benefits (*Pitt v. Hall*, 2 Blach. 229). Where a partner used all the facilities of his firm to devise improvements in the product manufactured by it, his patented inventions did not become the property of the partnership (*Belcher v. Whittemore*, 134 Mass. 330). Similarly in the case of employees, the courts have protected their personal rights to their own inventions, although developed at the expense of employers (*Barber v. National Carbon Co.*, 129 Fed. Rep. 370). In such circumstances, however, the partner or employee must usually grant a shop license to his firm, permitting the use of the invention without payment of a royalty. But this license need not be exclusive (same cases; also *Slemmer's Appeal*, 58 Pa. St. 156, *McClurg v. Kingsland*, 1 How. 202, and others), nor is it transferable upon dissolution of the corporation (*Peabody v. Norfolk*, 98 Mass. 40). There are also several cases in which it was held that the employer is entitled merely to the reasonable value of the assistance rendered in making the models and experiments, including the value of the employee's time (*Collar Co. v. Van Dusen*, 23 Wall. 563).

An employer may acquire a right to the inventions of his employees, if he engages them specifically as inventors. This condition must be clearly expressed in the contract of employment (*Hildreth v. Duff*, 143 Fed. Rep. 139).

If a patent is infringed upon through unauthorized use, the rightful owner may maintain an action for damages. The measure of his damages is the gain which the infringer has derived. This gain the claimant has the right to recover (*Mowry v. Whitney*, 14 Wall. 642 and others). The gain need not consist of a net profit; a smaller loss than would otherwise have resulted also reflects a gain from the use of the patent (*Mews v. Conover*, 125 U.S. 144, and *Celluloid Mfg. Co. v. Cellonite Mfg. Co.*, 40 Fed. Rep. 478).

A copyright is the exclusive right to reproduce, publish, and sell literary or artistic work. In this respect it is similar to a patent, except that the latter must be disclosed and belongs to the first person who does so in good faith, whereas an author's property in his work is not similarly restricted. To emphasize the difference, it is often said that if Milton had not written "Paradise Lost," no one else could have; but if Newcomen had not invented the steam engine, the same thought would have occurred to others, as in fact, it did.

The term for which patents are now granted in the United States is seventeen years, whereas copyrights are valid for twenty-eight years and may be renewed for a like period.

FRANCHISES AND GOING VALUE

A franchise expresses the goodwill of the commonwealth toward certain of its members, to whom it has granted certain privileges for their own and the public good. The most common form of franchise is that obtained by a company upon incorporation.

"Organization expense" is the name usually given to the cost of acquiring the franchise as well as to other outlays necessary in embarking upon an undertaking and in bringing about the decision to do so. All such expenditures are made only if it is reasonable to expect that avenues of profit will thereby be opened which would otherwise remain inaccessible.

The franchise of a public utility is the privilege of using public property in a business which could not be carried on without that privilege. "Going value" and "going concern value" are terms used in competitive business as well as in the public utility field in various senses. Usually, however, they are meant to represent the difference between the market or saleable value of an enterprise and its depreciated original cost or its reproduction cost. But whereas in the competitive field the essential similarity between goodwill and going value is not denied, it has been held that, in the case of a public utility, going value and franchise can not represent goodwill because "a monopoly has no goodwill, for its customers are retained by compulsion, not by their voluntary choice" (*Bristol v. Bristol Water Works*, 23 R.I. 278). To the same effect is the U. S. Supreme Court decision in *Wilcox v. Consol. Gas. Co.* (212 U.S. 19; 29 Sup. Ct. 192) and *Des Moines Gas. Co. v. Des Moines* (238 U.S. 113).

That a public utility has no goodwill may be true in the psychological sense, but it certainly is not true from the standpoint of value analysis. In order to secure the required flow of funds into the public utility field, it is necessary to set the regulated or allowable rate of return at a level higher than the normal return prevailing in the open money market. The difference creates goodwill. Franchise, going value and goodwill value are one and the same thing and can be explained only in terms of this excess return, which is perfectly legitimate so long as it is not further enhanced by chicanery and misrepresentation.

Franchise values were held admissible in tax cases, purchase and sale transactions and condemnation proceedings, but not for the purpose of rate valuations in *Spring Valley Water Co. v. San Francisco* (165 Fed. Rep. 666) and in *Monongahela Navigation Co. v. United States* (148 U. S. 312). And that is really the crux of the problem of public utility regulation:

> Earnings are dependent upon the rates exacted and hence the higher the rates, the more valuable the franchise and *vice versa*. Obviously, therefore, it would be futile to attempt to determine the reasonableness of a rate by any standard which is at all dependent upon franchise values for its dimensions. The concession that a franchise has value and is the subject of property rights does not at all militate against this principle (*Appleton. v. Appleton Water Works Co.*, 5 Wisconsin R.C.R. 215).
>
> The value of the use, as measured by the return, can not be made the criterion when the return itself is in question. If the return as formerly allowed be taken as a basis, then the validity of the State's reduction would have to be tested by the very rates which the State denounces as exorbitant. And if the return as permitted under the new rates be taken, the State's action itself reduces the amount of value upon which the fairness of the return is to be computed (*Fuhrman v. Cataract Power & Conduit Co.*, 3. N.Y.P.-S.C., 2nd Dist. 656, and *Second Minnesota Rate Cases*, 230 U.S. 352; 33 Sup. Ct. 729 to the same effect).
>
> A return can be expected only from investment and he that invests must part with something in the act of investing. The investment in property was made, not in the franchise, but under the franchise and on the faith thereof. The franchise is but a part of the power of sovereignty allotted to a private person for the benefit of all (*Consol. Gas Co. v. City of New York*, 157 Fed. 872).

In other words, the gift of the people should not be capitalized against the people.[15] "It is only when the theory and purpose of valuation are completely lost sight of, that going values thus considered can have any place in the appraisal for rate-making purposes. Such value adds nothing to the worth of the service and is no part of its cost."[16]

Nevertheless, there are many instances where going values have been accepted by the courts for rate-making purposes. In *National Water Works v. Kansas City* (62 Fed. 853) it was held that "the fact that it is a system in operation, not only with a capacity to supply the city, but actually supplying many buildings in the city—not only with the capacity to earn, but actually earning—makes it true that 'the fair and equitable value' is something in excess of the cost of reproduction." This theory, which makes going value a mere attribute of operation, has been dubbed the "barnacle theory."[17] The conclusion in *Omaha v. Omaha Water Co.* (21 U. S. 180) was to the effect that "going value shall be included in the valuation, if it actually exists," and in *Pillsbury v. Peoples Gas & Light Co.* (4 N.H.P.U.C. 391) the court stated that the property must be valued as a going concern.

Demand has also been made for the recognition of going value for rate-making purposes in the form of the excess of the market value of the plant above its appraised present value. Even if this theory is rejected, as in *Fuhrman v. Cataract*,[18] it is possible to include sums not represented by actual investment in the appraisal value. Goodwill values are sometimes claimed for efficiency of management, competency of supervision and other economies, which really means that, in the opinion of such claimants, rates ought to be based upon the incompetence displayed by some imaginary marginal producer. Recourse has even been had to the classic formula of the probability that customers will continue to come to the same company for service and attempts have ac-

---

[15] H. Floy: *Valuation of Public Utility Properties*, McGraw-Hill Co., New York, 1912, p. 132.
[16] H. Hartman: *Fair Values*, Houghton Mifflin Co., Boston, 1920, p. 182.
[17] *Ibid.*, p. 177.
[18] *Supra*, p. 326.

cordingly been made to value goodwill at so much per customer.

The so-called Wisconsin rule, which holds that going values in the form of deficits are costs properly capitalized on the same basis as other developmental expenses, has a limited validity in the sense that early losses, or in fact any deficiency below the allowable rate of return, ought to be set up as an item recoverable from future profits earned in excess of that rate. That does not justify permanent capitalization, however. A refinement of the Wisconsin rule is the "comparative plant method," which measures going value by pretending to construct an imaginary new plant with estimated developmental expenses and initial patronage. Development loss is then computed by finding the present value of the excess revenue of the actual plant over and above that of the imaginary one for an estimated initial period. This is one of the ways in which public utilities conform to the judicial dictum that "the burden of substantiating development losses rests on the utility.[19]

The capitalization of various forms of developmental expenses has been the subject of many decisions. Promoters' expenses may be so included upon showing their reasonable necessity and a resulting benefit of the service (*Edwards v. Glen Telephone Co.*, N.Y. 2nd Dist. P.U.R. 1916-B-940), but not if the holding company did the financing (*Herman v. Newton Gas. Co.*, N.Y. 1st Dist. P.U.R. 1916-D-825). Interest during the construction period was allowed in a reasonable amount of *Petalunia & S.R.R. Co.* (Cal. P.U.R. 1915-C-742). Bond discount is not usually recognized as invested capital, since in that case low interest-bearing bonds could be issued to make the amount as large as possible and then let it earn permanently the allowable rate in place of the mere market rate of interest.

With respect to goodwill, franchise, or going values in the case of sale, it is worth mentioning that their recognition in such an event will also lead to exploitation of the consumer. Nevertheless, the New York State Public Service Commission was recently held to have exceeded its powers when it ordered that property be stated at original cost, *i.e.*, cost at the time it was first devoted to public service, either by the accounting company or a prior owner. The Commission's orders were characterized as "more than general administrative or legislative rules," which "directly interfered with the private property rights of these respondents" (*New York Edison Co. et al. v. Maltbie et al.*, 1935. 279 N.Y.S. 949; 244 App. Div. 436).

THE VALUATION OF GOODWILL

Returning to the goodwill of unregulated enterprises, a few decisions concerning the value of goodwill may be reviewed. It was stated in *Austen v. Boys*,[20] 1859, that goodwill meant nothing more than the sum of money which the purchaser would be willing to give. If a business is such that when properly managed it will not yield enough to pay debts, it is not a desirable business, and its goodwill cannot be considered of any value to a prospective purchaser (*Halverston v. Walker*, 1910. 38 Utah 264) because goodwill is the chance of expectancy of securing a future profit (*In re Borden's Estate*, 159 N.Y. Supp. 346).

Conforming to this somewhat too broad concept, the practice of valuing goodwill in terms of annual profits arose. Thus in *Featherstonhaugh v. Turner* (25 Beav. 392) the goodwill of a successful surgeon was valued at two years' net profits. In *Millersh v. Keen* (28 Beav. 453) and *Page v. Ratliffe* (75 L.T. Rep. 371) valuations of one year and three years, respectively, were approved.

An important American case was *Washburn v. National Wall Paper Co.*, 1897 (81 Fed. 20), in which the court rejected the plaintiff's claim that sixteen times the profit for the eleven months ended May 31, 1892 was an excessive amount to pay. The goodwill of *Hearn's Estate*, 1917 (182 N.Y. 263) was appraised at five times the average profit of the six years preceding the death of the founder of Hearn's Department Store, while

---

[19] *Pillsbury v. Peoples Gas & Light Co.*, *supra*, p. 326.

[20] *Supra*, p. 317.

Temple Bowdoin's share of the goodwill of J. P. Morgan & Co. (1914) was valued at three times the average of the last ten years.[21] Other examples are *Matter of Silkman*, 1907 (105 N.Y.S. 872) and *Matter of Rosenberg*, 1908 (114 N.Y.S. 726), in each of which two years' profits were held the proper price of goodwill.

Von Au v. Magenheimer (110 N.Y.S. 629; 126 App. Div. 257) is considered a leading case because it explains the method of valuation which has been followed for a long time. According to the court there is no specific rule for determining the value of goodwill, but each case must be considered in the light of the surrounding facts. The question of value must be left to the jury, whose conclusions must rest on legitimate evidence establishing that value. The value of goodwill of a manufacturing company may be fairly arrived at by multiplying the past average net profits of a company by a number of years, such number being suitable and proper, having reference to the value and character of the business. But, when feasible, it is also proper to use the results of years subsequent to the sale and conclude therefrom with respect to the conditions prevailing at the time of the sale. The specific ruling in this case was that the goodwill in question was worth five times the average annual net earnings.

With respect to the years which ought to be averaged to obtained a representative annual net profit, it was decided *In re Welch*, 1912 (137 N.Y.S. 941) that "abnormal profits in one of the last three years should be disregarded." The averaging of the last three years has for a time been regarded as the standard method and is so mentioned in *Matter of Moore*, 1910 (69 N.Y. Misc. Rep. 535), although Surrogate Fowler in *Matter of Halle*, 1918 (170 N.Y.S. 898) insists on using an average of four years.

A better grasp of fundamental principles is displayed by the decisions which recognize that the value of goodwill depends, not upon profits, but upon excess profits. An English land tax case (*Reg. v. Grand Junction Rail Co.*, 4 Q.B. 18) prescribes that from the gross profits there are to be deducted the operating expenses, interest on capital invested, a percentage for depreciation of rolling stock and a fair profit for the tenant. The residual surplus approximates the annual rental value of the land, *i.e.*, the goodwill of the landlord, which is the subject of the tax.

The method outlined in *Von Au v. Magenheimer* above has been corrected in *Seaich v. Mason-Seaman Transp. Co.*, 1916 (156 N.Y.S. 579) as follows: "In determining the value of the goodwill by multiplying the average net profits by a number of years, such number being suitable and appropriate, the interest on the capital invested should be deducted from the net profits." To the same effect is *Pett v. Spiegel*, 1923 (2 N.Y.S. 650), where the value of goodwill was found by deducting 6% interest on investment from the average net profits of the preceding three years and multiplying the remainder by "the number of years indicated by the facts," *i.e.*, five. The goodwill of the New York jewelry firm of Tiffany & Co. was similarly computed, except that ten years were not considered excessive, in view of the fact that the company had been established for sixty years and had an excellent and wide reputation.[22]

The fair value of the owner's services ($100,000 p.a.) was deducted in addition to 6% interest on investment in *Matter of Flurscheim*, 1919 (176 N.Y.S. 694), to calculate the goodwill of the New York department store of Franklin Simon & Co. A three-year average of excess profits was multiplied by five in this instance. In *Kinderman v. Kinderman*, 1920 (183 N.Y.S. 897) the plaintiffs contended that excessive salaries had been paid to the officers, who were the sole stockholders. The court, however, held that such salaries were properly deductible from profits before computing goodwill as five times the average net profits for the preceding three years.

Finally, in *Matter of Brown*, 1925 (211 N.Y.S. App. Div. 662) various other adjust-

---

[21] *Commercial & Financial Chronicle*, December 2, 1922, pp. 2425–6.

[22] A. C. Ernst: "Goodwill and its Valuation," *Printers' Ink*, March 19, 1925, pp. 125 ff.

ments were made. The transfer tax appraiser had originally valued the goodwill at three times the three-year average of annual earnings not attributable to investment or to the personal services of the partners in a stock brokerage firm. This method was rejected and the referee's action approved in excluding from the average all speculative profits, less the value of services allocated to the speculative business. In addition, a two years' purchase of net (excess) profits was declared to be more equitable, inasmuch as the goodwill was personal rather than commercial.

The trend of the representative decisions here considered appears to be directed toward greater accuracy in the determination of excess profits. This effort to exclude all elements of a normal return due the factors of production from the base of the goodwill computation is in accord with economic principles.

THE AMORTIZATION OF GOODWILL

On the subject of writing down goodwill, the opinion of the courts appears to be that that is a matter of internal corporate administration, to be governed by the judgment of the directors. In *Wilmer v. McNamara*, 1895 (2 Ch. 245; 64 L.J. Ch. 516) it was held that "where the value of the assets of a solvent company has fallen below the normal amount of share capital, the company, in the absence of any special provisions in its articles or of a contract binding the company, is under no obligation to make good such depreciation in the value of the assets before declaring a dividend out of the profits. Depreciation in the value of the leases and goodwill of a company is a loss of 'fixed' as distinguished from 'floating' capital. The balance sheet of the company cannot therefore be impeached on the ground that it does not charge anything against revenue in respect of the depreciation of goodwill."

In the leading American case of *Washburn v. National Wall Paper Co.*[23] the court declined to pass upon the present value of the goodwill, declaring that "when the stock of a corporation has been issued for the goodwill of several separate business establishments and it is claimed that the value thereof has depreciated and that therefore the corporation has no right to declare a dividend, the court cannot determine that it has depreciated, in the absence of positive evidence of the value of such goodwill at the time of the issue of the stock and at a later time." Another American case declining interference with the value of intangibles is *Mellon v. Miss. Wire Glass Co.*, 1910 (78 Atl. 710; 77 N.J. Eq. 498), where it was held that "the corporation would not be compelled at the suit of the preferred stockholders to establish a sinking fund out of which to pay the par value of the preferred stock on dissolution of the corporation, on the ground that when the patents expired, in which nearly the whole capital stock of the corporation was invested, there would be no property out of which to pay the par value of the preferred stock; there being no obligation upon the corporation to do so in the absence of a contract."

There is even a case on record where goodwill written off was restored to the books in its original amount, in order that dividends might be paid out of the surplus so created. This step was endorsed by the court on the ground that it should never have been written off (*Stapley v. Read*, 1924, 93 L.J. Ch. 513). On the other hand, it was decided in *Fernald v. Frank Redlon Co.*, 1923 (140 N.E. 421; 246 Mass. 64) that "where goodwill, patents, etc. carried on the corporate books at $55,256 were of only nominal value and the directors reduced the item to $1, they violated no duty to the preferred stockholders, whose dividends were in arrears."

The obsolescence of goodwill due to Prohibition was given consideration in *V. Loewer's Gambrinus Brewing Co. v. Anderson*, 1931 (U.S.C.C. 352), permission being given for the amortization of its value over the period between the enactment of the law and its effective date.[24]

---

[22] *Supra*, p. 327.

[24] For a discussion of similar cases see: *Journal of Accountancy*, Editorials, March and April, 1930, pp. 161–66 and 241–43.

"GOODWILL IN ACCOUNTANCY"

Journal of Accountancy
(July 1937), pp. 28–50

Goodwill in Accountancy

BY GABRIEL A. D. PREINREICH

Definitions of Goodwill

As MAY be expected, accountants are interested chiefly in the value aspect of goodwill. Nevertheless, a few definitions appear to have been inspired at least in part by Lord Eldon and other nineteenth-century jurists. Thus it has been said that "goodwill is the monetary value placed upon the connection and reputation of a mercantile or manufacturing concern and discounts the value of the turnover of a business in consequence of the probabilities of the old customers continuing" (Lisle). It "may be taken as the typical form of immaterial assets . . . representing . . . the value of business connections, the value of the probability that present customers will continue to buy in spite of the allurements of competing dealers" (Hatfield). Other definitions describe it as "the value of the benefits or advantages which attach to a particular business, in addition to the actual value of the property used in its conduct" (Bentley) and as "the momentum acquired by a going business" (Couchman).

However, "unless a present or prospective future earning power or capacity larger than that of a newly established competing concern goes along with these elements, no one would be willing to pay anything for the goodwill of the old concern. Dormant or latent goodwill signifies the excess earning power that would exist, if it were not for poor management. The probability of the continuance of this advantage is the basic element in the valuation of goodwill" (Kester). "To have a sales value, goodwill should represent a substantial earning power in excess of ordinary interest on capital and the management salaries combined. The plea of bad management is overworked. Goodwill never attaches to a business which is not believed to possess possibilities of being made profitable" (Montgomery).

Several other writers emphasize the dependence upon excess profits. Goodwill is "the capacity to earn greater than ordinary profits" (Cole), "the profit-producing power of an established business beyond mere interest and replacement return" (Conyngton), "the capitalization of a differential profit which a par-

28

ticular enterprise enjoys" (Paton and Stevenson), or "the capitalized value of earnings in excess of a normal return" (Stone).

The basic thought underlying all these definitions is well expressed by Leake:

"Goodwill in its commercial sense is the present value of the right to receive expected future super-profits; the term 'super-profits' meaning the amount by which future revenue, increase or advantage to be received is expected to exceed any and all expenditure incidental to its production." That is the economic value-concept of goodwill.

Preliminary Steps in Valuation

The first point to remember in valuing goodwill is that the problem is concerned with the future, not with the past. It is necessary to look forward, not backward, because goodwill depends on future probabilities. But past events must usually be taken as a guide (Leake). However, "recorded earnings are notoriously unreliable and of varying significance, depending upon the circumstances of their determination" (Paton). Therefore, "the idea is to adjust the profits in such a way that an accurate figure is arrived at, which would have been the profit made for several years prior to the date of sale under such circumstances as will exist after the date of the sale" (Anonymous 1).

The translation of the record of the past into an estimate of the earning power of the future is achieved by paying attention to such factors as are enumerated by Stockwell: (1) Gross and net profits as compared with similar concerns, (2) trend of development, (3) future prospects, (4) operating expenses, (5) plant location, (6) labor conditions, (7) change of management, (8) are sales derived from articles sold under trade marks, brands, patents, copyrights, licenses or royalty contracts? or (9) has the name been associated with special quality? Browne lists the following additional points: (10) Tenure of premises and whether success depends on them, (11) future competition, (12) whether the business is steady or dependent upon a craze or fashion and (13) whether the earnings are due to the services of especially valuable employees.

In general, then, the preliminary analysis of earnings will be concerned with operating efficiency, the transferability and prob-

29

able duration of earning power and with opportunities for developing new sources of profit. With respect to transferability, Dicksee emphasizes the vendor's possible attitudes, while Kester and Freeman differentiate between patronage attached to the house, firm or institution and that adhering directly to the product. Relatively permanent earning power may be expected in case of a wide distribution in proportion to volume, when many different products are sold under a single trade name or if the business is in staple lines as distinguished from specialties (Freeman).

Taxation is also worth mention. "Some accountants contend that in ascertaining annual profits, income tax should not be treated as an expense of the business, while others are of a contrary opinion" (Dawson). Apparently "the value of the enterprise as a producer of taxes is not subject to purchase and hence may be ignored" (Paton). Since, however, "the purchaser takes on the burden of taxes" (Leake), he must carefully weigh the possibility that they may be increased. The act of "ignoring" taxes will therefore take the form of an appropriate adjustment of the estimated future earnings. The capitalization of future taxes against the vendor is a phenomenon observed already by John Stuart Mill.

"The next step is a critical appraisal of all the tangible assets of the enterprise, as they stand at the time that the value of the enterprise as a whole is being determined" (Paton). This step is necessary, because book values compiled in a balance-sheet do not, in general, reflect valuations from the viewpoint of a prospective buyer who has to take into consideration certain physical factors, such as "(1) The condition of the properties, (2) their ability to produce economically and effectively from a competitive standpoint, and (3) various engineering questions, such as whether the plant is designed so as to facilitate future enlargements, the modernness of apparatus and appliances and their adaptability to changes in technical processes" (Broad).

"The assets should be carefully scrutinized for items extraneous to the business" (Freeman). That is to say, unproductive assets (e.g., excess working capital) and groups productive in independent directions should be segregated to permit separate bargaining for each group on the basis of earnings similarly segregated. A number of writers mention the necessity of eliminating non-recurrent profits and go into more or less detail

30

concerning the procedure to be followed in specific circumstances cited by them (Cox, Dawson, Freeman, Kester, Kohler, Stone).

Methods of Valuation

The two principal methods employed by the courts have been described elsewhere in some detail,[1] so that only corresponding samples of thought on the part of accountants will be summarized.

The first of the two principal methods of valuation—that of averaging the entire net profits of several years and multiplying the result by a number of years which is "suitable and proper" [2] —is the only method mentioned by Dawson and De Zouche, and Cropper. The former suggest four years' purchase and the latter from one to three years for a professional business and two to five years for a trading concern. Several other textbook writers cite both the first method and the second or excess-profits method without discussing their respective merits. In this group, Cox's example of the first method uses a multiplier of three years, Bliss, and Curtis and Cooper use four years and Bell and Graham five years or more. Esquerré, Finney and Kester refer merely to a "certain" number of years. Walton and Finney hold that the first method is not so logical as the second, and Kohler correctly points out that the first should be used only when the capital invested has not been a material income-producing factor. Dicksee and Leake expound the same principle in greater detail.

The discussion of the excess-profits method (both by those who mention it as an alternative and those who do not refer to the first method at all) is marked by secondary differences of opinion. To avoid misunderstanding, the word "capitalize" will here be used only in the sense of dividing excess profits by the chosen rate of return. This means finding the value of a perpetuity at that rate. The process of computing the present value of a finite annuity will be referred to as "discounting."

Day expresses his conviction that "the most accepted method of computing the amount of goodwill is to take the total profits for the last five years and deduct from them five years' interest on the capitalization at 7 per cent. The balance is goodwill."

---

[1] Cf. Gabriel A. D. Preinreich: "The Law of Goodwill," *Accounting Review*, December, 1936. Pp. 327–29.
[2] *Ibid.*

31

Curtis and Cooper deduct 6 per cent. on capital and multiply one year's excess by six. Bell and Graham use 8 per cent. and five years in the same way.

Cole, Cox and Wildman subtract 6 per cent. interest on the invested capital from the net profits and capitalize the remainder at the same rate. Hatfield uses 8 per cent. in this manner and also points out that to capitalize at a given rate is equivalent to multiplying by the reciprocal number of years (i.e., 12½ years in his example or 16⅔ years in the former two).

A different group favors higher rates for capitalizing excess profits than for computing the normal return on the capital invested. For instance, Couchman considers 8 per cent. a fair return and capitalizes the excess at 15 per cent. Bliss uses 10 per cent. and 15 per cent., Eggleston 10 per cent. and 20 per cent., while Kohler suggests ranges of 6 to 10 per cent. and 10 to 20 per cent., respectively. Kester and Montgomery quote the method followed in appraising the stocks of the Press Publishing Co. (New York *World*) and the St. Louis *Post-Dispatch*, held by the Pulitzer estate. After various adjustments of net earnings, 6 per cent. interest on investment was deducted and the excess capitalized at 10 per cent. for both stocks. Walton and Bentley favor similar methods.

Finney mentions the capitalization of annual excess profits (i.e., their division by a rate) as one method and their multiplication by a number of years as another method. Esquerré confines himself to remarking cautiously that the rates used to capitalize excess profits are "said to vary between 5 per cent. and 50 per cent., but are . . . in reality connected in some way with a certain number of years' purchase of the excess itself." And Wildman clearly overlooks the reciprocal relationship between rates and years when he says that "as a means of valuing goodwill, this method . . . of capitalizing excess profits without regard to interest by what is known as the year's purchase method . . . seems fundamentally wrong."

A correct suggestion by Wildman is that the annuity of excess profits be discounted at the money rate. That is an alternative method, which is followed by Rorem, who uses 6 per cent. both as a normal return on capital and for discounting an annuity of five years' excess profits. Basset proceeds similarly, except that he prefers 7 per cent. and ten years.

32

A quotation from Paton may serve to clarify the basic principle:

"If the duration of the top layer of earnings is very conservatively estimated, it might be held that the investment in such earnings is no less secure than the investment in the layer matching the tangible assets and that the same rate of return may therefore be assumed in both cases. On the other hand, there is something to be said for the view that excess earnings are always more perilously situated than normal incomes and that a double dose of conservatism is desirable in estimating amounts which may reasonably be invested in prospective earnings of this type. From this standpoint the application of a substantially higher rate in the process of discounting the top layer is justified."

There is little theoretical merit in thus burning the candle at both ends. The question revolves around the risk, which may be expressed either in terms of years as a horizon of foresight or by adding an insurance premium to the money rate, but preferably not in both ways at the same time. The method of weighting the money rate for risk has been widely adopted, because it is well suited to the valuation of contractual obligations, to which the scope of the mathematical theory of investment has been well-nigh limited in the past. When the various considerations surrounding the goodwill of common stocks are approached, this two-in-one tool of analysis is not flexible enough. The mathematical analysis of goodwill as a probability is facilitated by divorcing the risk from the money rate and setting it up separately in terms of a future period. For this purpose, therefore, the horizon method is preferable to the capitalization method, although the latter is equally sound in theory, whether applied in the form of a weighted money rate, or in that of the reciprocal number of years.

The Treatment of Goodwill in Accounts

A great majority of accountants endorse the principle that goodwill ought to be recorded in accounts only if and only to the extent that it was paid for. Among those who are not content with making an unsupported statement to this effect, not all succeed in giving adequate reasons:

"Goodwill does not crystallize until a sale takes place and all attempts at intermediate valuation are idle. Indeed the only

33

excuse for the insertion of such an item as goodwill in accounts is that such an amount has actually been paid by the present proprietor of the goodwill of the business" (Dicksee). "Unless goodwill has been purchased from a predecessor, it should not be regarded as a live factor on the company's books" (Koehler). "The reason for this is that the purchaser has demonstrated his belief in the existence of goodwill by paying cash for it" (Gilman). "Accounting practice prudently, though perhaps illogically, forbids the firm which created goodwill to place in the balance-sheet any value on the clientele which it has built up and which it could at any moment sell for a large sum. This conservative restriction is doubtless necessary to prevent a harmful exaggeration" (Hatfield).

These comments do not touch the kernel of the matter, which can be laid bare only by examining what Hatfield considers illogical. The thought is expressed by Greendlinger thus: "If there are two similar companies and one has changed hands, there is no reason why one balance-sheet should state goodwill and the other not." To this it is not enough to reply that "the effect would be to forestall the future" (Leake). The essential thing is that the respective owners of the similar companies are not in the same position. Although the net business profits of both are the same, one has invested a greater sum of money than the other, and that is what their balance-sheets should show. By comparison with the earning records, the basic fact is disclosed that a dollar invested in one business is less productive than a dollar invested in the other. "The actual rate of return is the significant fact for the proprietor. He wishes to know just what the capital fund in his possession is yielding and if the rate is reduced to a nominal level by the capitalization of a part of the income, the actual situation is covered up" (Paton and Stevenson). "To register on the books a capitalization based on earning capacity is not only to register an unnecessary figure, but to bury the actual cost of the assets" (Cole).

It is well known, of course, that many a business man desires to cover up the situation and bury the actual costs. "The ratio of return to nominal capital might be abnormally high. For business reasons it might be to his advantage to increase his capital in accordance with the goodwill acquired and thus decrease the rate of return on the investment. In the same manner

34

a corporation might find it advantageous to reduce the apparent return on its capital stock by setting up goodwill and distributing the surplus arising therefrom by a stock dividend" (Wildman).

So long as such an asset remains offset on the credit side by a correctly described appraisal surplus, the situation is at least fully disclosed, but the eradication of the record by means of a stock dividend is most objectionable.

Couchman outlines the method of recording the purchase price of a business in part as follows: (1) The purchaser of a group of mixed assets may distribute that sum to the assets acquired without regard to the value at which they were carried on the books of the seller, and (2) if the aggregate purchase price exceeds the proper value of the other assets acquired, the difference may be recorded upon the books of the purchasing company as goodwill. But ". . . it must be borne in mind that in many cases the value decided upon for goodwill represents simply the difference between the book value of the business sold and the price paid for it, which may be the result of a compromise between bid and asked prices having little relation to any theoretical methods of computing goodwill" (Bliss). "In ordinary American practice, the accountants have assumed the existence of goodwill whenever the tangible property purchased is less than the par value of the stock issued therefor" (Hatfield).

"Because of the very widespread habit of overcapitalizing . . . a goodwill account is used very commonly to carry . . . the contra of watered stock, which is overcapitalization. Thus it is the difference between the property value of the issued stock . . . and the par value of that stock" (Bentley). As long as business reasons continue to be stronger than theory, this form of disclosure is welcome, because "it is manifestly better bookkeeping to show overcapitalization as goodwill than to bury it in such an asset as 'plant' or in some other tangible fixed asset" (Bentley). But "American corporations have very generally not set forth goodwill as a distinct item in the balance-sheet" (Hatfield), at least not in statements accessible to the general public.

The path of least resistance out of this conflict between theory and practice is to hold that "the treatment of intangible fixed investments in actual business is very largely determined by the company's financial policies rather than by accounting theory. The creation of goodwill . . . etc. . . . are questions that are

35

settled by the financial management and not by the application of some standard accounting principle. . . . Accounting procedure can only accept the situation as it exists" (Bliss). "So long as the item is separately stated, it is scarcely desirable that he (the auditor) should interfere with the discretion of the management" (Dicksee).

The importance of the goodwill account is often minimized on the ground that "the amount is absolutely meaningless, except as an indication of what the goodwill may have cost in the first instance" (Dicksee). The original cost, however, is too significant to be dismissed in this manner, even though it is perfectly true that "such statement is not intended to convey any guarantee that its present worth is fairly represented by the amount at which it appears" (Cropper). "The profit-and-loss record is the best evidence of it—that should guide us as to its valuation and not the value carried on the balance-sheet" (Kester), because "so far as fixed assets are concerned, a balance-sheet does not pretend to be an index of value. What it does purport to do is to record actual expenditure not hitherto charged against profits" (Anonymous 2).

The Amortization of Goodwill

On the subject of writing off goodwill—whether described as depreciation, amortization or extinguishment—Hatfield has attempted to point out two opposing camps: "Among accountants favoring the writing off of goodwill are Bell, Leake, Pixley, Webner and Wildman, while Cole, Couchman, Dicksee, Finney and Montgomery hold that it is unnecessary or even improper." Actually, this classification is neither comprehensive nor accurate enough. Most writers who, at first sight, seem definitely opposed to amortization, can conceive of reasons why goodwill ought to be written down after all. Many remarks are either of the cautious "yes and no" or the neutrally aloof and non-participating "some say yes, some say no" variety. Other authors go on record with equal emphasis on both sides of the question, but there are also not a few who are convinced that some plan of amortization is necessary.

The negative side is stressed in the following excerpts:

"If a business purchases the goodwill of another business, obviously the charge is a perfectly legitimate one and it should be carried as a permanent asset not subject to depreciation or

36

extinguishment" (Bentley). "It is such an elusive asset that it is not subject to wear and tear and the principles of depreciation certainly cannot be applied to it as to other items" (Montgomery). "When the transfer of goodwill involves an asset actually recorded on the books of the vendor . . . there has been an actual purchase of goodwill and there is no reason why it should be amortized. Goodwill of this nature has nothing to do with earning power. There appears to be no sane reason why organic goodwill, having been built up slowly, painfully and at great cost, should be put to death through the process of amortization" (Esquerré).

"Goodwill represents property to which the owner possesses a tenure in perpetuity and unless the nature of the business is such that the value of the goodwill must of necessity become reduced as time goes on, no depreciation can be said to take place" (Anonymous 3). "Ordinarily it need not be depreciated, especially if the organization makes reasonable efforts to maintain its good name among its customers. However, there are organizations which have apparently depended upon a good name previously created, rather than upon present success. In such cases goodwill is doomed to an early extinction" (Couchman). "If the special advantages purchased are permanent, the asset goodwill evidently need not be depreciated. Peculiar efficiency and monopolistic advantages, however, are seldom permanent factors and hence the problem of depreciation arises in most cases. When the advantages purchased disappear, goodwill should be written down" (Paton and Stevenson).

The main bulwark of opposition is the celebrated paradox which has been quoted and paraphrased by almost every writer on goodwill for the last fifty years. Couchman puts it with slogan-like brevity: "If you can write it down, you need not; if you cannot, you should." In other words, "the existence of earnings sufficient to write it off justifies its retention" (Montgomery), because "as long as the earnings of an enterprise equal those contemplated at the date of purchase, one cannot well say that there has been any depreciation in its value or that any provision for such depreciation need be made" (Bennett). "When profits are small, it would hardly be logical to write off any amount less than its decreased value, yet the profits at such a time are hardly sufficient to stand so heroic a treatment" (Kester). The answer to the paradox may be summarized as follows:

37

"It is sometimes loosely said that if the profits of a business are well maintained, the value of the goodwill cannot diminish. That is not necessarily always the case, because the value of goodwill at any time depends upon future prospects, and these may be deteriorating, even while profits are maintained. Supposing, however, that the value of the now-existing goodwill is not less than the value of the goodwill which existed at the date of purchase, yet it is equally necessary gradually to write off the cost of the earlier existing goodwill, because part of this cost has expired" (Leake). Purchased goodwill is a "portion of the business income which . . . has been prepaid to the vendor . . . [and] . . . does not represent physical assets available for the redemption of common stock in case of dissolution. That the intangible equity of the common stock should be replaced in due course by a tangible equity is a principle of finance and business economics" (Esquerré). "Eventually dividends will be paid out of capital, if the goodwill is not depreciated" (Yang).

Another argument against the amortization of goodwill is that "if written off, a secret reserve might be created; therefore no objection can be offered to its retention at cost" (Montgomery). "What is really effected by the process is to create a reserve fund without stating it as such—or in other words a secret reserve" (Dicksee). But "the dropping of goodwill from the balance-sheet is no secret, since any one can see that it is not there. The difference between charging off a building and charging off goodwill is that a business does not necessarily have to own a building and its absence from the accounts would imply that it did not own one" (Walton). That is to say, every business must have goodwill attached to it in an amount which may be positive, zero or negative, depending upon future prospects.

"Accountants of the more conservative school recommend that goodwill be depreciated over a term of years" (Cox), although many hold that "nothing need be done, unless the concern is desirous of being very conservative" (Bell and Powelson). "Depreciation does not occur in goodwill . . . [but] . . . writing off goodwill is a conservative practice" (Bliss). "Goodwill purchased is a permanent asset, not subject to depreciation or extinguishment . . . [but] . . . prosperous firms in many cases will write off this asset on account of its questionable actual value" (Bennett). "There is usually no logical reason for writing it off. [Nevertheless] the best course for all purposes is to retain

38

goodwill in the accounts at a nominal amount . . ." (Kester). "The original cost is rarely written down and should be stated in the balance-sheet at cost. . . . however, the directors may wisely decide to enhance the financial strength of the undertaking by reducing the book value of the goodwill" (Cropper).

In such circumstances some accountants are of the opinion that the same end can be more advantageously attained by creating a reserve fund (Cropper). "Goodwill does not depreciate, but rather improves with old age so long as the profits are maintained and to my mind the best course is in most cases to allow the goodwill to stand in the balance-sheet at cost and to gradually set aside out of profits a special reserve, until such reserve shall equal the cost of the goodwill" (Dawson). "Patents, goodwill and franchises are very much akin to one another. . . . Provided that the principle is admitted of building up a substantial reserve fund against whatever portion of the capital is invested in this class of assets, it would seem reasonable to merge the three items into one and treat them as part of the permanent invested capital of the business, which may be left to continue at its original value, as long as the business is a going concern" (Dickinson). Dicksee remarks that "the chances are that they will find it rather embarrassing to disclose this cost price at a subsequent date and thus there is a very powerful argument in favor of the amount standing to the debit of goodwill being written off with all convenient speed." Guthrie prefers a reserve fund, but agrees with Dicksee that the depreciation of goodwill should be left to the management.

A minor question is whether or not the amortization of goodwill ought to be charged against profits. It is said that "goodwill should be charged off, not against current profits, but against the capital invested" (Gilman); ". . . the amounts written off are not in any sense charges against revenue, but should take the form of appropriations of profits" (Cropper); ". . . anything which is credited to the goodwill account must be a premium set aside out of profits and not a charge against profits" (Dawson).

The merit of these statements hinges entirely upon whether it is desirable for the owner to earmark certain investments of business funds as personal and private items. The essential fact is that the purchaser "has prepaid income which he will actually receive during a series of years, but which will not constitute his

39

own earnings. As soon as the periods of earnings covered by the goodwill have expired, the new investor will enjoy the totality of the business income. In the meantime he will have periodically and proportionately amortized the debit account which recorded the prepayment of what both parties to the contract . . . have understood to be the vendor's earnings" (Esquerré). In general, it is simpler for the owner to hold that—along with plant and other fixed assets—"goodwill has been paid for in advance on revenue account, for the purpose of enabling the gross revenue to be earned, in which process all these things waste and are inevitably, though perhaps slowly, destroyed" (Leake). "When payment is made on the probability of excess earnings, the purchaser has paid a price for the tools of business operation. Hence the depreciation of intangible assets should constitute a charge against . . . operations" (Yang).

As to the method of amortization, Gilman believes that "the number of years' profits which have been purchased determines the number of years over which the goodwill shall be charged off." But "it is unfair to deprive the management of income for that period, when goodwill was acquired for the benefit of a greatly extended time" (Guthrie) and the suggestion is accordingly made of doubling the period, i.e., charging off only half-a-year's purchase annually. Wildman recommends that goodwill be written off "on the basis of life according to the most conservative estimate." A more specific suggestion is that "the cost may be written off over a period of from five to ten years" (Bell and Powelson). And Day is perhaps too definite when he says that "goodwill should be written off the books during five subsequent years by charging off one-fifth against each succeeding year."

"In calculating the amount to be depreciated, the method of computing an annuity is sometimes employed" (Cox). "Strict logic requires, at least where the price of goodwill is calculated as representing the present value of a series of excess annual profits, that it should be written off as any terminable annuity" (Hatfield). In other words, goodwill should be treated like a bond premium (Gilman and Walton). It follows that, when goodwill is computed by the years' purchase (of excess profits) method, "the purchaser has in fact bought the right to an expected annuity for a longer term of future years, although he may have

40

measured the value of this right as being equal to the amount of the profits for the last three or five years" (Leake). A valuation made by the years' purchase method must, therefore, be converted into the corresponding annuity, in order to determine the amounts chargeable against each succeeding year's profits. In addition "the judgment of the purchaser at the time of purchase must be deemed correct" (Yang), although that is an assumption altogether contrary to practical experience.

Changes in conditions subsequent to the date of purchase are considered in the suggestion that "goodwill paid for . . . should be amortized as the super-profits are realized" (Roth). This may mean either that the entire excess profits of succeeding years be credited to goodwill until it is extinguished, or a more flexible method of annual appropriations recommended by many of the older writers.

Created Goodwill

"Expenditures which are made by a corporation before it can begin business, are usually classified as organization expenses and . . . are properly treated as capital expenditures" (Eggleston). On the other hand "it is a fallacy to assume that . . . incorporation expenses, etc., have any of the attributes of an asset; and so the sooner the cost appears in the expense account, the better" (Montgomery). "In strict theory, the value of these costs will last as long as the corporate existence" (Kester). And since such expenditures have been incurred for the purpose of making profits which could not have been obtained in another manner, there appears to be little reason for insisting that organization expense differs in essence from purchased goodwill.

"Where it is clearly foreseen that the new undertaking must necessarily be run at a loss before it can be built up into a profit-making concern, such initial loss may be treated as the cost incurred in establishing the goodwill of the undertaking" (Dicksee). "There does not seem to be a valid objection to the charging of the operating shortcomings of what might be called the 'probation period' of a newly established business to an account which would record the cost of obtaining the goodwill of the community" (Esquerré). "Such expenses are charged to some such account as 'establishment outlay' . . . until the developed or expanded business reaches a point where the expense of ob-

41

taining new business can be paid out of the profits" (Stockwell). "A person buying an established business would be willing to pay for the capitalized values of the sums by which the actual earnings of a new business would fall short of the normal earnings of a developed business" (Yang).

"Whenever, however, expenditure upon advertising is capitalized, it is important to bear in mind that a business established by advertising will ordinarily require advertising for its maintenance" (Dicksee). "A distinction is made between what may be considered a normal value of advertising necessary to maintain a given volume of trade and the presumably greater amount of advertising necessary to increase the amount of sales, especially that necessary to establish a market for a new product" (Hatfield). "No capitalization of advertising costs should be passed by the accountant, unless the increased asset value is unquestionable or unless any other treatment would work an injustice to anyone or present unfair records of operating results of various accounting periods" (Couchman). When this principle is neglected "the balance-sheet showing the large deficit and the later balance-sheet showing the increased profit are both false" (Montgomery).

In general, "an auditor may pass the carrying forward of any legitimate expenditure which has been incurred solely for the benefit of future business, provided that in his judgment the setting up of a deferred charge and its consequent inclusion as an asset are justified by its probable value to the future business" (Montgomery). But the future periods benefited by deferred charges vary in length according to the nature of the charge. An analysis and classification of expenditures during the developmental period is therefore preferable to an indiscriminate capitalization of initial losses.

"The justification for this capitalizing of deficits is greater in the case of public utilities than in ordinary commercial enterprises" (Hatfield). The reason is that a public utility is entitled to a stated fair return, so that deficits, whether developmental in character or not, partake of the nature of accounts receivable from consumers. Reimbursement out of subsequent profits in excess of the allowable rate of return is therefore proper, although permanent capitalization is not.

42

As a rule, accountants are inclined to be quite strict in auditing deferred charges. "More than one enterprise has been wrecked by the failure to look preliminary or establishment expenses squarely in the face. The temptation to state the current operations in such a way as to show a profit was too strong; so those concerns have gone along from year to year, the burden increasing instead of diminishing, until the inevitable day of reckoning, when it was realized that liabilities cannot be liquidated with capitalized expenses. If the business is not successful, there will be no future profits to which the deferred items can be charged. Therefore the auditor should use every argument he can muster to induce his client to absorb these expenses as soon as possible" (Montgomery). This attitude is proper, but it should be remembered that the arguments are fully as applicable to that goodwill which the same auditors often accept as permanent. An admittedly genuine investment in goodwill and the various forms of deferred charges differ only in degree, not in kind, and therefore the only moot question is the rate or manner of extinguishment, not its necessity.

Reorganizations

In most accounting textbooks the elementary partnership problems form an important part of the discussion on goodwill. The typical procedure is to begin with the sole proprietor A, who takes unto himself a partner B. Later the two together admit C. One of the three then dies and his estate has to be liquidated, or else he merely retires and sells his interest to D. In all these situations, Dicksee proceeds systematically by first setting up the entire goodwill which the business is deemed to possess, as determined by a bargain concluded for a portion of it. The change in ownership is then recorded and the goodwill written off again in the ratio in which profits and losses are to be shared thereafter. The method of settling privately for the goodwill is also considered, it being pointed out that the resultant differences in the final capital accounts are offset by the payments which have not passed through the books.

Other accountants treat the subject in the same way, except that they are generally opposed to the total elimination of goodwill. The objections which have been raised against that procedure are discussed by Yang, whose observations may be sum-

43

marized as follows: (1) The question is whether or not the present owners have actually incurred business costs. Failure to recognize such costs would occasion an understatement of assets and an overstatement of revenue during the existence of the proprietors. (2) If the degree of change in ownership is not substantial, it might be improper to conclude, from the value of a part, the value of the whole goodwill. (3) The proportionate recognition of the entire goodwill would imply an accruing of future income, the depreciation on which would convert a portion of real earnings into capital. (4) If, however, goodwill is not recognized proportionately, the new partner would have to make an individual calculation to apportion his share of the profits between real earnings and what to him is but capital returned. (5) There is a natural inclination on the part of business men to increase the value of their assets, when there is a chance to do so. Dicksee himself admits that "it is in many cases perhaps expedient that the value of the retiring partner's share should be stated in the accounts as an asset, so as to avoid disturbing the amounts standing to the credit of the continuing partners. But it seems clearly desirable that such an item should, if possible, be got rid of at once."

If the expenditure of business funds has resulted in the acquisition of goodwill, the cost must evidently be absorbed prior to the date of liquidation, in order that the owners' investments be recoverable in full. The amortization of written-up goodwill is a form of saving which leads to liquidating values in excess of the original investment. If that be the purpose, it can be accomplished by simpler means. As for the new partner, to whom the goodwill represents actual cost, he is merely the ancestor, in point of evolution, of the investor who buys common stock in the market and is obliged, as a matter of course, to keep his own records. All elementary partnership problems, indeed, are valuable chiefly because they present simple analogies to corporate complications and often furnish the guiding thread through a maze of technicalities.

The natural inclination of business men toward inflated valuations is never more apparent than upon incorporation, when the legal theory of the separate entity provides the welcome excuse. Accordingly goodwill usually receives liberal recognition, even though no actual change of ownership has taken place and, there-

44

fore, no need for valuation has arisen. Accountants are usually confronted with a fait accompli in this respect.

In the case of consolidations, the situation is more complicated, because the earning power of the enterprises to be united must be considered when apportioning the stock of the new company. The general approach has been indicated; in many instances the valuation methods preferred by the various authors have been taken from illustrative consolidation or merger problems presented by them. The final steps are: (1) issuance of stock for the appraised value of the so-called tangible fixed assets plus the audited value of current assets; (2) deduction of an agreed rate of normal return from the audited and adjusted net profits; (3) capitalization or discounting of the excess profits to determine their fair present value; and (4) allocation of a second block of stock in proportion to the goodwill so computed. When two classes of stock are used, it is customary to issue preferred stock for assets and common stock for goodwill.

Dicksee and Leake strongly oppose capitalization of goodwill and suggest various remedies. Shares without par value have been in use for some time. When preferred stock is issued for assets, common stock without par value is entitled to all excess profits without the necessity of stating goodwill on the balance-sheet. The alternative plan consists of letting "the shares be issued at such a premium as would amount to the price to be paid to the vendor of the goodwill" (Dicksee). That would be sound theory, well adapted to take deception out of cash transactions, but it is poor sales-psychology and therefore unworkable. Leake also proposes redeemable shares, in order to amortize the goodwill in conformity with its original valuation, while Dicksee would state goodwill on the balance-sheet only if it could not possibly be omitted, and then only in a form making it clear that it was only discount on stock, after all.

Trading on the Equity

"Some authorities contend that it is better to use the average total assets—rather than the average tangible assets, less liabilities—employed in the business, as a basis for applying the interest element. It is claimed . . . that the variable factor of 'trading on the equity' is thereby eliminated and that a more nearly accurate valuation of the real goodwill is obtained" (Montgomery).

45

In so far as this comment refers to current liabilities, it may be observed that the custom of granting cash discounts for prompt payment makes it expensive to trade on the equity by holding up bills. The practice is therefore resorted to only by those who are in financial difficulties. Before computing the value of such businesses it will be more logical to determine the normal volume of current liabilities as a preliminary step in valuation. No enterprise can operate without having some current liabilities and therefore the "real goodwill" cannot be ascertained by starting with an assumption contrary to fact. For valuation purposes, current liabilities should be offset against current assets, with or without adjustment, as indicated by the circumstances.

"Corporations sometimes issue bonds because . . . a larger return is made on the funds thus borrowed than the interest rate paid. This is called 'trading on the equity' " (Kester). But "The value of the enterprise as a whole . . . is not affected by the nature of the sources of the funds supplied, by the form of capitalization. . . . There are two main possibilities, . . . on the one hand, earning power may be expressed in terms of the final amount after all charges accruing to the residual proprietary interest, and . . . on the other hand earning power may be stated from the managerial, all-capital point of view" (Paton).

Even when purchase means no more than the acquisition of a majority of the common stock, the prospective purchaser of an enterprise will look upon it from the all-capital point of view in the sense that he has his own ideas on the subject of trading on the equity. He is less interested in what the common stock is paying under the present capital structure than in what he can make it pay. And that depends primarily on what the business as a whole is paying. The record of the past must again be translated into an estimate of future prospects before computing the goodwill of the common stock in the usual manner from those estimates.

An extreme form of trading on the equity is the promotion of reorganizations and consolidations by selling to the public a full line of assorted securities in a new company. By using the proceeds to buy one or more enterprises previously secured through options and reserving the majority of the voting stock for themselves, promoters have in the past reaped handsome cash profits, in addition to retaining control over what they have sold.

46

The Goodwill of Holding Companies

"Goodwill may be defined as the purchase price of the control of excess earning power. Minority holdings in intercompany stock do not give rise to goodwill" (Newlove). That is, not on the consolidated balance-sheet. "The positive goodwill calculated . . . meets three requirements. A purchase has been made, the control element exists, and the potential excess earning power may be assumed, as a purchaser expects to receive his money's worth of the tangible (recorded book value) and intangible (goodwill) assets. The positive goodwill . . . is universally accepted, the disputes involving only the negative goodwill" (Newlove).

"In preparing a consolidated balance-sheet, the investment account is replaced by the things it represents. Therefore that portion which represents subsidiary net assets is eliminated; and the portion which represents excess payment . . . appears in the consolidated balance-sheet" (Finney). "Goodwill upon the consolidated balance-sheet may be said to be the algebraic sum of the goodwill items purchased from the subsidiaries by the holding company" (Bennett). But Newlove holds that "if a company's stock can, under ordinary market conditions, be purchased for less than its book value, some of the assets of that company are inflated. This inflation is in the assets of the company which is being analyzed and therefore this negative goodwill has no effect on the goodwill of the other companies." Dicksee expresses the same thought: "The mere fact that a company's shares were quoted at a discount would imply that it has lost some of its tangible assets, as well as the whole of its goodwill."

The last two opinions constitute a reversion to the pure property or capital value concept of accounting valuations. An inflation in tangible asset values may be present, but that is a matter for audit and adjustment. The mere fact that goodwill is negative does not prove that inflation exists. A balance-sheet, after all, can do no more than state figures resulting from an acceptable method of interpolation between original cost and salvage values. The goodwill is negative whenever prospective earnings fall short of the money rate on the interpolated values. For the same reason, the purchase of assets for less than their

47

admittedly proper balance-sheet value is not necessarily a "lucky buy" warranting a credit to capital surplus, although that is Newlove's alternative conclusion.

When stock is exchanged for stock and "the book value of the shares acquired is less than the book value of the shares issued, it is evident that goodwill has been purchased, unless . . . the shares issued are not worth their book value" (Sunley and Pinkerton). That is, unless the book value of the shares issued is based upon improper accounting methods resulting in overstatement, or unless the book value of the shares acquired is based upon incorrect accounting methods resulting in understatement, or unless the exchange of stock was effected on the basis of market prices manipulated in favor of the subsidiary, which is less frequent than the reverse. Apart from these possibilities, the difference between the book value of the shares issued and the shares acquired is the difference of the goodwills attaching to the respective blocks of stock. But even if the difference includes impurities of one sort or another, the book value of the stock issued by the holding company measures the total cost of the transaction to it and the investment should be recorded at that figure. To use any other method would be to repudiate one's own yardstick. That yardstick may indeed be false, but if so, it should be audited and corrected, not simply disregarded. To record a purchase at the market value of the stock issued for it amounts to writing up one's own goodwill not purchased.

"Goodwill created by the purchase of stock of a subsidiary company is determined definitely at the date of purchase, and remains unchanged ever afterward" (Bliss). "If the holding company has handled its investment accounts on an accrual basis, i.e. so that they reflect the holding company's share of the profits, losses and dividends of the subsidiaries, the consolidated goodwill is determined by finding the difference between the respective investment accounts and the book value of the portion of the subsidiaries' net worths owned by the holding company. If the investment accounts are carried at cost . . . the consolidated goodwill is determined in the same manner as at the date of acquisition. The book value of the subsidiaries' shares at that date and not on the date of the consolidated balance-sheet should be taken, because only the former book value was acquired" (Kester).

48

When the percentage of control over a subsidiary decreases, a corresponding portion of the goodwill originally acquired must be written off. If the cost of an increase in percentage is greater or smaller than its book value, the difference should be added to or deducted from the consolidated goodwill. Finney, Kester, Newlove, and Sunley and Pinkerton give illustrations of such adjustments.[3]

Goodwill Insurance

"The man who causes the world to 'make a path to his door' creates goodwill. A policy of insurance, payable to the firm, written on the life of a man who has been instrumental in building up such a business is, in a measure, capitalizing . . . such a personality" (Hunter). Life insurance as a goodwill problem is also mentioned by Guthrie, and Dicksee recommends it as a convenient means of liquidating goodwill upon the demise of a partner. He points out the proper way of defraying the cost of this insurance: "The equitable plan is to charge each partner with his due proportion of the cost of insuring the lives of each of his co-partners" (Dicksee). Thus, if A, B and C share profits and losses in the ratio of 3:2:1, B and C are to share the premium on A's life at the rate of 2:1, A and C that on B's life at 3:1 and A and B that on C's life at 3:2. The same principle evidently applies to private corporations, whose officers are also its stockholders. In public corporations, on the other hand, the net premium is a business expense, although not recognized as such by Federal income-tax regulations.

Conclusion

The outstanding characteristic of modern accounting literature on the subject of goodwill is its barrenness. Quotations taken from two papers written almost fifty years ago can be used to summarize most valid conclusions published since then. Limitations of space preclude a detailed demonstration, but the fact becomes evident upon perusal of a prize essay by J. H. Bourne [4] and an article by Francis More.[5] The latter has even made the valuable suggestion noted only by Hatfield "to split

---

[3] For graphic illustrations of the same basic problem see: Gabriel A. D. Preinreich: *The Nature of Dividends*. New York, 1935.

[4] "Goodwill," *Accountant*, Sept. 22, 1888. Pp. 604–5.

[5] "Goodwill," *Ibid.*, April 11, 1891. Pp. 282–7.

49

up excess profits into two or more parts and assign a value to each part. An excess of 5 per cent. over the ordinary rate is more likely to be maintained than an excess of 10 per cent. . . . and so on." This treatment, although cumbersome in the form suggested, shows an excellent understanding of goodwill as a probability, the theory of which is worth developing.

The only topics not covered by Bourne and More are created goodwill and the technique of consolidated balance-sheets. The capitalization of preliminary expenses and developmental deficits appears to have been first mentioned by Dicksee in 1897. Intricate corporate family relationships are a more recent development, but their analysis involves merely an extension of old principles.

[NOTE.—Limitations of space prevent inclusion of a list of about 150 references submitted by the author with this article. Any reader who wishes the references may obtain them from the author or from the library of the American Institute of Accountants.—*Editor*]

50

"VALUATION AND AMORTIZATION"

The Accounting Review (September 1937),
pp. 209–226

The Accounting Review

VOL. XII   SEPTEMBER, 1937   No. 3

VALUATION AND AMORTIZATION

GABRIEL A. D. PREINREICH

WHAT IS A BALANCE SHEET?

MANY accountants appear to have no very definite notion of what a balance sheet is. Forthright opinions on the subject are rare; by inference, however, two main trends of thought may be distinguished, one of which is based on the capital-value or property concept and the other on the investment or amount-of-money-advanced concept.

The former is exemplified by the so-called fundamental equation: Assets minus liabilities equal net worth. Numerous remarks on the subject of accounting valuations clearly show that their authors were guided at least temporarily by the idea that a balance sheet is or ought to be a statement of the worth of the business. This comment applies to all who would write up good will not purchased or who hold that, if purchased, it need not be amortized until it is actually worth less than it cost. That patents need not be amortized, because they are, in time, supplanted by good will, and that if a company's stock is quoted at a discount, its balance sheet must be inflated, are further samples of the same trend of thought. Inconsistencies are the rule, rather than the exception. For instance, many who subscribe to these views when discussing so-called intangibles would not uphold them with respect to what they consider tangible assets. On the other hand, those who by no means endorse the capital-value concept, sometimes make statements which sound as if they did. Leake, among others, says that "unfortunately it cannot be assumed as a matter of course that the assets or the liabilities of a joint stock company are stated in the balance sheet at their full and fair values" and refers to the "more or less common knowledge that the value of the assets is either greater or less than stated in the balance sheet."[1]

The fallacies of the value idea are discussed by May: ". . . accounting is not essentially a process of valuation, as some writers on accounting and some economists conceive it to be. Primarily, accounting is historical in approach, with valuation entering into it at times as a safeguard. The emphasis is on cost, though where an asset is intended for sale and its selling value is known to be less than cost, the lower figure may be substituted for cost . . . The fact is that the word 'value' has come to be used to describe what is a mere figure—'book figure' would be more accurate than 'book value' . . . A balance sheet in which one asset is stated at book value, another at replacement value, a third at liquidation value and a fourth at going concern value, does not yield a figure that can be described as net worth . . . This does not mean that the balance sheet is valueless, but only that it is a highly technical production, the significance of which is severely limited and has in the past often been greatly overrated."[2]

The foregoing excerpts and the rest of the article from which they were taken may explain fully what a balance sheet is *not*, but they certainly remain silent on what it *is*. *Yang* also devotes a great deal of space to the theory of accounting valuations without reaching more than a negative conclusion.

[1] *Cf.* P. D. Leake: *Commercial Goodwill*, Sir Isaac Pitman & Sons, Ltd., London, 1921.

[2] G. O. May: "The influence of accounting on the development of an economy," *Journal of Accountancy*, Jan., 1936, pp. 15–21.

According to him, "a balance sheet is an expression of opinion, a hypothetical magnitude arrived at through a series of complicated and arbitrary computations."[3] Better are the definitions he quotes: "We may look upon annual balance sheets as statements that apportion in a *reasonable* way all payments, whatever their nature, over the whole period during which an undertaking continues to derive advantage from them."[4] "A display to those, such as creditors or proprietors, who have advanced values to a business, showing what has been done by that business with the values so advanced."[5]

The last two descriptions express the investment or amount-advanced concept of the balance sheet, but even they emphasize merely what has been done, not what the result is or ought to be. Modern accounting methods still adhere to the plan followed by Columbus, when he started out by dead reckoning in a "reasonable," *i.e.*, general westerly direction, knowing only whence he came, with perhaps some notion of how far he had come, but without ever being aware of where he was. Since a reasonable westerly direction may lie anywhere between northwest and southwest, it is essential to mention that the accountant's real goal is the liquidating value of the business, to be reached upon the unknown date of liquidation. In other words, *the task is to connect original cost with liquidating value in a way which will give due consideration to both risk and time.* Cost is an advance concept and liquidating value a value concept, each of which is paramount on its date. Between the two dates, both share in determining the course to be followed, the relative importance of the former declining and that of the latter increasing gradually. Only if bearings are continuously taken, not only backward, but also forward, will the course steered come near the true direction. In that case the balance sheet will measure, not the worth or capital value of a business, but the amount of money invested

in it at a given stage of the transition. And that is the highest purpose which it can serve, although it may also be adapted to simpler and more generally useful ends.

For certain assets independent methods of taking bearings forward have been developed to a remarkable degree, especially by statisticians and engineers. Many accountants could undoubtedly profit by a study of these methods, even though they are familiar with the general principle that "the accounting function in relation to capital assets is to measure and record, not the fluctuations in their value, but the extent to which their usefulness is exhausted through age or use and to make proper charges against income in respect of such exhaustion, based on the cost of the property exhausted, with the intent that the property shall stand on the books at its salvage value when the term of its usefulness is ended."[6] Uncoördinated methods, however, can lead to no satisfactory result, no matter how great their individual merits may be. What is still lacking is a bird's-eye view of the problem as a whole. Not only must each asset stand on the books at its salvage value when its usefulness is ended, but all assets taken together must be written down to their liquidating value by the time the company's life is ended. This period of life is an uncertainty, which the market regards in terms of the "horizon"(that future point of time beyond which the investor is unable or unwilling to look). Any asset's expectancy of usefulness is, therefore, limited by the horizon. Beyond that limit only its exchange value may be considered.

TANGIBLE AND INTANGIBLE ASSETS

As *Hatfield* has pointed out, "the phrase is not particularly appropriate and, except by enumeration, the separation between tangible and intangible assets is not easily made. There is no real difference between them as regards tangibility, materiality or realness."[7] That is to say, the term "asset" does not

---

[3] J. M. Yang: *Goodwill and Other Intangibles*, Ronald Press Co., New York, 1927.

[4] E. M. Carter: "What is an annual balance sheet?" *Accountant*, Oct. 22. 1910, p. 566.

[5] C. B. Couchman: *The Balance Sheet*, Journal of Accountancy, Inc., New York, 1924.

[6] May, *op. cit.*

[7] *Cf.* H. R. Hatfield: *Modern Accounting*, D. Appleton Co., New York, 1916, pp. 107–118; and *Accounting, Its Principles and Problems*, D. Appleton Co., 1932, pp. 111–129.

refer to all the inherent or acquired characteristics of material or immaterial property, but only to their aspects as investments. Assets are valued only for their services and this valuation is necessarily governed by two fundamental economic phenomena: risk and interest. So far the attention given by accountants to these basic factors has been quite inadequate and inconsistent, the result being that dubious mixture of conservatism and recklessness, which is commonly called "accounting theory," although it is truly a mere collection of partly obsolete and contradictory conventions or working rules, recopied and reexpounded faithfully year after year.

In theory, differences between assets are limited to differences in the services expected from them either in use or in exchange. The principal criteria are total quantity, intensity, and time-shape of the stream, together with the degree to which each is capable of modification. In practice, there is another important difference: The specific services of some assets can be readily identified and measured, while those of others can not—especially if they are combined into a single productive unit. Valuation of the former is accordingly possible by the direct method, *i.e.*, by the discounting process, whereas the best that can be done for the latter is to value them indirectly, *i.e.*, to maintain a record of what their future services have cost.

Canning has done valuable work in defining direct and indirect valuation,[8] but his thoughts are not always carried to their logical conclusion. With respect to accounts receivable, for instance, he points out that they ought to be discounted for the period of their turnover. He overlooks that cash on hand or a demand deposit bearing no interest is likewise worth its face value only at the moment when its service is rendered, *i.e.*, when it is spent. Cash being thus subject to discount for its own turnover, it follows that accounts receivable must be discounted for the sum of both periods. Rapidly moving merchandise or finished goods can also be valued by the direct method, but it again

follows that the discount deducted from "selling price less selling expenses" must cover not only the turnover of the inventory, but the sum of all three turnovers. The suggestion that liabilities should also be discounted for the delay in payment is entirely in order.

In general, accountants give adequate attention to risk in valuing current assets, so that the main question there concerns interest alone. As will appear later, it is proper to omit interest for certain purposes. In any event the treatment of current assets and liabilities could be responsible for only a small fraction of the discrepancies which have rendered the typical balance sheet so meaningless that no one cares to define it. The principal problem is the treatment of the so-called capital assets and the various forms of deferred charges. Examples are illustrated and discussed in subsequent paragraphs.

DEPRECIATION

Leake describes depreciation, in part, as "fall in the exchangeable value of . . . assets."[9] If he had stopped there, he would not only have conformed to etymology, but would also have defined one of the essential bases of accounting valuation. To say that depreciation is the "fall in the exchangeable value of wasting assets, computed on the basis of cost expired during the period of their use in seeking profits"[9] is contradictory, because original cost less cost expired gives, not exchange value, but merely use value, which may, and usually does, differ from exchange value. By his insistence that " 'expired capital outlay' is an exact definition of depreciation",[10] the concept of exchange value is definitely abandoned. Depreciation in this generally accepted sense has nothing to do with exchange value, but is merely concerned with the gradual extinquishment of cost; a task better described as amortization. Whether wasting assets be called tangible or intangible, the same thing, *viz.*, the cost of services not yet rendered, must remain on the books, so that it is il-

---

[8] J. B. Canning: *The Economics of Accountancy*, Ronald Press Co., New York, 1929.

[9] P. D. Leake: *Depreciation and Wasting Assets*, Sir Isaac Pitman & Sons, Ltd., London, 1917, p. 1.
[10] *Ibid.*, p. 5.

logical to describe the extinguishment of certain assets as depreciation and that of others as amortization.

THE METHOD OF AMORTIZATION

The cost of any capital asset may be analyzed into the present worth of its ultimate selling price plus the present worth of an annuity, each item of which consists of the

investment. If it is not essential that the balance sheet should record the true investment, interest may be omitted in the distribution.

The foundation for amortization is a curve showing the decline in the exchange value of an asset during the course of its useful life. By marking on this curve the point at which its usefulness is expected to come to an end,

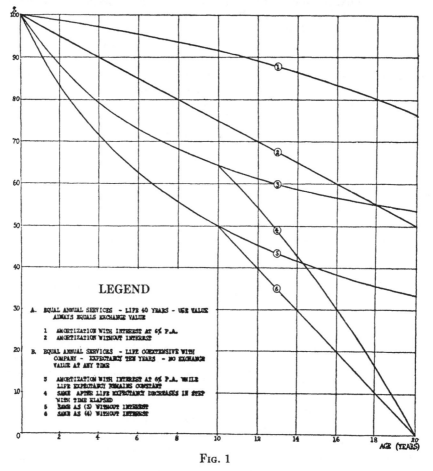

LEGEND

A. EQUAL ANNUAL SERVICES - LIFE 40 YEARS - USE VALUE ALWAYS EQUALS EXCHANGE VALUE

　1　AMORTIZATION WITH INTEREST AT 6% P.A.
　2　AMORTIZATION WITHOUT INTEREST

B. EQUAL ANNUAL SERVICES - LIFE COEXTENSIVE WITH COMPANY - EXPECTANCY TEN YEARS - NO EXCHANGE VALUE AT ANY TIME

　3　AMORTIZATION WITH INTEREST AT 6% P.A. WHILE LIFE EXPECTANCY REMAINS CONSTANT
　4　SAME AFTER LIFE EXPECTANCY DECREASES IN STEP WITH TIME ELAPSED
　5　SAME AS (3) WITHOUT INTEREST
　6　SAME AS (4) WITHOUT INTEREST

Fig. 1

cost of that unit of service to be rendered. The proper figure at which the asset should be stated in successive balance sheets is therefore obtained by discounting both the remaining service-costs and the ultimate selling price down to the successive dates. The difference between two consecutive summations is the net amortization, which may readily be separated into a charge for services rendered and a credit for interest on the

the allocation of cost to services and liquidating value is determined. The form of this real depreciation curve differs widely for different assets. In some cases, exchange value practically equals use value, while in others it drops immediately to zero. Between these extremes lie all other cases, where exchange value declines more or less rapidly to a salvage value or to zero, sometimes long before the asset has outlived its usefulness.

This behavior of exchange values is explained by the more or less specialized utility of assets. Some are equally useful to anyone, whereas others can serve only their original owner. In general, second-hand equipment commands only a restricted market controlled by the buyer, so that the entire remaining use value can seldom be realized upon sale. Amortization must be computed with due regard for these variations.

EXAMPLES OF AMORTIZATION

A leasehold which has been subleased for its entire term may be taken as a fairly good sample of an asset commanding an exchange value practically equal to its use value to the sublessor. Curve (1) in Fig. 1 shows the amortization line connecting its original value with a final exchange value of zero forty years later. The ordinates of this curve were obtained by finding that forty-year annuity which $1 will purchase at 6% *per annum* and plotting the worth of the decreasing number of payments still due on the successive dates. The amortization of such an asset will be entirely independent of the life expectancy of the business itself, since the curve of depreciation (exchange value) and the curve of amortization (investment or use value) follow the same law. The ordinate of the curve will represent either cost or fair market value, dpending upon whether the asset is being valued indirectly or directly.

The opposite extreme is illustrated by organization or preliminary expenses, which have no salvage value. In such a case, amortization will depend entirely upon the life expectancy of the company. Assuming it to be ten years, the first year's amortization will be the difference between an eleven-year annuity worth cost and the present worth of its ten remaining payments. If at the end of the second year the life expectancy of the company is still ten years, the original cost must be reapportioned over twelve years and ten such payments discounted. Continuing from year to year, the investment level drops with decreasing speed as shown by curve (3) in Fig. 1.[11] When liquidation becomes a

definite future event, instead of merely a risk to be provided for, no revision of the apportionment will be made and the amortization curve (3) will bend toward zero ten years hence, as indicated in Fig. 1 at the ten-year point (curve 4).

As the third example, an item of equipment may be selected which has a long life and is subject only to comparatively slow depreciation. The exchange value, for instance, may not reach scrap value for forty years, although it will always be lower than use value. Statistical research shows that the mortality of physical property is subject to the same laws which govern human lives, except that the correspondence between the theory of probability and practical experience is closer because the phenomenon of high infant mortality arises only in the case of human beings.[12]

The mortality curve shown in Fig. 2 (1) is a cumulative frequency distribution of a special kind,[13] which appears better adapted to the problem than the cumulative normal curve of error. The ordinates show the chance of survival *per centum* at the various ages marked on the axis of abscissa. By summing up the entire area below the mortality curve, the average life (3) of the asset is obtained, which is in this case twenty years. When the asset is new, that is its life expectancy. As it grows older, the expectancy remaining at successive ages is found by

value, but a life coextensive with that of the company and if the annual services are equal in magnitude, the figure C_t at which it ought to be stated in the balance sheet, is:

$$C_t = C_0 \frac{1 - \dfrac{1}{(1+i)^n}}{1 - \dfrac{1}{(1+i)^{n+t}}}$$

In this formula i is the money rate, n the life expectancy or horizon of the company, and t the number of times (years) the expectancy was revised, *i.e.*, extended, since acquisition of the asset. Applying the theory of limits to the special case $i=0$, the same formula without interest becomes $C_t = C_0 n/(n+t)$. This formula is applied in Fig. 1 for the construction of curve (5).

[12] *Cf.* E. B. Kurtz: *Life Expectancy of Physical Property*, Ronald Press Co., New York, 1930.
[13] The cumulative curve VII (a form of the Pearsonian curve I) used by Kurtz. *Ibid.*, p. 90 and table 50, p. 170.

---

[11] If C_0 be the cost of an asset having no exchange

computing the area of the mortality curve to the right of each age. The result, *per centum* of the total area, is plotted horizontally by adding it to the age on the level of the corresponding chance of survival. This gives the probable life curve (2). For instance, if the asset has reached the age of

on the right. The next step is to compute the remaining cost (6) at all ages. It is done by multiplying the remaining services (4) by the difference between 100% and the exchange value *per centum* (5) and then adding the latter again. If the investment is desired, interest must be considered in the computa-

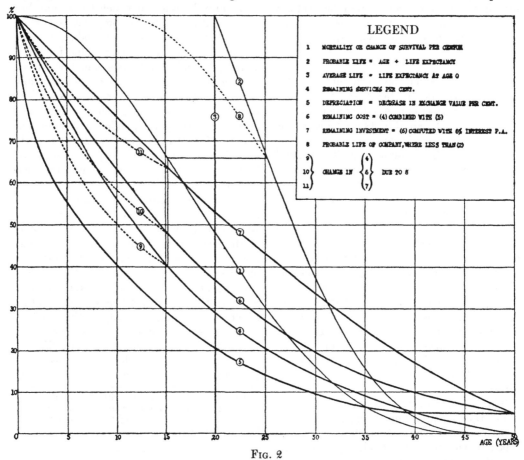

FIG. 2

ten years, it may be expected to live $12\frac{1}{2}$ years longer; if it has survived twenty years, its expectancy is eight years more; and so on until the maximal age is reached. The sum of expectancy and age is the probable life. Terminology and method are the same as those used in human mortality studies.

The life expectancy at successive ages divided by the corresponding probable life gives the remaining services of the asset in terms of a total of 100%. This information is plotted vertically in Fig. 2 (4), descending from the upper left hand corner toward zero

tion. This phase of the problem does not appear to have received as much attention from engineers, perhaps because they are not primarily interested in investment valuations. The theory has been outlined in the preceding section entitled, "The Method of Amortization," but may be illustrated by concrete data. At the age of twenty years, for instance, the asset is expected to last eight years longer. Presumably, therefore, it will be sold at the age of 28 years when, according to the depreciation curve (5), it will be worth 11.2% of its original cost. Discounting this figure at 6% for 28 years gives 2.09%, which means that 97.91% of the total cost must be allocated to 28 years of service. One payment of a 28-year annuity which 97.91 will purchase is 7.3 and the present worth of eight such payments is 45.5. Adding the present value of 11.2 due eight years hence, *viz.*, 7.0, results in the answer required, namely, that the investment in the asset at the end of the twentieth year is 52.5% of its original cost. Upon repeating the computation at suitable intervals, the investment or amortization curve (7) can be plotted.

If the life expectancy of the company is more than twenty years, there will be no interference with the independent calculation of amortization. Assuming, however, for the sake of illustration, that it is only ten years, the expectancy of the asset must be reduced to that figure, wherever it is greater. The upper portion of the mortality curve has accordingly been recopied ten years to the right (8) to supplant the corresponding portion of the probable life curve. The resultant indentions of the remaining service, cost, and investment curves are shown as dotted lines, which extend to about the fifteenth year.[14] Beyond that age the life expectancy of the asset is below ten years, so that the company's life has no further effect, unless its expectancy has also decreased in the meantime.

COMPOSITE AMORTIZATION

In Fig. 2 only a single and slowly wasting item of equipment was considered. It might have dropped out of service at any time, the probability of such an event being expressed by the mortality curve. What has been done there was to make only that provision for amortization which is "probably" sufficient, but not necessarily so. In the case of a large plant, consisting of many similar items of machinery, the problem is somewhat different. The more numerous the items are, the closer will the number of those actually dropping out of service correspond to the number called for by the mortality

curve. For locomotives, rolling stock, pumps, telegraph poles, *etc.*, a most remarkable correspondence between theory and practice has been observed.[15]

The amortization of a composite plant is illustrated in Fig. 3. Individual units are continuously discarded and replaced. Upon disposal all units have only a scrap value of 20% regardless of their age; the depreciation curve (5), therefore, is a horizontal line. The mortality (1) and probable life (2) curves are similar to those of Fig 2, except that the average life is only ten years. The rate at which units drop out of service is shown at the bottom of the chart; the replacements of the original units form the basic frequency distribution (8) the summation of which is the mortality curve. In addition to original units, replacements must also be replaced, so that the replacement rate (9) gradually stabilizes itself around the 10% level, corresponding to the average life of ten years.

The remaining service (4) remaining cost (6) and amortization (7) curves have been plotted as outlined for Fig. 2. Each block of annual replacements will have reached a different stage in this respect. At the end of the tenth year, for instance, the plant will be composed of about 48% of original units, plus 52% of the first year's replacements, plus 59% of the second, plus 67% of the third, and so on, the weighted total being always 100%. Correspondingly, the original units will represent a remaining service of 29%, a cost of 43%, and an investment of 50%; the first year's replacements, a remaining service of 31%, a cost of 45%, and an investment of 51%; and so on. The averages of all these data, weighted by the size of the respective blocks, give the composite service, cost, and investment remaining in the entire plant. The composite services without scrap value have not been plotted; the two other curves (10) and (11) start in the upper left hand corner of the chart, reach their lowest points at the end of the tenth year and become gradually stabilized at a slightly higher level, corresponding to an average age of 5.1 years and an average

---

[14] In strict mathematical theory this method is not entirely correct, but will serve as a satisfactory approximation.

[15] *Cf.* Charts and tables of actual experience presented by Kurtz, *op. cit.*

life expectancy of 6.2 years. These figures are obtained by tracing the level of the composite remaining cost from the infinitely distant future back to the remaining cost curve of a unit, proceeding from there along the 5.1 year ordinate to the mortality curve and drawing the horizontal line of probable life at that point. The same result will be obtained by tracing the level of the composite investment curve to the unit investment curve. The intersection lies on the same 5.1 year ordinate.

pany's life expectancy into the problem will not reduce the plant to its scrap value, but will merely maintain it at the proper number of years' distance from scrap. The drop of the level is not proportionate, because the original cost had to be distributed over a shorter probable life, and in the case of the investment curve the scrap value was also

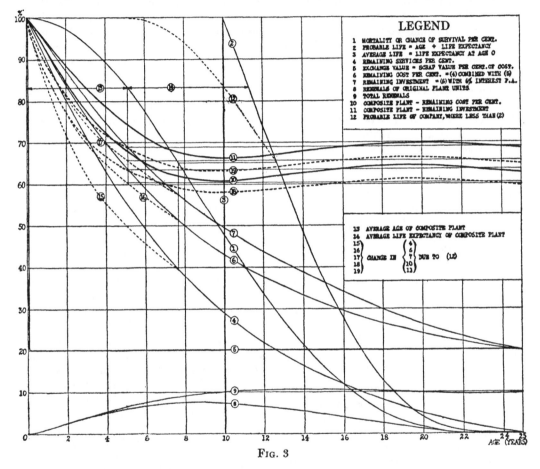

FIG. 3

tained by tracing the level of the composite investment curve to the unit investment curve. The intersection lies on the same 5.1 year ordinate.

Ordinarily the company's horizon is not apt to be less than ten years; nevertheless, to show what would happen if it were less, say five years, the cost and investment curves have been computed for this assumption also. It may be seen that their trend is again horizontal; introduction of the com-

discounted for a shorter period. The result is a higher present worth for both services and scrap which partly offsets the reduction in the length of the annuity discounted. The scrap value assumed in Fig. 3 has a great influence in this respect, because it is unusually high. If the plant is expanding, the compound amount of expansion must be added to the replacements. This will give an ascending trend to both the replacement and the cost or investment curves.

AMORTIZATION OF INVESTMENTS IN GOODWILL

If goodwill has been purchased on the basis of a careful and unbiased calculation, the data so obtained may be used for purposes of amortization. All that is necessary is to sum up the area below the discounted mortality curve to the right of each age and plot vertically the result *per centum* plus compound interest for those ages. Goodwill conceivably behaves like a large number of small original plant units taken together. Individual units will drop out of service in accordance with the mortality curve. The only difference is that good will has no scrap value. The plotting of the probable life curve and the computation from it of the curves of remaining services (cost) and investment per unit at successive ages are similar to the principles explained above. Multiplying the last curve by the number of units still in service, *i.e.*, by the ordinates of the mortality curve, produces the total investment curve.

Reference to the composite plant charted in Fig. 3 inevitably leads to the question of whether or not it is possible to replace goodwill in the same manner in which plant units are replaced. Theoretically it ought to be possible; in practice, however, the successive items added will seldom be sufficiently numerous or uniform. It seems preferable, therefore, to let each item of purchased or created good will and other deferred charge stand separately on its own merits, subject to corresponding amortization. The limitations imposed by the company's own life expectancy must be observed in all cases.

When purchased good will is not *bona fide*, but represents mere overcapitalization, there is a great deal to be said for *Canning's* insistence that "there is no possible excuse for perpetuating a gross blunder or the results of a misdeed in asset valuations."[16] That is particularly true in the public utility field, where the misdeed becomes a permanent source of revenue. In competitive business, accuracy is a goal equally worth striving for, but even if corporation laws were drastically revised, there would always remain a range

---

[16] *Op. cit.*, p. 248.

of reasonable doubt within which the valuations made might be suspected, but not upset. For this reason I do not agree that to distribute overvaluation over a future period is a statistical error for which no valid excuse can be presented.[16] On the contrary, the knowledge that amortization is as certain as the proverbial death and taxes, will itself restrict opportunities for abuse. To the investor, on to whom the organizers have unloaded the stock, the fictitious valuation is an actual investment. All he must understand is that the cake of excess profits has been eaten and that only the crumbs were left for him. It is the omission of adequate amortization from prospectuses forecasting future profits, which magnifies these crumbs into a semblance of the cake which he will never enjoy.

Until allegedly *bona fide* computations of good will can be checked by reference to statistical data and until abuses in reorganization can be effectively stopped, it may perhaps be best to treat all such deferred charges as if they were organization expenses having a life coextensive with that of the company. Uniformity will at least be gained in this manner.

TIME-SHAPE OF SERVICES

To simplify the presentation of the actuarial theory of life expectancy in Figs. 2 and 3, the services of various assets were regarded as evenly distributed over their useful lives. In practice, that is seldom the case. Two main types of behavior may be distinguished in this respect. Certain assets have a more or less limited total capacity for rendering service, the average of which is known from experience. If the intensity of their use or exploitation varies greatly from time to time, it will be better to base the mortality study upon units of production in terms of the total expected. That is done in several industries. The considerations which tip the scales in favor of one method or the other can not be discussed here. Suffice it to say that if the abscissa of the mortality curve measures production units instead of time, a scale of time distorted in accordance with expected variations in productive intensity must, nevertheless, be superimposed upon it to permit the computation of the investment remaining in the services not yet rendered.

Another class of assets has a capacity for service which is limited only by the opportunities for rendering it. Those commonly described as "intangibles" are in this group, *viz.*, patents, trade marks, copyrights, preliminary expenses, *etc.* As the recorded cost of such assets is frequently not *bona fide*, the inclination to refer to their services as "burdens" may be difficult to resist, but the change in name does not invalidate the general principle of amortization, intent upon insuring the stockholder's recorded equity against loss from liquidation. These services or burdens must be distributed in accordance with the opportunities to render them or the ability to bear them, whichever terminology be preferred. In other words, if the company is growing, the rate of growth should be considered. For this purpose the single horizon may no longer be an acceptable indicator of risk, because expansion has its own horizon. The distribution may accordingly be governed by a two-horizon method. Until research sheds more light upon the risk involved, the expansion horizon can only be estimated, but a careful estimate will give a more accurate result than mere scorn for all theory.[17]

The two main types of assets and their subdivisions deserve a great deal more attention than can be given them here. Assets with a limited total capacity for service often show a gradual decline in efficiency, so that their successive annual services may not be considered equal, even if opportunities for rendering them do not vary. The rate of decline will then influence the distribution.[18]

Patents and copyrights expire within certain legal limits, but their true expectancy of service may justify a distribution over a shorter period. On the other hand, if the life expectancy of the business is shorter than that period, the residual exchange values on the horizon enter into the problem. The life expectancy of trade marks and trade names is limited by that of the company and there is no scrap value wherever the legal rule prevails that assignments in gross are void.[19] The illustrations given in preceding paragraphs indicate the general approach, which must be suitably modified for special cases.

APPRECIATION

Exchange values need be considered only as of the future dates when exchange is expected to take place either in the normal course of business or by way of insurance against the risk of liquidation. General hints have already been given about the valuation of current assets and liabilities. From them it is possible to deduce the rules governing other cases; for instance, when demand deposits earn a low rate of interest or when accounts, notes, and bonds receivable or payable call for a higher or lower rate than the one used in their valuation.

The exchange value of machinery, equipment, *etc.*, on the date when their sale is contemplated is ordinarily so small a portion of the original cost that normal fluctuations of exchange values will have only a negligible influence upon the apportionment of cost to services. It will seldom be necessary to revise the original estimate of scrap value for a composite plant. Gains or losses are, instead, absorbed currently, as they arise. The

---

[17] The recognition of expansion (x) will change the formula of note 11 into the following, wherein $h=$ horizon of excess earnings and $k=$ horizon of expansion:

$$C_t = C_0(1+x)^t \frac{\dfrac{x}{i}\left(\dfrac{1+x}{1+i}\right)^k + \left(1-\dfrac{x}{i}\right)\dfrac{(1+x)^k}{(1+i)^h} - 1}{\dfrac{x}{i}\left(\dfrac{1+x}{1+i}\right)^{k+t} + \left(1-\dfrac{x}{i}\right)\dfrac{(1+x)^{k+t}}{(1+i)^{h+t}} - 1},$$

This expression may be suitably reduced.

[18] Maintenance and repair charges as well as taxes and insurance may properly be considered in the computation of the net services rendered in successive periods. See Harold Hotelling: "A General Mathematical Theory of Depreciation," *Journal of The American Statistical Association*, Sept., 1925, pp. 340–353. For the sake of giving a plausible illustration, Hotelling assumes that repairs depend upon age, and taxes and insurance upon residual value. This does not justify Canning's criticism (*op. cit.*, p. 298) that the integral equation presented by Hotelling will work only in the assumed case. The equation states the general problem in terms of symbols representing the variables as unknown functions of time. If anyone does not like the known functions tentatively substituted, he may readily substitute others acceptable to him. The solution will fit the case he has in mind.

[19] *Cf.* my article on "The Law of Goodwill," Ac-COUNTING REVIEW, Dec., 1936, pp. 317–329.

greater the number of units in service, the less significant the distortion of earnings arising from this source.

More attention must be given to single large and slowly wasting items of investment. The extreme example is land, the cost of which often represents the present worth of perpetual service. Even then, however, the technique of apportionment is the same as for other assets. Under the investment-concept of the balance sheet the difference between cost and the net selling price looming upon the receding horizon must be distributed over the services rendered between the date of purchase and the horizon. So long as the trend of land values is horizontal, the charge for each annual service equals the credit to interest on investment and the land remains recorded at cost. If the trend is rising, the cost of each service is less than the credit to interest on investment, and the difference may be added to the cost of land. Should the slope of the trend equal the combined rate of interest and taxes, the services will cost nothing.

For cost accounting purposes appreciation may be disregarded, but it constitutes nevertheless a gain connected with manufacturing, until the point is reached where the selling price upon the horizon would pay for a comparable location plus the expense of tearing down the plant and moving the equipment. If no such action is taken, the company will thereafter be engaged in two separate ventures: one manufacturing and the other a real estate speculation, each of which calls for separate records. In the manufacturing division the book value of the land must be kept at the balancing point, which will change with changing opportunities for removal.

The real estate venture may be recorded by either the direct or the indirect method; preferably by both, supplemented further by copious explanation.[20] The direct method will consist of tracing the changing present worth of the selling price and deducting the value recorded in the manufacturing division. As for the indirect method, it will be limited to capitalizing taxes and assessments not chargeable to manufacturing and to compounding interest on these expenditures. Or interest may be omitted in both instances. In an extreme case the facts will generally be easier to understand than the method of their recording. This should be borne in mind because any method is valuable only in proportion to its ability to simplify facts, and to permit conclusions to be drawn from them.

The date of sale which will yield the greatest profit is located at the point where the declining rate of appreciation becomes equal to the combined rate of interest and taxes on the value estimated by the direct method. This date is the logical horizon for manufacturing purposes, unless it is so far distant that the risk of manufacturing calls for a shorter period.

When the purchasing power of money shows a definite trend of change or fluctuates too widely, it may become necessary to adjust accounts by reference to some general price index.[21] The true appreciation or depreciation of a specific asset can then be measured more accurately.

A different form of appreciation occurs when exploration is rewarded by a valuable discovery. The same technique of apportionment could again be applied and would furnish a mathematically correct presentation, but such a method of gradual negative amortization would, nevertheless, look highly artificial and contrary to common sense. It is far more reasonable to adopt the position that exploration is one kind of business activity and the exploitation of discoveries quite another. Reorganizations have been effected for less weighty reasons. And even if the legal corporate entity happens to remain unchanged,[22] there can be no valid ob-

---

[20] In discussing this subject, I have in mind an extreme case within my own experience, where the land rose about a hundredfold in value while the company continued manufacturing operations at a declining profit. In the end practically the entire value of the stock was attributable to the land.

[21] *Cf.* H. W. Sweeney: *Stabilized Accounting*, Harper & Bros., New York, 1936.

[22] I again have in mind a case within my experience, where an oil well was discovered and appraised at forty times the cost of the land and its exploration. A share was quoted in the market at forty-three times the capital paid in and the first years profits equalled twice the recorded book equity.

jection to a careful allocation of the rewards to their respective sources. For this reason I do not quite understand why *May* calls discovery values "perhaps the most phantastic of all,"[23] unless he means merely that there is too much room for fancy in the appraisal.[24] All appraisals, of course, are "for experts of good character only,"[25] but the play of fancy will be greatly restricted by well-defined and enforced principles of amortization fully understood in advance.

INTEREST AND ITS LIMITATIONS

It is a curious phenomenon that many writers, in discussing the place of interest in valuation, devote more space to witty, but misleading remarks than to an exposition of its limitations. Interest can not be disposed of merely by saying that "it is as absurd as trying to correct for the earth's rotation in a snowball fight" or that "all we should have to do to earn rate i forever would be to abandon the plant." And when the "muddy pool of interest" is mentioned, it is difficult to resist the temptation of retorting that the appearance of muddiness may be due to the condition of the eye rather than to that of the pool.

expired life, the discounted excess profits plus the recorded value will always give the true fair market value, even though both the investment and the excess profits are measured incorrectly. This statement is a simple theorem of arithmetic.

Risk being disregarded for the time being, the only basic facts are the life of the asset and the proceeds of its services. Let us place the life at four years and let us assume that the proceeds are $500, $600, $900 and $700 for the successive years. Valuing now the asset at any random figure and filling in annual amortization (cost) likewise at random, a table may be completed as follows:

TABLE 1

Prin-cipal	Services		Profit		
	Cost	Pro-ceeds	Total	Normal	Excess
$1,000	$ 300	$ 500	$ 200	$ 50	$ 150
700	100	600	500	35	465
600	200	900	700	30	670
400	400	700	300	20	280
—	$1,000	$2,700	$1,700	$135	$1,565

Or, if preferred—

TABLE 2

Principal	Services		Profit		
	Cost	Proceeds	Total	Normal	Excess
$200,000	$ 20,000	$ 500	$— 19,500	$10,000	$— 29,500
180,000	80,000	600	— 79,400	9,000	— 88,400
100,000	30,000	900	— 29,100	5,000	— 34,100
70,000	70,000	700	— 69,300	3,500	— 72,800
—	$200,000	$2,700	$— 197,300	$27,500	$— 224,800

The opponents of interest really have an argument stronger than any of those which they have mentioned so far, to my knowledge. A fundamental truth about accounting is that, given perfect and unlimited foresight, no matter at what value an asset is placed on the books and no matter in what haphazard way it is amortized over its un-

The random figures of amortization may be taken to represent more or less profound theories of distribution. Irrespective of their merit, the fair market value of the asset can be computed correctly from either table. It is $2,373.75. If interest were used in the distribution of cost, the answer would still be the same. It follows that interest may be disregarded in the process of preparing accounting statements which have only the limited purpose of permitting a correct appraisal of the fair market value.

---

[23] *Op. cit.*, p. 17.
[24] See the recognition and measurement of discovery value under successive revenue acts and treasury regulations.
[25] Canning, *op. cit.*, p. 305.

The inclusion of interest has only one primary advantage: The true investment and the true goodwill can be separated only by allocating both cost and interest to future services. When used jointly with a measure of risk, interest will, therefore, partly remedy the complaint that "book figures may be reasonably satisfactory for current assets, but the recorded data of fixed property are usually inadequate for the purpose of a qualitative analysis of earning power."[26] But if risk can be omitted from consideration and if only the sum of investment and goodwill is desired, almost any method will give the correct primary result.

The rate of interest to be used is evidently the riskless rate which the market itself uses in valuing common stocks. The average level of that rate can be determined with sufficient accuracy[27] to preclude any wide di-

THE GENERAL BUSINESS RISK

To introduce the concept of risk into the valuation problem means to limit perfect foresight to a short future period. This is merely a way of averaging unlimited, but imperfect foresight. Typical examples have already been presented graphically, but a review by figures appears indicated. To save computation, a very simple example must be selected. A certain amount of harmless distortion will result, which may serve to emphasize the principle involved.

Let the unit to be valued consist of an asset having a fixed ten-year life and of another having a life coextensive with that of the company, whose expectancy is limited to five years. Each asset cost $1,000. Under accounting methods now in vogue the table of amortization would be as follows:

TABLE 3

| Year | Book Value | Services | | Profit | | | Apparent Market Value |
		Cost	Proceeds	Total	Normal	Excess	
1	$2,000.00	$ 100.00	$ 250.00	$ 150.00	$100.00	$ 50.00	$2,041.09
2	1,900.00	100.00	220.00	120.00	95.00	25.00	1,912.09
3	1,800.00	100.00	180.00	80.00	90.00	− 10.00	1,827.55
4	1,700.00	100.00	160.00	60.00	85.00	− 25.00	1,797.67
5	1,600.00	100.00	180.00	80.00	80.00	—	1,805.92
6	1,500.00	100.00	200.00	100.00	75.00	25.00	983.62
7	1,400.00	100.00	220.00	120.00	70.00	50.00	832.80
8	1,300.00	100.00	240.00	140.00	65.00	75.00	654.44
9	1,200.00	100.00	260.00	160.00	60.00	100.00	447.17
10	1,100.00	1,100.00	220.00	−880.00	55.00	−935.00	209.52
	—	$2,000.00	$2,130.00	$ 130.00	$775.00	$−645.00	—

vergence of opinion. And if the rate and amount of interest included in asset figures are disclosed, adjustment by interpolation is an easy task for anyone who prefers a slightly different rate. The requirement of full disclosure will also eliminate temptation.

[26] W. A. Paton: "The valuation of the business enterprise," *Accounting Review*, March, 1936, pp. 29–30. That portion of the complaint which refers to the change in the purchasing power of money will, of course, remain in force and calls for separate correction. *Cf.* note 21.

[27] For instance, by analyzing well known seasoned stocks which have long been earning less than the money rate. The horizon can there be considered infinite, and, therefore, their yield must equal the money rate, subject only to minor disturbing factors, which can be eliminated if a sufficient number of observations is analyzed.

The computation of the apparent fair market value is based, in accordance with the assumption, upon the next five years' excess profits ahead at each successive date. It may be seen that this method of bookkeeping grossly overstates the market value until the end is in sight. Thereafter the figures are correct. When books are kept in this manner, the market will sooner or later learn to disregard them. Appraisal on the basis of rumors and "tips" is the natural consequence.

If risk is now considered, but interest is still omitted, the following figures will be obtained:

TABLE 4

Year	Book Value	Services		Profit			Correct Market Value
		Cost	Proceeds	Total	Normal	Excess	
1	$2,000.00	$ 333.33	$ 250.00	$— 83.33	$100.00	$—183.33	$865.79
2	1,666.67	238.10	220.00	— 18.10	83.33	—101.43	815.80
3	1,428.57	178.57	180.00	1.43	71.43	— 70.00	808.96
4	1,250.00	138.89	160.00	21.11	62.50	— 41.39	857.45
5	1,111.11	111.11	180.00	68.89	55.56	13.33	944.05
6	1,000.00	200.00	200.00	—	50.00	— 50.00	983.62
7	800.00	200.00	220.00	20.00	40.00	— 20.00	832.80
8	600.00	200.00	240.00	40.00	30.00	10.00	654.44
9	400.00	200.00	260.00	60.00	20.00	40.00	447.17
10	200.00	200.00	220.00	20.00	10.00	10.00	209.52
	—	$2,000.00	$2,130.00	$ 130.00	$522.82	$—392.82	—

Every line of this table is taken from corresponding primary tables prepared by using a different combination of foresight and hindsight for each. For instance, the second line of Table 4 is the second line of a six-year table combining one year of hindsight with five years of foresight. Similarly, the ninth line involves eight years of hindsight and two years of foresight. The fair market values now found are correct, but they must be calculated from the primary tables, not from Table 4 itself.

If it is desired to separate investment from goodwill, the ten primary tables must be computed by using interest in the distribution of cost. The result will be:

TABLE 5

Year	Book Value	Goodwill	Market Value
1	$2,000.00	$—1,134.21	$865.79
2	1,705.97	— 890.17	815.80
3	1,496.44	— 687.48	808.96
4	1,339.74	— 482.29	857.45
5	1,218.23	— 274.18	944.05
6	1,121.38	— 137.76	983.62
7	918.43	— 85.63	832.80
8	705.34	— 50.90	654.44
9	481.60	— 34.43	447.17
10	246.67	— 37.15	209.52

For the purpose of the example, the horizon had to be assumed. Actually, it depends partly upon the nature of the business, partly upon special information relative to the future and partly upon the rate of return and the changes expected in it. A secondary advantage of including interest in the computation is that, by correctly stating the investment in the services expected, it will eliminate that part of the error in estimating the risk which is due to incorrectly computed rates of return.

The amortization enforced by the horizon of the business is a premium paid for insuring the book equity against loss upon liquidation. As in the case of natural persons, the company does not actually expect to die so soon; nevertheless, the horizon measures the risk that it might. The correctness of the premium charged in a given case may be checked roughly by using what appears to be an appropriate horizon for the computation of the market price from book figures. Until the legal phrase "suitable and proper"[28] can be made more definite by applying statistical methods, a range of doubt will remain open; in many instances, however, the discrepancy is so great that it can be immediately spotted.

THE FORMULA-REVERSAL TEST

To illustrate the application of the valuation formulae, let us select at random the unexpired portion of the primary table upon which line 3 of Table 5 is based (Table 6).

The negative good will at the beginning of the third year is $687.48. The average excess profit for each year, therefore, is one payment of an annuity which that sum can purchase, viz., $—158.79. Subtracting normal profits gives an average net loss of $83.97. Accordingly, the fair market value may be computed as follows:

[28] Cf. Note 19.

$$-158.97\frac{1-\dfrac{1}{1.05^5}}{.05}+1,496.44=808.96$$

From this method, it is not proper to jump to the conclusion that the horizon refers to

all. If the asset will ultimately be reduced to salable scrap, only the present worth of that can receive consideration. The horizon-theory or liquidation insurance presented in this article rests ultimately upon the equivalence or interchangeability of the three formulae, or two viewpoints.

TABLE 6

Year	Book Value	Services			Profits		
		Amortization	Cost	Proceeds	Excess	Normal	Total
3	$1,496.44	$ 270.81	$ 345.63	$180.00	$−165.63	$ 74.82	$− 90.81
4	1,225.63	284.36	345.64	160.00	−185.64	61.28	−124.36
5	941.27	298.58	345.64	180.00	−165.64	47.06	−118.58
6	642.69	313.51	345.64	200.00	−145.64	32.13	−113.51
7	329.18	329.18	345.64	220.00	−125.64	16.46	−109.18
	—	$1,496.44	$1,728.19	$940.00	$−788.19	$231.75	$−556.44

excess profits only and not to the life of the business itself. The computation can be readily converted into

$$-83.97\frac{1-\dfrac{1}{1.05^5}}{.05}+\frac{1,496.44}{1.05^5}=808.96.$$

Now, the formula states clearly that the entire investment is repayable upon the horizon. Both varieties of the formula, of course, express a fiction obtained by substituting earnings, *i.e.*, "standard income," for the actual stream of services coming in.[29] The fiction was created for the purpose of permitting the investor to rely upon the recorded book equity and to compute the capital value from it. Figures closer to reality are used in the service formula preferred by economists. The average service in the example is $345.64−$158.79=$186.85. Therefore—

$$186.85\frac{1-\dfrac{1}{1.05^5}}{.05}=808.96.$$

Here the book equity is not mentioned at

When the annual volume of production is not constant, the averaging process is somewhat more complicated. If the increase is such that the fitting of a compound expansion curve is reasonable, the rate of expansion may be so found. A fairly accurate expansion rate can also be derived from the gross (undepreciated) book value of a composite plant, after it has been in operation long enough enough to have a stable renewal rate (see Fig. 3). By dividing an annuity growing at the expansion rate into the present worth of excess profits, adding the normal profit of the first year and dividing the result by the book equity at the beginning, the average earning rate is obtained. Alternatively, the net cash dividend rate (subscriptions, assessments, *etc.*, being considered negative dividends) may be computed and added to the expansion rate to find the earning rate. Choosing now an appropriate horizon, the appraisal can proceed.[30]

[29] Irving Fisher defines standard income as "that income which capital can yield without alteration of value." Cf. *The Nature of Capital and Income*, p. 333.

[30] The service formula is as follows, when $r=$ earning rate, $x=$ expansion rate, $r-x=$ services, $a=$ amortization and $s=$ scrap value:

$$P=\frac{r-x+a}{x-i}\left[\left(\frac{1+x}{1+i}\right)^n-1\right]+s\left(\frac{1+x}{1+i}\right)^n$$

The formula of amortization is:

$$a=(1-s)\frac{x-i}{1-\left(\dfrac{1+i}{1+x}\right)^n}$$

The assumption here is that the horizon (n) of earning and expansion rates is the same. If that is unlikely, the amortization can be obtained from a two-horizon formula.

Comparison of the appraisal so derived from past book figures with the trend of market prices for the same period makes it possible to estimate with a fair degree of accuracy, first, that portion of the book equity upon which redemption service has been maintained and, second, what the true return would have been under full redemption service.

SUMMARY OF THE INVESTMENT-CONCEPT

The investment-concept of the balance sheet may be restated briefly as follows:

1. Asset figures are obtained by either the direct or the indirect method of valuation. The difference between the two is that the former proceeds backward from the next future starting point of the operating cycle, whereas the latter moves forward from the last starting point. This point is the moment when cash is disbursed.

2. The dividing line between direct and indirect valuation is the line of realization. Above the line, assets are stated at their fair market or capital values, while below it merely unexpired past costs (including time-cost) are recorded for the purpose of submitting them to the market for appraisal on the basis of their earning power.

3. The exact point where the realization line ought to be drawn depends upon conditions prevailing in different industries; these conditions determine the degree of accuracy with which the value of future services can be foretold. The degree of accuracy, in turn, determines the choice of the method. In most cases, inventories will be found next to the line, on either or both sides of it.

4. It is not necessarily true that any asset capable of direct valuation should be so valued. Uniformity of classification will often be preferable. In many cases services in exchange are best valued by the direct method and services in use by the indirect method.

5. Each asset has its own horizon or life expectancy. The horizon of current assets is the sum of all turnover periods which separate them from the date when their proceeds are again disbursed (*cf.* page 211). The expectancy of the so-called fixed assets can be found from mortality studies.

6. Paramount over all horizons of individual assets is the life-expectancy of the company itself. Beyond the limit so set, an asset can not be expected to render services in use, but merely a final service in exchange.

The horizon of the business enterprise is the least definite element entering into the investment concept, but a very essential one, upon which research is sorely needed. Fortunately a high degree of correlation evidently exists between this horizon and the "average life"[31] of the principal items of equipment used in industry, because the more or less substantial nature of such equipment is determined chiefly by the prevailing business risk. For this reason the horizon of an enterprise is not apt to interfere with the independent amortization of plant assets so long as normal operating conditions exist. Its principal practical significance is probably limited to actually impending liquidation and to the amortization of assets or burdens having an indefinite life.

OTHER BALANCE SHEET CONCEPTS

The capital-value, property, or true-net-worth concept of the balance sheet is strenuously opposed on the ground that appraisal is not a function of accounting. This position is probably well taken although—wherever business risks are not adequately considered in selecting the type of equipment, *i.e.*, where the horizon of the business is shorter than the "average life"[31] of such equipment, the best way of disclosing how amortization was determined would be to compute annually *Canning's* "master valuation account."[32] In this manner it could easily be shown what the capital value of the business would have to be if the assumptions made in keeping the books were correct and if last year's profit were considered a correct average in the sense explained in the section entitled, "The Formula-Reversal Test." Indeed, if such a test were appended to every balance sheet which is nowadays blandly certified, the frequently ludicrous discrepancy between actual market quotations and the result of the test would forcibly call

---

[31] *Viz.* life expectancy at the age zero. *Cf.* the preceding section entitled "Examples of Amortization."

[32] *Op. cit.*, p. 42.

attention to the fact that something is radically wrong either with the market or with the books and the methods by which they are kept. A single test might not be conclusive; within a few years, however, it would inevitably appear who is right and who is not.

Quite apart from this suggestion it must be admitted that the investment concept can render valuable service in the public utility field by placing regulation on an unequivocal basis. That seems true especially because in the general case the horizon of earnings could be considered infinite, so that only the minor problem of the expansion horizon would remain. Furthermore, public utilities are entitled to a stated fair return, so that deviations from it are really assets or liabilities, as the case may be.

In all cases where it is not essential to measure the exact investment and the exact rate of return from year to year, interest may immediately be omitted. This will cause only a small conservative bias in estimating the horizon. The main problem of the horizon still remains, however, because when foresight does not extend beyond the "average life"[31] of the most durable asset, the shifting of the horizon from one set of services to the next makes it impossible to compute the fair market value from successive reports. This was pointed out with reference to Tables 4 and 5. Assets or deferred charges having an indefinite life always create this error, and this is the true, although perhaps not generally realized reason for the rule often preached, but seldom practised, that purchased goodwill, etc., ought to be separately stated on the balance sheet.

The mere segregation of such items will do no good, however, unless every reader of a balance sheet fully understands what that form of disclosure means. Another horizontal line has in effect been drawn, separating self-liquidating assets from those which are excluded from gradual redemption and are branded instead as ultimate deficits. If all assets having an "average life"[31] longer than the corporate horizon are placed below the line of redemption service and are thereby excluded from consideration in the valuation

process, the remainder of the book equity and the excess profits computed thereon in successive years will regain their faculty of giving the true fair market value, subject only to errors of foresight, but to no mechanical flaw of procedure.

The policy of banishing certain capital expenditures below the redemption line can be carried much further. A great deal, for instance, could be said in favor of the idea that items above the line shall present liquidating values only, *i.e.*, net selling prices of all assets looming either upon their own horizons or upon that of the company, whichever be shorter. Upon acquisition the cost of an asset could be apportioned immediately to both sides of the line. Depreciation tables, based upon market statistics of second-hand equipment—not upon any theory of use value to the present owner—would be needed for the annual adjustment of the figures above the line. The amount of the adjustment could be transferred below or written off altogether, since for valuation purposes what happens to it is irrelevant. The income account, in turn, would have to emphasize the net potential service, *i.e.*, sales less operating, selling, and administrative expenses, but excluding all depreciation or amortization. This requirement is observed in an old practice now frowned upon; that of stating depreciation at the end and not in cost of sales. For valuation purposes accounts would thus revert to the fundamental formula of capital value based upon services, for which the balance sheet would furnish the second term and the income account the first. For this purpose, however, reinvestments must also be deducted from the balance of the income account. Actually, therefore, only positive or negative cash dividends enter into the formula.

Above the redemption line, which now extends to the income account also, the fiction of standard income would thus be abandoned, but that does not mean that it can not be retained with respect to the entire balance sheet and the entire income account to whatever extent such a course may seem desirable. In accordance with this theory, accountants of the old school were in the habit of gradually "rearing up" reserves against capital expenditures by appropriating profits. In so doing, they introduced no error into the valuation formula based upon services, since the transaction took place below the redemption line. Only an improvement in the method of disclosure could have been suggested to them, namely that of stating separately the future selling prices of all assets. How the remainder of cost is recorded is entirely optional.

When "during the 1920's, accountants fell from grace and took to readjusting capital values to an extent never before attempted,"[33] their cardinal sin was failure to disclose the redemption line and to call proper attention to its significance. This omission amounts to a warranty that such adjustments do have a bearing upon the capital value of an investment, although that is not true. So long as revaluation, however questionable, is limited to manipulating debits and credits

---

[33] May, *op. cit.*, p. 16.

below the redemption line, the resultant harm is traceable directly to ignorance of its existence and ignorance of the economic law of capital value. On the other hand, when entries are passed between assets below the line and that portion of the income account which is above the line, the result is a misrepresentation or falsification of ascertainable facts.

Under the investment concept of the balance sheet the redemption line will disappear because full redemption service commensurate with risk becomes obligatory. That is a great advantage because there can be little doubt that the complications surrounding the line facilitate fishing in troubled waters. In the last analysis, however, no balance-sheet concept or other accounting principle can provide a safeguard unless it is applied in an intellectually, as well as legally, honest manner. That, incidentally, is a matter which might well receive a bit more attention from professional broadcasters on professional ethics.

"ECONOMIC THEORIES OF GOODWILL"

Journal of Accountancy (September 1939), pp. 169–180

Economic Theories of Goodwill

By Gabriel A. D. Preinreich

I

COMPARISON of the writings of the principal economists shows that they are approaching the topics they wish to discuss on different levels of analysis.

"On the basis of human nature, as conceived by Bentham or Ricardo, the real forces which control human conduct are pleasure and pain. Commodities are important, because they are sources of pleasure and pain. Money is important as a means of getting commodities. And finally, welfare or happiness is a net balance of pleasurable feeling experienced in the long run.

"You can treat human behavior by giving an account of it in terms of pleasure and pain; or in terms of what men do about commodities; or what men do about money; or with reference to the happiness they get in the long run." [1]

The theory of pleasure and pain is no longer formally accepted, either in its seven dimensions originally described by Bentham or the four retained by Jevons. Nevertheless, traces of hedonistic psychology are distinctly discernible in the works of later economists, even of those who profess to discard it altogether. Marshall merely lessens the emphasis by speaking of "gratifications and sacrifices" and Fetter's "psychic income" and "desirable results in the realm of feeling" are closely akin to pleasure. Similarly the concept occurs in the utility calculus of the Austrian School, in Davenport's "human desires" or "paying dispositions and willingness to labor and wait," in Fisher's "real income" and "impatience," in Hobson's "human costs" and "human

utilities," and to some extent even in Veblen's "tropisms" and "preconceptions." The level of pain and pleasure, as subsequently modified by emphasis upon instincts and habits, may be called the psychological level.

The commodity level in the strict sense was used extensively by the classical economists. Analyses often carried out in terms of corn, etc., were concerned chiefly with production and the distributive shares derived from it by land, labor, and capital, the concept of the entrepreneur being added somewhat later. The description "production level" will be preferable for present purposes.

The money level of analysis is based upon the premise that economics should remain "innocent from contamination by psychological concepts" (Walras), because it is "the science which treats phenomena from the standpoint of price" (Davenport). Cassel demands "the direct construction of economic theory on the basis of a theory of prices" and even Marshall says that "money is the centre around which economic science clusters." Since "money is the one convenient means of measuring human motive on a large scale" (Marshall), a strong tendency has arisen to avoid an analysis of the motives themselves.

Finally, the welfare level deals in the main with problems of social justice and morality. It may therefore also be called the "ethical level." John Stuart Mill believed that, although the laws of production were unchangeable, the distribution of wealth depended upon the laws and customs of society determined by the ruling classes. These "are very different in different ages and countries and might be still more different, if mankind so chose." Karl Marx, basing his work in part on the study of the British "Blue Books," was concerned princi-

---

[1] W. C. Mitchell: *Lectures on Types of Economic Theories.* Columbia University. Mimeographed 1931, p. 174.

169

pally with social abuses. Veblen has a great deal to say about "capitalistic sabotage" and "conspicuous waste" under the present industrial system, which concentrates on "making money rather than making goods." He analyzes the "dissonances which have often been represented as the harmonies of modern economic organization" and attacks the philosophy of Christian apologetics advanced in its justification. Hobson similarly denounces the philosophizing fallacy of orthodox economists and is bent upon finding ways and means of maximizing human utilities, while minimizing human costs. Patten also deals at length with methods of improving the distribution of what he calls the "national dividend."

The development of the modern concept of goodwill has followed analysis on the levels described.

II

In the psychological sense, goodwill is a state of mind, an inclination to favorable judgment, and the willingness to associate. It is often said that it springs from such sources as honesty, courtesy, reputation, liking, or faith. For instance:

"Goodwill is established for a good, when purchasers learn to like it and call for it in preference to similar goods. So also is goodwill established for a firm when, through tactful, prompt, and honest dealings, a collective friendliness is created, which insures future patronage."[2]

Goodwill thus appears as the result of a bargain. If both parties are satisfied, they remain inclined to continue the relationship. Veblen[3] and Hobson[4] likewise define goodwill as the reputation, business standing, or favor which

the entrepreneur enjoys in the eyes of the public.

On the other hand, it is shown by the general use of the word "customers" and, in a more restricted sense, of the term "habitués," that business relations are often maintained through mere custom and habit. This aspect of goodwill is emphasized by Ely:[5]

"Goodwill is to be attributed, in a large measure, to the economic inertia and friction which results from the fact that buyers are guided to a very large extent by custom and habit rather than by conscious choice."

Taussig[6] describes goodwill as the habit or custom which leads men to deal with a particular enterprise in preference to others of the same kind. And Sidgwick[7] has defined custom as ". . . the tendency to do as one has done before and as others do. Men continually get less for their money, goods or services, because they exchange them, not in the best market, but in the market they have been used to frequent." Similarly according to Hadley,[8] "It is a mistake to draw fine-spun deductions as to the motives which guide buyers in their choice, when three-quarters of the buyers exercise no choice at all."

As the complexity of business enterprises increased, it became apparent that the bargain between them and their customers is not the only kind necessary for success. Bargaining also takes place with the landlord, the employees, and the financial community. In these transactions, the criteria of friendliness, courtesy, honesty, etc., as well as custom and habit, play an equally important part. It is accord-

[2] J. R. Turner: *Introduction to Economics.* C. Scribner's Sons, New York, 1917, pp. 483–4.
[3] Thorstein Veblen: *Theory of Business Enterprise.* C. Scribner's Sons, New York, 1904, p. 170.
[4] J. A. Hobson: *Evolution of Modern Capitalism.* C. Scribner's Sons, New York, 1912, p.246.

[5] R. T. Ely: *Outlines of Economics.* Macmillan Co., New York, 1927. 4th rev. ed., p. 524.
[6] F. W. Taussig: *Principles of Economics.* Macmillan Co., New York, 3rd rev. ed. 1921, p. 175.
[7] H. Sidgwick: *Principles of Political Economy.* Macmillan Co., London, 1883, p. 392.
[8] E. R. Hadley: *Economics.* G. P. Putnam's Sons, New York, 1896, p. 70.

ingly recognized that there are three kinds of goodwill: commercial, industrial, and financial, of which the last is better known as credit. And, since initiative is necessary to success in business, the conclusion is reached that the various forms of goodwill can, to a great extent, be created by the entrepreneur alone. This logically leads to theories which consider goodwill as an internal economy arising in the form of surplus value in the process of production.

III

Although the classical economists do not appear to have referred to goodwill by name, the basic concept is inherent in their analysis of surplus or rent. Originally, land was considered the only factor of production capable of yielding a surplus, and thus Ricardo derived his well known theory of rent from the application of labor and capital to land. To put it briefly and incompletely, he starts from the premise that, in the beginning, only land of the highest fertility was taken under cultivation, yielding just enough to remunerate the farmer. With the growth of population, the increasing demand for farm products raised their price and made it profitable to extend cultivation to land of lower fertility. Equal effort devoted to better-grade land already in use then yielded a surplus, but competition forced farmers to surrender it to the landlords, who could now demand a rent for all land better than that on the margin of production.

Since land was originally free, the surpluses appropriated by the landlords are payments for their goodwill in permitting the use of the land. The distribution of the total payments within the chain of successive landlords was effected through the successive selling prices, which represent future goodwill in capitalized form.

Subsequent study of Ricardo's theory of rent has demonstrated, first of all, that "fertility" must be considered a generic term, embracing all forms of possible differential advantage. Furthermore, it was found that the principle of scarcity which he recognized only with respect to "fertile" land is equally operative in the case of capital and labor in the sense that the pressure of demand for goods, whether agricultural or industrial, forces the employment of gradually less efficient labor and capital (machinery), the respective productivities of which are lower in proportion to their cost than the productivity of those already employed. Accordingly, labor and capital of more than marginal efficiency will also yield differential rents in much the same manner as better-grade land does. Rent or goodwill thus becomes an almost universal phenomenon, arising in all cases where business activity of any description, including trade, enterprise, and professional work is carried on with the aid of advantages not enjoyed by the marginal producer, whose costs tend to determine price, because his coöperation is necessary to satisfy the demand.

As already noted by Richard Jones, Ricardo's contemporary, the actual rents paid seldom correspond to the theoretical surplus of land, because the forms of land tenure are economic institutions varying according to the time and locality. In the same way, the "composite quasi-rents" created by other factors of production are "divisible among the different persons in the business by bargaining, supplemented by custom and notions of fair play." [9]

In a general way the situation can be illustrated by Marshall's familiar diagram (shown on page 172).

The rate of production of a commodity is measured along OX and its unit price along OY. The demand curve is DD_1, showing at what rate the commodity will be consumed at the corresponding prices, and SS_1 is the "par-

---

[9] Alfred Marshall: *Principles of Economics*. Macmillan Co., London, 1930, p. 626.

ticular expenses" curve, i.e., a form of supply curve, where the owners of differential advantages of production are arranged from left to right in the order of magnitude of the advantages enjoyed. Thus, the most efficient producer's units costs are represented by OS, those of another, less efficient, by

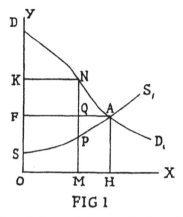

FIG 1

MP, and those of the marginal producer by the market price HA. Cost, in this sense, comprises adequate remuneration for all factors of production, including the wages of management and a normal return on the investment. Adding all individual rates of output together, the total rate (per unit of time) of the cost of production is represented by the area OHAS, for which compensation is received at the rate OHAF. This yields a producers' surplus or efficiency return SAF, which is shared in accordance with the differential advantages commanded by each producer.

Corresponding to the producers' surplus, the consumers also obtain a surplus FAD, which may be considered a representation of the goodwill of those who would have been willing to pay more than HA for a unit of the commodity.

The same diagram may also be used to visualize the bargains between factors of production and their employer. For instance, if SS₁ is taken to represent unit costs of labor arranged in the order of the laborers' relative efficiency, the area SAF is industrial goodwill accruing to the employer. The same form of goodwill arises, if the doses of capital invested in machines of different efficiency are arranged in the form SS₁. The financial goodwill of the employer could be shown by so arraying rates of interest payable of his mortgages and debentures. Reversing the reasoning, the laborer can be looked upon as a consumer in a wage-bargain [10] who would be willing to give effort worth OD to the employer for the first small unit OF of his wages, but can just be induced to give a final effort worth HA for its equivalent. In this case, his consumers' surplus is FAD, since he does not find it necessary to give that effort. Further examples along these lines come readily to mind.

Efforts by the entrepreneur to increase his differential advantages by increasing the efficiency of the business may next be mentioned. Apart from improvement in purely technical processes óf production, advertising falls under this heading, in so far as the greater volume of business resulting therefrom lowers the cost per unit, including the cost of advertising. All psychological factors known or believed to create goodwill may be cultivated at some expense, for instance through the employment of well bred and well dressed salespeople, tastefully furnished showrooms, credit, delivery, and other courtesies extended to customers. In the field of industrial relations, working conditions can be made more pleasant and a sense of solidarity, duty, and mutual understanding promoted. Profit-sharing methods may provide an incentive to greater efficiency.

Consolidation of competing enterprises will often increase the differential advantages of efficiency, although the opposite result is also frequently achieved.

[10] J. R. Commons: *Industrial Good-Will.* McGraw-Hill Co., New York, 1919, p. 18.

According to Veblen:

"A large proportion of the nominal collective capital resulting in such cases is made up of the capitalized goodwill of the concerns merged. This goodwill is chiefly the capitalization of the differential advantages possessed by the several concerns as competitors in business and is for the most part of no use for other than competitive business ends. The differential advantages possessed by business concerns as competitors disappear when the competitors are merged, in the degree in which they cease to compete with rival bidders for the same range of business. To this aggregate defunct goodwill (which in the nature of things can make only an imaginary aggregate) is added something in the way of an increment of goodwill belonging to the new corporation as such."[11]

The way in which goodwill becomes defunct is perhaps better explained by Ely:

". . . when it is sold at a fair price, the purchaser acquires no peculiar power of getting unusual profits. For him the price paid for goodwill is an investment and he has to deduct interest on the investment, before he can count his income as profits. In short, he has to start afresh, with no differential advantage." [12]

A state of affairs worse than that frequently results from consolidation. The burden of securities issued in payment of alleged goodwill often becomes oppressive. That, however, is no reason to deny that new economies may be open to consolidations, which have not been available to its original members. For example:

"So far, however, as goodwill is expressed in terms of credit, this consolidation may create a value larger than the canceled goodwill of the amalgamating units; the credit of the new corporation may be larger than the added credits of the old ones." [13]

---

[11] Op. cit., pp. 126–7.
[12] Op. cit., p. 524.
[13] Hobson: Op. cit., p. 246.

Probably more important are increases of goodwill through consolidation in industries which, normally, can operate their plants only at a fraction of their full capacity. The wastefulness of competition in such circumstances is sometimes so evident that public policy demands its suppression and the substitution of a regulated monopoly. To the extent that such regulation is successful, the resultant economies go to swell the consumers' instead of the producers' goodwill.

The various forms of "produced" goodwill may be classed as internal economies of production, so long as their effect is that of increasing efficiency. It will often be found, however, that many plans are at least in part aimed at the appropriation of a portion of the consumers' surplus, including in this sense the surplus or goodwill of employees or the investing public as consumers in the wage, interest, or dividend bargain. This introduces the ethical concept, which may be considered next.

IV

From the viewpoint of business ethics, the tendency is to draw a sharp dividing line between the earned profits of efficiency and the unearned scarcity profits of exploitation. In other words, everyone is said to be entitled to the fruits of his superior skill and ability to produce at lower costs than his competitor, but not to the results of a manipulation of prices.

That advertising may not always be classed entirely as an internal economy of efficiency is recognized by various economists:

"An important obstacle to the play of competition sometimes arises from custom and goodwill—from brands, labels and trade-marks. Where producers and consumers are separated by a long chain of intermediaries, the consumers often look to some external familiar mark in deciding which among

173

competing products they will select. Hence the immense part played in business by advertising.

"He who has induced many people to get into the way of buying a particular brand, may sell at a price higher than that of his competitors or sell in greater volume and with more steadiness. No doubt this advantage does not come by accident, but is created by shrewdness, patience, persistence." [14]

Ely likewise thinks it a noteworthy feature of modern business that manufacturers influence ultimate consumers through direct advertising of particular brands which are important factors in gaining or holding the patronage of consumers. He concludes that "the goodwill of a large manufacturing establishment thus comes to be in some cases as valuable a possession as a monopoly franchise." [15]

It is doubtful whether the fact that shrewdness, patience, and expense are necessary to build up this monopoly may be advanced to justify its creation and perpetuation. A series of unfair trade practices, such as misrepresentation of merits, origin, etc., fictitious grading of identical goods, and the like also belong in the category of exploitation through advertising, but are considered far more reprehensible. A slight adjustment of price above cost may even be maintained irrespective of advertising because:

". . . in many small transactions, for customers to buy always at the lowest price would result in a waste of energy disproportionate to the gain. Hence, aside from the influence of custom and habit, there may often be rational ground for the continued patronage of particular establishments and the continued purchase of particular goods which customers have found to be trustworthy." [16]

It is evident that in so far as goodwill is perpetuated through custom, inertia,

or stupidity, it may easily be exploited. Carelessness is said to be the principal characteristic of the ultimate consumer.[17] On the other hand:

"In the large transactions of wholesale jobbing and manufacturing establishments the element of goodwill is not entirely absent, but the vigilance of expert buyers and the mere size of the ordinary transaction (making even small differences in size important) tend to reduce it to a minimum." [18]

The ownership of a patent may lead either to economies of efficiency or monopoly profits, depending upon whether it protects a productive process or the product itself. In the latter event the greatest scarcity returns are sometimes obtained by refusing to sell the product and leasing it instead.

The exploitation of the factors of production controlled by the entrepreneur, i.e., land and labor, is recorded in the pages of economic history and need not be described here. Consolidation of business enterprises as a source of exploitation profits may be reviewed instead. Under the heading of consolidated goodwill, economists appear to have given consideration chiefly to the ingredients of which the capital of the new enterprise is composed. Veblen mentions that:

". . . the goodwill of Mr. Carnegie and his lieutenants, as well as of many other large businessmen connected with the steel industry, has also no doubt gone to swell the capitalization of the great corporation. But goodwill on this higher level of business enterprise has a certain character of inexhaustibility, so that its use and capitalization in one corporation need not, and indeed does not, hinder or diminish the extent to which it may be used and capitalized in any other corporation." [19] ". . . what

---

[14] Taussig: Op. cit., pp. 177–8.
[15] Op. cit., 2nd ed., pp. 447–8.
[16] Ibid., 4th ed., p. 524.

[17] E. S. Rogers: *Goodwill, Trademarks and Unfair Trading.* A. W. Shaw Co., Chicago, 1914, p. 66.
[18] Ely: Op. cit., 2nd ed., pp. 447–8.
[19] Op. cit., p. 127.

may be called the working capital on which this higher finance proceeds is made up chiefly of two elements: the solvency (and consequently potential credit) of the men engaged, and the goodwill of these men." [20]

Hobson is more outspoken about the exploitation of the investing public:

"The vendors, promoters and underwriters of a company are not unnaturally given to calculating in the first place how much they individually and collectively can get out of the business enterprise or in other words, how little they can leave to the ordinary investing public, whose capital they want to attract. It is their profit and not the interest upon the shares of the investors that is the originating motive of most companies." "By overvaluing the earning capacities of the various plants of amalgamating businesses, of the patents and especially of the goodwill and other invisible assets, they may bloat out the capital value of the company to the utmost, distributing among themselves in vendors' and promoters' shares and in other payments as much of the more vendible stocks as they can conceal, substituting in this capitalization the consideration of immediate vendibility for future earning capacity." [21]

That such abuses often occur, is well known, but it must be admitted that, at least occasionally, companies are formed for purposes other than the sale of nonexistent goodwill to a gullible public. Aside from efforts to increase productive efficiency, consolidations are resorted to principally in order to restrict competition and gain control over prices.

Let us assume that, in the industry represented by figure 1, there are two rival groups, OM and MH. If the latter group were eliminated, the former could demand a price MN for its product, thereby appropriating that portion of the consumers' surplus which corre-

[20] Ibid., p. 169–70.
[21] Op. cit., pp. 245–6.

sponds to the area FQNK. If the group OM proposes to buy out the group MH, it appears to follow that the latter will demand a price for its goodwill, which is based not upon the area PAQ, but rather upon FQNK. In fact, the price asked may be even higher, depending upon whether the group OM can subsequently further exploit its monopoly by discarding its own least efficient plants (i.e., moving the point M toward the left) to make the area SPNK a maximum.

This nuisance value of an independent producer may cause the group OM to start a price war instead. The respective

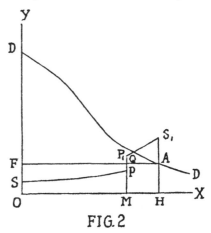

FIG. 2

costs of the two alternatives will depend in part upon the shape of the demand curve DD_1 and that of the curve of differential advantages SS_1. If the demand is inelastic (i.e., DD_1 steeply descending) and the differential advantages comparatively small (i.e., SS_1 slowly ascending), the odds will favor a price war. Conversely, an elastic demand and great differential advantages are arguments in favor of purchase. Complications arise, however, because the curve SS_1 represents merely the relative advantages of producers corresponding to a given scale of production, when the aggregate rate of production is OH. For a greater output SP moves lower if production conforms to the law of increasing re-

175

turns, or higher, if the law of diminishing returns is operative.

In the first event (see figure 2), group MH will be driven out of business in the ordinary course of competition at little or no cost to group OM, which may actually increase its producers' surplus (i.e., SPQF in figure 2 may be larger than in figure 1), while group MH incurs a deficit QAS₁P₁.

On the other hand, if the law of diminishing returns controls production on that scale, the cost of underselling may become prohibitive. In that case (figure 3), group OM must assume a deficit FQPS in addition to sacrificing its surplus SPQF (see figure 1), in order to inflict a total loss of QAS₁P₁ plus PAQ (figure 1) upon group MH.

ings up to a certain point of maximal efficiency. Thereafter costs tend to increase again. Supply curves may be considered fixed for short periods, although they are subject to change, whenever the volume of productive facilities available is changing. Gradual developments could be represented by a three-dimensional diagram, with time as the third coördinate. Demand and supply would then appear in the form of surfaces.

After a monopoly has been obtained, production can be adjusted so as to result in a maximum of revenue. Marshall shows the method [22] by subtracting the supply curve from the demand curve to obtain the monopoly curve

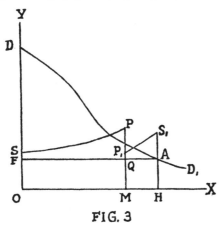

FIG. 3

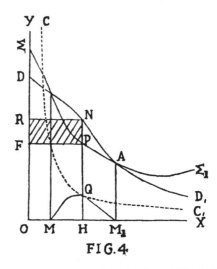

FIG. 4

The several positions of the curve of differential advantages SS₁ in figures 1 to 3 conform to a supply curve somewhat similar to ΣΣ₁, illustrated in figure 4. This curve is constructed by measuring along OY the average unit costs which result, when the rate of production is measured along OX.

Although supply curves vary in shape not only with different commodities, but also with each individual enterprise producing the same commodity, figure 4 shows a type which occurs frequently. In most instances a small output entails high unit costs and increased production brings great sav-

MM₁ (figure 4). The abscissa OH of the point of tangency of a rectangular hyperbola (constant revenue curve) CC₁ and the monopoly curve expresses the rate of production required to obtain the maximal monopoly revenue FPNR. The same answer can be obtained in a simpler manner by constructing cumulative curves of demand and supply, subtracting one from the other, and noting the highest point on the resultant cumulative monopoly curve. The maximal revenue is then expressed by

[22] Op. cit., p. 480.

176

an ordinate, instead of by an area, as in figure 4.

The extent to which monopoly can be exploited in practice depends upon circumstances. In earlier days price wars were frequent, but the growing tendency toward governmental regulation has made powerful combinations afraid of the publicity attendant upon ruthless practices. Interests in control of certain industries are now content with compromise benefits far short of the theoretical maximum. In fact, the power to fix prices is occasionally used with such restraint as to permit the smaller independent producers to earn a fair return on their share of the total business. By thus retaining competitors at the margin of production, the controlling producer is able to claim that his own large profits are not derived from the exploitation of a monopoly, but merely from the differential advantages of efficiency at his command. The argument may help to postpone the enrolment of the industry among public utilities. In terms of figure 1, it is better to enjoy the surplus SPQF and attempt to justify it by pointing to the marginal cost of production HA than to put group MH out of business, only to have one's surplus reduced by regulation. The illustration shows that it is impossible to draw a sharp boundary line between efficiency and scarcity profits. Whether or not it is fair to the consumer to allow the less efficient producers to remain in business, could be answered only on the basis of the three-dimensional analysis just mentioned.

The conclusions of the welfare school of economics on the subject of goodwill are summarized by Foreman:

". . . value itself is not goodwill. It is simply the price of the privilege of carrying on without interference commercial intercourse with the public. When this fact is recognized, much trade restraint will fall to the ground as illegal coercion; and by making a proper distinction between the rights of the producer and those of the consumer, a natural division may be drawn between the profits of efficiency and the unearned profits of goodwill." [23]

It is quite true that trade is restrained to a considerable extent by the liberal capitalization of goodwill, when existing enterprises are reorganized or consolidated, because the necessity of earning a fair return upon the inflated investment tends to raise the supply curve. Nevertheless, it would be difficult at present to obey literally the same writer's injunction that:

"The main duty of accountants should lie . . . in computing the present and prospective profits of efficiency, which the courts have declared just and legal." ". . . this should preclude the capitalization of such [exploitation] profits as an intangible asset." [24]

V

Although goodwill may not always be "good" in the social or ethical sense, the term is in general use to designate the capital value of all periodic surpluses accruing to an enterprise in the regular course of business, whether or not they are efficiency or exploitation profits. These surpluses, as illustrated in the diagrams, are returns in excess of the normal return on the investment, since a normal return is included among all other costs for the purpose of drawing the supply curve and the curve of differential advantages.

The value of goodwill may be obtained in the course of computing the capital value of a capital good. As Fisher explains in great detail, the act of investing consists of the purchase of a capital good, in order to enjoy the flow of services or income which it will yield. The future value of all items of income making up the flow must then

[23] C. J. Foreman: *Efficiency and Scarcity Profits.* University of Chicago Press, 1930, p. 240.
[24] Ibid., pp. 199–200.

177

be translated into present values by discounting.[25] In other words, the value of a capital good equals the discounted value of all future services which it is expected to yield in the course of its useful life. The difference between value and cost is the goodwill in terms of money.

The connection between the cost and the value of a capital good is only an indirect one, which is illustrated by

represents the original investment in, or the cost of the capital good. This money is spent and gone; all the investor now owns is the right to receive—at future dates shown horizontally—the sums of money expressed by the vertical dimension of the diagonally shaded bars. By discounting each payment separately at the prevailing rate of interest for the period involved, the value of the capital good is found.

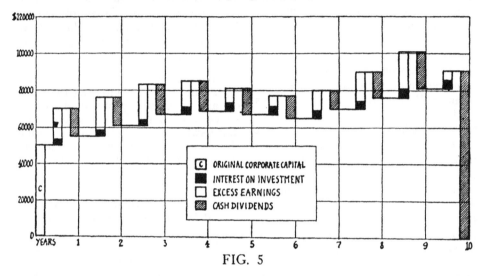

FIG. 5

figure 1. The demand curve DD_1 for a given type of capital good is determined by its consumers in accordance with what they think they can obtain from it in the way of services. Supply, on the other hand, tends to be determined in the long run by the marginal producer, whose cost HA equals the market price. To the marginal consumer, cost and value are equal, but all other consumers obtain a surplus, which measures the value of the goodwill attaching to a given capital good in the particular circumstances of its employment by a given owner.

In terms of money, the problem is better presented by figure 5. The long unshaded bar C at the extreme left

[25] Irving Fisher: *The Theory of Capital and Income.* Macmillan Co., New York, 1912.

It should be carefully observed that the term "services," which Fisher and other economists use interchangeably with "income," denotes all sums which the owner pockets for his own use, including in this sense the ultimate selling price of the capital good, if any. In the case of a complex capital good, such as a business corporation, "services" mean cash dividends, as long as the stockholder remains passive. If he sells some of his original or dividends shares, subscription rights, etc., the proceeds also constitute "services."

Services shaded diagonally in figure 5 may now be compared with earnings determined in accordance with accounting principles by deducting from gross sales or other revenue all costs and expenses incurred, *except interest on the investment.* These earnings—which ac-

178

countants consider synonymous with net profits or income—are represented by the partly black and partly unshaded bars of figure 5. The difference between earnings and services is the capital gain (loss). Since capital gain so defined is not a service, and since the value of a capital good equals the discounted value of its services, it follows that capital value cannot be computed by discounting earnings. Neither can goodwill. This

course of operations. Accordingly, interest at the prevailing rate must be allowed on the original invested capital as well as upon its subsequent increments, before the remainder of earnings can be considered "excess earnings." These interest items are shown in black in figure 5. Upon discounting, at the same rate of interest, the unshaded bars left atop the black ones, goodwill is directly obtained. To restate the principle, the

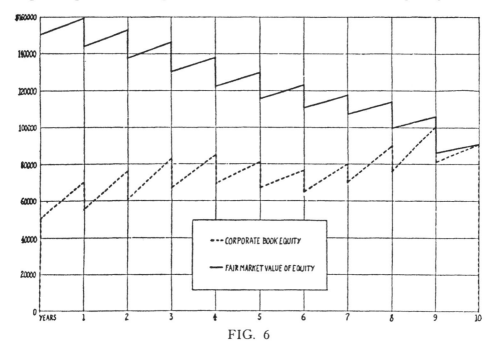

FIG. 6

basic principle is sometimes overlooked in accounting and legal practice.[26]

Goodwill can be computed, however, from "excess earnings" or "superprofits," i.e., earnings in excess of a normal return upon the investment, as indicated at the outset. The investment consists not only of the original cost of the capital good, but also of all capital gains subsequently reinvested in the

aggregate present value of all white bars equals the aggregate present value of all diagonally shaded bars at the time zero, or at the beginning of any other period, if the corresponding ordinate is used in lieu of C.

In order to show the connection between capital value and the book value determined by accounting methods, figure 5 has been redrawn as figure 6, giving consideration to the fact that earnings accrue gradually, while dividends are distributed suddenly.

On the books, the investment is increased by annual earnings be they great or small, and decreased by the

[26] For a detailed discussion of legal and accounting practices in determining goodwill see: Gabriel A. D. Preinreich: "The Law of Goodwill." *Accounting Review.* December, 1936, pp. 317–29 and "Goodwill in Accountancy." THE JOURNAL OF ACCOUNTANCY. July, 1937, pp. 28–50.

cash dividends distributed. Capital value, on the other hand, increases merely at the rate of interest between distributions. Figure 6 thus illustrates Ely's statement that, if goodwill is sold at a fair price, it becomes an ordinary investment to the purchaser and does not give him any peculiar power of getting unusual profits.[27] The price will be fair, in the sense that it will correspond closely to the value determined by the discounting process, whenever nearly perfect foresight is possible, as for instance in the case of a gilt-edge bond, the premium commanded by which is

nothing but goodwill. To generalize the principle, it may be said that *no investment can yield either more or less than the money rate, if all data, upon which its value depends, are known.*

The data necessary are: (1) the amount of each payment; (2) its due date and (3) the rate of interest. In most instances where goodwill is known by that name and in many where another term is commonly applied to it, the date upon which its value depends cannot be foretold with a reasonable degree of accuracy. The value of goodwill then becomes a problem to be treated by the methods of the theory of probability.

---

[27] Cf. the passage to which note 12 refers.

THE DEPRECIATION
PROBLEM

"THE PRINCIPLES OF PUBLIC UTILITY VALUATION"

The Accounting Review (June 1938), pp. 149–165

THE PRINCIPLES OF PUBLIC-UTILITY DEPRECIATION

Gabriel A. D. Preinreich

I HAVE read Professor Perry Mason's monograph on the "Principles of Utility Depreciation"[1] with great interest and consider it as valuable a contribution to the literature of accountancy and public utility regulation as can be made by the traditional discursive method of presentation and by what is still essentially a "single machine" approach. Un-

fortunately, the subject is far too complex for these limitations. To give its students a bird's-eye view of the main problem unobscured by innumerable conflicting opinions, decision, rulings, etc., it is necessary to make, first of all, an introductory comparison of representative methods of depreciation, as applied to a composite plant consisting of many similar items of equipment which are continuously replaced.

[1] American Accounting Association. Chicago, 1937.

After demonstrating, how the "rate" chargeable to the consumer is determined by the method in various circumstances, it is in order to investigate the theoretical requirements, which the "true" method must fulfil. Finally, the enormous practical difficulties may be pointed out and compromises discussed.

Before beginning the exposition, it is also advisable to define the senses, in which the principal terms will be used. The "rate-base," in general, is evidently the "fair value, on which the utility is to earn its prescribed rate of return."[2] In a study limited to depreciation, all extraneous elements may be neglected, so that it is permissible, at least *ad interim*, to define the rate-base as the depreciated cost (book value) of the plant. The "rate," similarly limited in meaning, then becomes the sum of capital consumption and a fair return on the unconsumed plant investment, divided by the time-service units produced or rendered.

When comparing depreciation methods with each other without criticism, it is convenient to consider the entire annual output of the plant as one unit and to express the "rate" per centum of a suitable investment figure. For a discussion of static conditions, the original cost of the plant is most suitable; inquiry into dynamic changes, such as expansion and change in replacement costs, prompts the use of a figure which would have been the undepreciated cost of the equipment now in service, if replacement costs had always remained at their original level. When it becomes necessary to distinguish between various rate concepts, this rate will be called the "annual plant rate."

In addition to the terms defined, a name is needed for those assets which represent an accumulation of depreciation or capital consumption charges paid by the consumer in excess of plant replacements ac-

tually made. The designation "idle assets" seems appropriate, because they do not render any public service and consequently can not claim any remuneration from the consumer. That is the fundamental principle, which must be understood at the outset. Professor Mason does understand it,[3] but his examples and their discussion eventually confuse both the reader and himself on that point, as will be demonstrated later. Whenever idle assets are able to earn on the outside a rate of return equal to that due the plant investment, it is obviously immaterial, whether they are included in the rate-base or not, provided that their income is correspondingly considered or disregarded in the "rate" calculation. What should be emphasized is that ordinarily the idle assets earn only a lower rate of return. If they are nevertheless included in the rate-base, the consumer is improperly forced to contribute to the income of the capital which he has already repaid. That improper depreciation methods may have practically the same effect, is a matter which must be deferred until the theory of the true method is set forth.

I

Discursive methods supplemented by tabulations of debits and credits are quite inadequate for the purpose of showing how various depreciation methods determine the book value of the plant and the "rate" chargeable for its use. The problem involves lengthy mathematical calculations based upon the mortality theory of physical property.[3a] The results, however, can be presented simply and concisely in graphic form.

Without going into mathematical details, it may be said that the rate, at which

[2] *Ibid.*, p. 86.

[3] *Cf.* p. 88: "The investors are not entitled to a return on both the existing and the exhausted capital."

[3a] See my paper: "Annual Survey of Economic Theory: The Theory of Depreciation," *Econometrica*, July, 1938, pp. 219–241.

"machines" installed at the same time gradually drop out of service, ordinarily forms a frequency distribution of the Pearsonian type I. For the calculation of the graphs here presented, a simple curve of this type was used, which corresponds closely to that computed by Edwin B. Kurtz and found applicable to his group VII, comprising seventeen different kinds of industrial property out of a total of fifty-two examined by him.[4] In a theoretical discussion, almost any other bell-shaped frequency distribution serves equally well, since the general appearance of the resultant curves is very similar in all cases.

In Fig. 1 the original cost of the plant is represented by the 100% ordinate, while time is extended along the abscissa. Curve 5 is the basic frequency distribution, from which all curves of all four figures are derived. The reversed summation of the frequency distribution is the mortality curve (6). It shows, what proportion of the machines installed at the time zero is still in service on any subsequent date, up to the assumed maximal age of twenty years, when there will be none left. To maintain the original number of machines in service at all times, it is necessary to replace them at the rate indicated by the unbroken curve 7. It may be seen that the replacement curve gradually changes into a horizontal line, the ordinate of which is the reciprocal of the average life of all machines. In this case, the average life is eight years (vertical line 8), obtained by substituting a parallelogram of equal area for the area enclosed by the mortality curve and the coordinate axes.

The depreciation methods to be compared are: 1. the retirement method (here called a depreciation method purely for convenience of language); 2. the annuity method (equivalent to the sinking fund method, when only one rate of interest is used); 3. the straight line method and 4. the diminishing balance method. Four examples illustrate the behavior of these methods:

A. Static conditions. The number of machines in service remains constant. Replacement costs equal original costs.

B. The number of machines in service remains constant. Replacement costs increase at 2% per annum.[5]

C. The number of machines in service increases at 5% per annum.[5] Replacement costs equal original costs.

D. The number of machines increases at the rate of 5% per annum. Replacement costs increase at 2% per annum.[5]

In all four examples a scrap value of 10% of the purchase price is assumed. These examples still simplify actual conditions greatly, but they lead nevertheless to a number of important conclusions which may be read in an affirmative as well as a negative sense, depending upon whether the rates of change assumed are positive or negative.

Example A—Figs. 1 & 2—Unbroken lines applicable only

Under the retirement method the book value (1) of the plant always equals its original cost, since this method is based on the fallacious claim that a machine which serves as well as when it was new, can not be worth less than it cost. The three other methods recognize that value depends not only upon present service, but also upon the future period, during which it will be maintained.

The straight line method obtains the unexpired cost of the original machines at any chosen age by summing up the

---

[4] *Cf.: Life Expectancy of Physical Property.* Ronald Press Co. New York, 1930.

[5] All rates mentioned in this article are described for brevity as rates per annum, but it should be understood that the forces of annual rates are meant.

areas of both the mortality curve and the frequency distribution to the right of that age and adding 90% of the first summation to 10% of the second. The composite book value is then found by making the same calculation for each small block of replacements and adding the aggregate to the book value of the original machines. Repetition of the procedure for successive ages yields the composite book value curve 3.

The annuity method leading to curve 2 operates in the same manner, except that the value of both future services and scrap proceeds is simultaneously discounted; the rate used in the figure being 7% per annum.[5]

The diminishing balance method is a somewhat crude attempt to recognize a decline in the value of services, as a machine grows older. The procedure is again the same, except that it is based upon a mortality curve so transformed as to make the depreciation rate, applied to the composite book value curve 4, a constant. In the graph, the rate used is 28.78231% per annum.[5] It reduces the book value of a single machine from 100% of cost to 10% in eight years. This method may be of little importance in the public utility field, but is presented nevertheless, because it makes the picture more or less symmetrical. The book value level determined by it happens to be about as far below the straight-line level as the retirement level is above that of the annuity method. The levels, i.e. the axes around which the oscillations of the book value curves diminish rapidly in amplitude, are marked on the right-hand margin of Fig. 1.

Figure 2 shows the four rates of composite depreciation determined by the four methods, as well as the corresponding four "rates" chargeable to the consumer. All rates of composite depreciation are obtained by computing the slopes of the book value curves, reversing the signs

and increasing the four results uniformly by 90% of the rate of replacements. The "rate" owed by the consumer is then found by adding a 7% return on the appropriate book value to each depreciation curve.

It may be seen at once that, under static conditions, any method of depreciation will eventually[6] result in the same charge to operations, viz. a charge at 90% of the rate of replacements. In the meantime, however, widely different levels of book value are established, so that the "rates" must correspondingly differ. Their ultimate levels are indicated in Fig. 2. It is particularly noteworthy that, under the annuity method, the "rate" is a horizontal line, i.e. it is altogether independent of the age of the plant. Under the straight line method, the depreciation is a horizontal line, but the "rate" is too high in the beginning and drops gradually a bit below the annuity "rate." These relationships are the only ones pointed out by Prof. Mason.[7] He holds, moreover that "to adjust the rates from time to time . . . is untenable as a matter of practical administration, and there is no logical reason why rates charged for service should be lowered."[8] Thus, he takes it for granted that the "rate" commanded by the straight line method is always a horizontal line on the level from which "rate"-curve 3 starts in Fig. 2. This line is the axis toward which the "rate" of the retirement method gravitates. It combines the effect of straight line depreciation with that of an undepreciated rate-base.[8]

---

[6] The adverbs "eventually" or "ultimately" must be so often employed hereafter, that it is necessary to clarify them. Speaking mathematically with reference to the problems discussed, they often mean the infinitely distant future. Practically, the statements qualified by those adverbs are true either entirely or very substantially (i.e. beyond five decimals) after four or five average life periods have elapsed. In some cases they are true even before the end of the first such period.

[7] *Op. cit.*, pp. 66–67.

[8] *Ibid.*

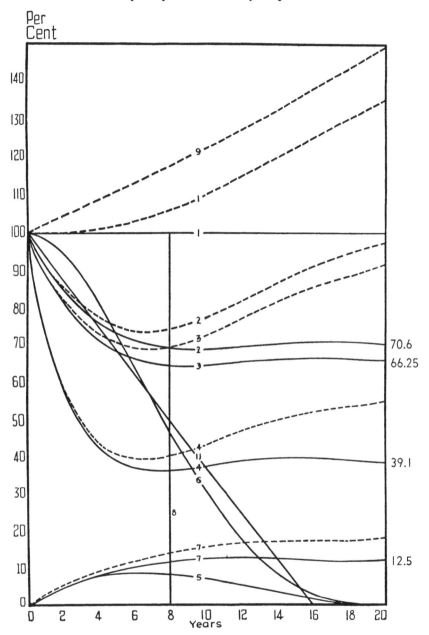

FIGURE 1.—Vertical scale represents per cent of cost of original plant. Smooth lines indicate static conditions. Broken lines include increase in replacement costs at the force of 2 per cent per annum.

Composite-book-value curves: (1) Retirement method; (2) Annuity method at the force of 7 per cent per annum; (3) Straight-line method; (4) Diminishing-balance method.

Auxiliary curves: (5) Basic frequency distribution; (6) Mortality curve; (7) Rate of replacements; (8) Average life = life expectancy of a new machine; (9) Index of replacement costs; (11) Limit of shape of possible other mortality curves. The opposite limit is (8).

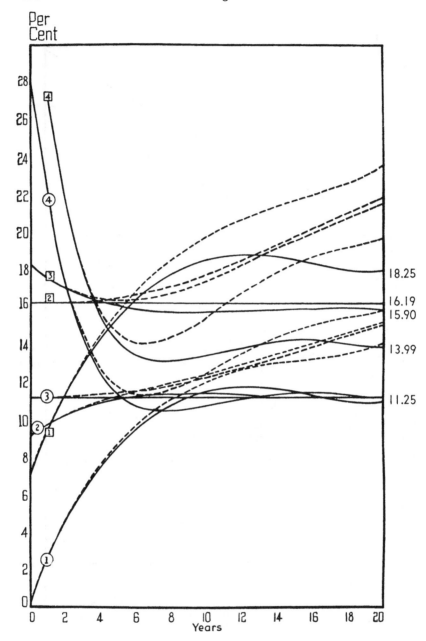

FIGURE 2.—Vertical scale represents per cent per annum of cost of original plant. Smooth lines indicate static conditions. Broken lines include increase in replacement costs at the force of 2 per cent per annum. Circles around numbers indicate rates of depreciation per annum. Squares around numbers indicate the sum of depreciation rates and a fair return at the force of 7 per cent per annum on the respective book values.

1. Retirement method; 2. Annuity method at the force of 7 per cent per annum; 3. Straight-line method; 4. Diminishing-balance method.

Example B—Figs. 1 & 2—Broken lines applicable only

The index number of replacement cost is shown as curve 9. The calculation of all four book value curves follows the procedure described for static conditions, except that the rate of replacement is first multiplied by the index. All curves obtain upward trends which ultimately reach equal proportions (2% p. a.), when measured in terms of the static levels. In amount, of course, the book value by the retirement method increases fastest and that by the diminishing balance method least rapidly. Depreciation charges must in the end differ in the opposite sense, because one method postpones them to a greater extent than another. This development is clearly disclosed by the depreciation curves of Fig. 2. They were obtained by taking the slopes of the book value curves, reversing the signs and increasing each result uniformly, not only by 90% of the rate of replacement (multiplied by the index), but also by the rate of growth of the scrap value.

When replacement costs increase, depreciation charges increase also, but the diminishing balance method leads the rise, while the retirement method brings up the rear. The straight line method's depreciation remains proportionately the same, i.e. it is the product of the unbroken horizontal line 3 of Fig. 2 by the dotted line 1 of Fig. 1.

The "rates" prevailing under increasing replacement cost are again found by adding each of four different conceptions of a fair profit to the respective measurements of capital consumption. Among the "rates," that of the annuity method remains proportionately unchanged; the others approach slightly toward it. An index increasing only at the rate of 2% per annum is not sufficient to wipe out entirely the ultimate differences, but it lessens the discrepancy existing under entirely static conditions.

Example C—Figs. 3 & 4—Unbroken lines applicable only

In Fig. 3 the 100% ordinate no longer represents the original cost of the plant, but the undepreciated cost of all the machines in service at any given time, when their number increases at 5% per annum and when replacement costs are static. The relationship between Figs. 1 and 3 is clarified by the 5% discount line (10) in Fig. 3. This line is equivalent to the horizontal 100% line of Fig. 1. It shows the original cost of the plant for comparative purposes.

Calculations of the four book value curves are now made for the third time along the lines first indicated, except that the rate of replacements and additions, which must now be used (curve 7 of Fig. 3), differs materially from the corresponding rate (7) plotted in Fig. 1. Instead of starting at the origin, it starts with an ordinate of 5% and increases rapidly in terms of the scale prevailing at the time zero. In Fig. 3 the real rate has been discounted, i.e. multiplied by line 10 and thus shows an ultimately horizontal trend on a level of 15.8% which is lower than the sum of 5% expansion and the level of 12.5% reached by curve 7 in Fig. 1.

The book value curves of Fig. 3 similarly represent the real ascending curves discounted at the expansion rate. By this device they have been made comparable to the book value curves of Fig. 1 in terms of the respective undepreciated costs prevailing when replacement costs are static. It is apparent that, under any method but the retirement method, the book value of an expanding plant stabilizes itself at a higher proportion of its undepreciated cost than the book value of a static plant. This must be so, because an expanding plant contains a greater proportion of relatively new machines. The average age is less and the average service-expectancy is correspondingly greater. That the amplitudes of oscillations are smaller is a secondary, but still interesting phenomenon. Its cause is the greater influx of new machines, which offers a wider scope for the automatic stabilizing process from the very start.

The depreciation curves of Fig. 4 were calculated by finding first the true slopes of the book value curves, viz. the slopes before applying the discount indicated by line 10. After reversing the signs, 90% of the true (undiscounted) rate of replacements and additions was added along with the rate of growth of the scrap value. The result was discounted and plotted. To obtain the "rates," a 7% return on the true book values was also added before discounting.

It must be clearly understood that discounting at the rate of expansion is merely a plotting device adopted for the purpose of reducing Figs. 2 and 4 to a common denominator. While the respective vertical scales of Figs. 1 and 3 measure different concepts which merge only at the time zero, those of Figs. 2 and 4 mean the same thing at any point of the horizontal time-scale. They measure sums of money due per annum for the use and gradual repayment of each dollar originally invested in the plant, or of such a larger sum which subsequently replaced or matched that dollar in rendering equal service.

Figure 4 shows that expansion causes an eventual discrepancy in the trends of depreciation rates, which occurs in the same sense as that caused by an increase in replacement costs in Fig. 2. The charge decreases materially for the retirement method, and slightly for the annuity method. For the straight line method it remains unchanged and for the diminish-

ing balance method it increases a good deal as compared to the curves of example A.

Among the four "rates," that of the annuity method remains unchanged, while the others are much closer to it than under static conditions. It can easily be shown mathematically that, when all other conditions are as assumed, but the rate of expansion exceeds 6.00%, the four rate levels will ultimately be reversed in order. In other words, a public utility expanding faster could claim the highest "rate" under the diminishing balance method and only the lowest under the retirement method. It is interesting to note that one of the few public utilities adhering to the straight line method of depreciation, the American Telephone & Telegraph Co., has in the past had an average expansion rate in excess of 9% per annum. It is thus probably better off than if it had insisted upon the use of the retirement method, as many utilities in the same position still do.

Example D—Figs. 3 & 4—Broken lines applicable only

A 2% annual increase in replacement costs is now combined with 5% annual expansion. In the recalculation of book values, the rate of replacements and additions must again be multiplied by the index number of replacement costs. After applying the expansion discount for plotting purposes only, the resultant curves look very similar to those of Fig. 1, except that they begin their rise faster in proportion to levels which are higher. (N.B. The difference between the ordinates of curves 9 and 1 is less throughout Fig. 3 than in Fig. 1.) The discrepancy of depreciation rates is greater than in any of the three preceding examples. When a 7% return on the book values is now added to the respective rates of depreciation, it so happens that all four methods call for

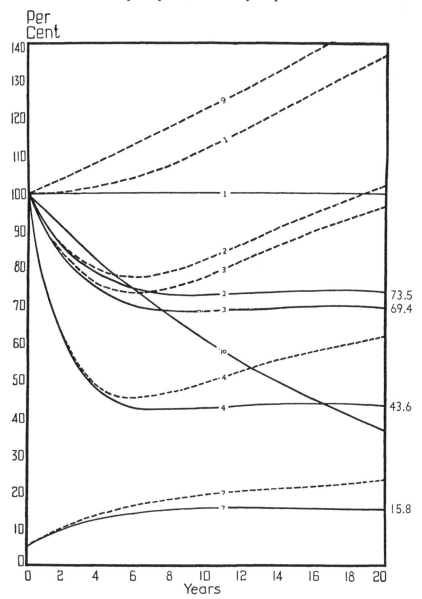

FIGURE 3.—Vertical scale represents per cent of cost of plant in service at any time *t*, when number of machines expands at the force of 5 per cent per annum and when replacement costs remain at the level of original costs. Smooth lines indicate static replacement costs and plant expansion at the force of 5 per cent per annum. Broken lines include increase in replacement costs at the force of 2 per cent per annum.

Composite-book-value curves: (1) Retirement method; (2) Annuity method at the force of 7 per cent per annum; (3) Straight-line method; (4) Diminishing-balance method.

Auxiliary curves: (7) Rate of replacements and additions; (9) Combined index of expansion and replacement costs; (10) Original cost of plant. True ordinates of all curves have been discounted at the force of 5 per cent per annum before plotting.

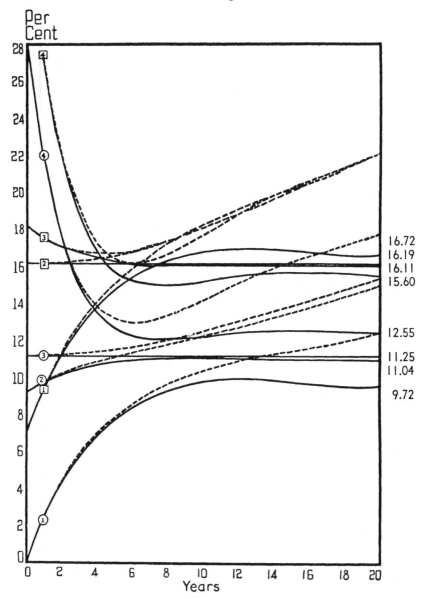

FIGURE 4.—Vertical scale represents per cent per annum of cost of original plant, chargeable at any time t per the original number of machines. Smooth lines indicate static replacement costs and plant expansion at the force of 5 per cent per annum. Broken lines include increase in replacement costs at the force of 2 per cent per annum. Circles around numbers indicate depreciation rates per annum. Squares around numbers indicate the sum of depreciation rates and a fair return at the force of 7 per cent per annum on the respective book values.

1. Retirement method; 2. Annuity method at the force of 7 per cent per annum; 3. Straight-line method; 4. Diminishing-balance method.

almost exactly the same ultimate "rate." That is purely an accident resulting from the assumptions. It shows, however, that if either the rate of expansion or the rate of increase in replacement cost had been chosen higher, the retirement method would have found its "rate" at the bottom, while that of the diminishing balance method would have been on top. The other two methods would have changed their respective positions simultaneously.

It does not seem necessary to add a fifth example to cover the case, where the pertinent portion of the rate-base is defined as the depreciated present reproduction cost of the plant, instead of as the

depreciation rate, unless the discussion is carried on in terms of a single machine only. It is quite true, however, that "the problem of providing funds to finance replacements should be treated as quite distinct from that of handling depreciation."[10] It is possible that the first statement is also meant only in this sense.

The financial problem of providing for replacement leads to many opinions on idle assets, which deserve clarification. The relevant parts of four balance sheets, say for the end of the sixth year and for the straight line method, can be readily taken from the plotting calculations of Figs. 1 and 3 as follows:

	Example A	Example B	Example C	Example D
Idle Assets..........................	$ 33.444	$ 31.063	$ 5.654	$ 996
Plant.............................	100.000	102.872	134.986	140.408
	$133.444	$133.935	$140.640	$141.404
Depreciation Reserve................	$ 33.444	$ 33.935	$ 40.640	$ 41.404
Equity..........................	100.000	100.000	100.000	100.000
	$133.444	$133.935	$140.640	$141.404

depreciated historical cost. Undistorted graphs of this situation can easily be drawn by discarding all broken lines in all graphs and multiplying all unbroken lines by the index of reproduction costs (9). When this is done, "rates" will result, which may be described either as the sum of depreciation charges based upon present reproduction cost plus a 7% return on the rate-base, or as the sum of depreciation charges based upon reproduction cost at the time zero, plus a 9% return on the rate-base.

The analysis presented up to this point refutes Prof. Mason's oft repeated statement that "there is no fundamental relationship between depreciation and replacements."[9] No matter what the depreciation method may be, the replacement rate always enters directly into the

In example A, the idle assets will always be offset exactly by the depreciation reserve, but Fig. 1 shows that practically none of these assets will ever be needed. A utility in substantially this position will accordingly engage in the investment business, while claiming simultaneously under single-machine ideology that "if it is realized that each item of property has its claim on the accumulation, then . . . no part of the reserve can be useless—every cent will eventually be required."[11] The trust fund doctrine, the risk of obtaining funds when perhaps needed, etc., are advanced for the purpose of securing the inclusion of the idle assets into the rate-base as a necessary replacement or sinking fund.

Whether these arguments are accepted

---

[9] *Op. cit.*, pp. 19–20.

[10] *Ibid.*, p. 69.
[11] *Op. cit.*, p. 76.

or rejected by the regulatory bodies, it will also be maintained that "the reserve created under the more complete method [than the retirement method] is largely useless in that it gives the utility control over more funds than it needs to take care of the situation."[12] The fault lies partly with corporation laws, which prevent the return of unnecessary capital. The correct principle appears to be the one which I have elsewhere called the "principle of good management," according to which the corporate directors must neither retain idle funds, nor distribute any which can be productively reinvested.[13] It should be pointed out nevertheless that, under conditions of moderate expansion and a moderate increase in replacement costs, a public utility permitted to use the retirement method will in the long run get control over more funds than if it were not so favored. It does not complain, however, because it is free to distribute the excess in cash dividends, without sacrificing any part of its higher earning power.

Both the graphs and the above comparative balance sheets show that the importance of the idle asset problem diminishes with expansion and increased reproduction costs. None the less, a careful definition of "replacement funds" and "sinking funds" is needed, before subscribing to Prof. Mason's conclusion that "the fund is a necessary part of the property of the utility and should not be excluded from the rate-base; it may be considered as part of the 'working capital'."[14] He recognizes that "the amount of the fund need not and should not be as large as the reserve for depreciation as long as there is enough variety in the property,"[15] but that is not definite enough. In examples B, C and D the fund must always be smaller than the depreciation reserve, but it is idle nevertheless, until it disappears altogether. The limit up to which any replacement fund or sinking fund might reasonably be considered a rate-base asset is given by the oscillating discrepancies observed in practice between the theoretical and the actual rates of replacement. A good indication of the size of such fluctuations can be gained from the books of utilities adhering to the retirement method. Their reserves for such a purpose rarely exceed one per cent of the plant account.

II

Toward solution of the problem of how to find the "true" method of depreciation, Prof. Mason contributes nothing beyond a recommendation that the subject be studied. That is probably the greatest shortcoming of his work, because the public-utility field is the only one which offers a chance, be it ever so small, for the practical application of the true depreciation theory. No justice can possibly be done to this subject without the extensive use of mathematics and therefore I shall here attempt merely to outline the general trend of the argument.

The starting point is the economic theory of capital value. It is well established that the capital value of any investment is the sum of the discounted values of all future services expected from it, including in this sense the ultimate proceeds of liquidation. Thirteen years ago, Prof. Harold Hotelling started out

---

[12] *Ibid.*

[13] *Cf.* my book: *The Nature of Dividends.* New York, 1935, pp. 9–10 and 175 f. Not to distribute reinvestable funds may mean in practice either no distribution at all, or stock dividends, or a combination of cash dividends and subscription rights.

[14] *Op. cit.*, p. 81. The next sentence, that "a larger income must be permitted on the main operating property in order to compensate for the deficiency of earnings of this part of the invested capital," is apparently intended as mere corroboration because even from Prof. Mason's viewpoint, the argument could be advanced only if the fund were excluded from the rate-base. If it is included anyway, one of the two wrongs which supposedly make a right is canceled.

[15] *Ibid.*, p. 80.

on this basis and made some genuine contributions to the subject.[16] Their value, however, is somewhat impaired by the unfortunate assumption that the capital value of a new machine is its cost. If that were true, no one would wish to struggle with the many alphabetical and other handicaps of business enterprise, so long as safe bonds are available. The connection between the capital value and the cost of a new machine is by no means a direct one. The market price oscillates around a balancing point determined marginally by the least efficient pair of producers and consumers of such machines. In the general case, the capital value is therefore apt to be higher than the cost, although, in the course of constant fluctuation, the reverse is not impossible. Be that as it may in a special case, it follows immediately that the transition from the capital value to the book value of a single machine can be achieved by using the same formula of capital value, but substituting the rate of profit for the rate of interest used in the discounting process. Regrettably enough, it also follows that the true book value (unexpired cost) on any subsequent date can be calculated only if the rate of profit is known in advance, at least in terms of a known function containing an unknown parameter.[17] The public utility

industry comes closer to meeting this requirement than the field of unregulated enterprise.

To continue the discussion in the simplest terms, I must assume contrary to fact, that the rate of profit equals the prescribed rate of fair return. The elements entering into the net service may be analyzed next. For this purpose, the previous limited definition of "rate" must be discarded and a more comprehensive definition adopted. For a single machine the "true rate" is that constant price per unit of service charged to the consumer which, when multiplied by the rate of production and after deduction of all operating expenses, will produce the fair net rental or service. The fair net rental, in turn, is that flow of service which, when inserted into the book value formula applicable to the time zero (i.e. the capital value formula with profit substituted for interest and zero substituted for the variable time-symbol), will result in original cost less the discounted scrap value.

It should be of particular interest to accountants that the term "operating expenses" includes every business expense except depreciation. None may be omitted, except those which vary in exactly the same manner as the rate of production. If there are any which fulfil that requirement, they may be eliminated against the sales, which is the product of the "true rate" by the rate of production. The depreciation calculation will remain correct; the "rate" so obtained will, however, fall short of the "true rate" by the pro-rata shares of all expenses eliminated. These can be readily added to the answer. When both the rate of production and all expenses are considered constant and equal for all machinery, the elimination can be carried to the limit and the annuity method results. If, in addition, a whole year's output is considered as a unit of service, the resultant "rate" is the annual plant

---

[16] "A General Mathematical Theory of Depreciation," *Journal of the American Statistical Association*, September, 1925.

[17] When the profit function is unknown, the edifice of theory must be erected on the highly artificial foundation of perfect foresight extending up to the death of the enterprise, thus assuming as known all the total production surpluses of each successive machine in the long chain of replacements. Even then, however, the problem is indefinite, because the distribution of each surplus over the life of the respective machine remains optional. A continuous rate-of-profit curve fitted to the successive blocks of production surpluses is the general answer, which permits of different solutions.

Any depreciation method ever devised amounts merely to a conscious or unconscious assumption of the form of the rate-of-profit curve. Prof. Hotelling's assumption happens to be that costs move parallel to sales and is therefore anything but a "general" theory.

For the mathematical demonstration see *op. cit.* in note 3a.

rate ⟨2⟩ of figs. 2 and 4. In addition, the consumer must be charged with his pro-rata share of all expenses.[18]

The next point to be introduced is the value-theory of discarding. Prof. Hotelling[19] derives it from the formula of capital value by showing that the investment will be best conserved, if the machine is discarded at the moment when it barely earns the rate of interest on its scrap value. That is true enough for a single machine which is not to be replaced. When considering a chain of replacements extending into the dim future, the value of the whole chain or what is left of it must be made a maximum, not the value of a single machine. When the rate of profit is unknown, that immediately leads to speculative comparisons between the machine now in service and those which will be on the market at the time when the question of replacement becomes acute. Since, however, I have assumed that the profit actually equals the fair return, the answer is simple: the machine must be discarded and replaced, when it barely earns the rate of profit on its scrap value.

The value-theory of discarding is based upon the assumption that a machine is certain to last longer than it can be operated profitably, i.e. that at least some expenses directly connected with its operation will gradually rise to prohibitive levels. That need not always be the case. It is conceivable that a machine may be profitable until the moment when it suddenly falls to pieces, like the late Justice Holmes' famous "one-hoss shay." Practically speaking, expenses may remain almost constant for a long time and then begin to rise so rapidly as to make it clear that the end has come. In such cases discarding has a physical, rather than a value aspect, and the future date of scrapping ought to be known from experience.

Disregarding the latter eventuality as the simpler one, there are in the general case three equations, viz.: 1. the book value formula applicable to the time zero; 2. the same formula for any time between zero and the date of discarding; and 3. the equation which defines the fair return on the scrap value in terms of the sales at the time of discarding, less the rates of all expenses as of the same date. The three unknowns are the book value at any time other than zero, the "true rate" and the date of scrapping. Equation 2 contains all three unknowns, while equations 1 and 3 contain only the last two. These equations can be solved simultaneously as outlined by Prof. Hotelling,[20] bearing always in mind that the fair return must be used in lieu of the rate of interest employed by him. Otherwise all three answers will be wrong.[21]

For purposes of the solution, perfect foresight is necessary up to the end of the machine's life, as far as the rate of production and all expenses are concerned. An analysis of the latter may accordingly be

---

[18] I am still neglecting items extraneous to the discussion, such as a fair return on rate-base assets other than the plant, modifications caused by senior capital, etc. In this sense, the "true rate" is not yet the true one, nor can its product by the rate of production be described as sales. When all these complications are considered, it will follow that the utility is entitled to the fair return only on that part of the common equity, which is invested in rate-base assets. To the extent that the investment is furnished by senior capital, the rate-base may claim merely a return equalling the hire of such capital. The "prudent investment" concept thus leads to the definition of the rate-base in terms of equities rather than assets. It logically extends the field of regulation to the entire capital structure and the proportions, which its component elements ought to bear to each other.

[19] *Op. cit.*

[20] *Op. cit.*, p. 347.

[21] When Prof. Hotelling's book value formula is used for keeping the books of a machine which earns more than the rate of interest, it further follows that the books so kept will report an enormous profit per centum of the scrap value, at the very moment, when the machine is discarded for the reason that it earns barely the rate of interest. That is to say, his assumption of the form of the rate-of-profit curve is inconsistent with the data which determine the moment of scrapping. *Cf.* note 17 above.

made to an almost unlimited extent. All will depend upon outside influences too numerous to mention; some in addition upon the rate of production which, in turn, depends upon the general economic situation as well as special developments. Taxes and insurance, finally, might possibly be considered to depend upon the book value to be found. Whenever the dependence is linear, insurance and taxes may be crossed off the list of expenses deductible from sales, their rates on the book value being added instead to the fair return used in the discounting process. A more complicated relationship creates difficulties which are not always surmountable.

Prof. Hotelling's theory ends at this point. With the amendments suggested, it becomes acceptable for public utility purposes as far as single-machine analysis goes. Next, the findings must be made applicable to a large number of machines installed at the same time, i.e. to the original plant. Curve 6 of Fig. 1 shows that every machine drops out of service at a different time. If it be assumed that the mortality curve was obtained by value-analyses of many machines, or at least that sporadic value-analyses have tended to confirm the results of physical inspection, it follows that certain expenses and probably also the rate of production must differ widely from machine to machine. The functions expressing these elements of calculation accordingly contain another variable, namely the life of the machines (date of scrapping), which varies from zero to twenty years in Fig. 1. This variable may be expressed as the reversed mortality formula, meaning that the equation is so changed as to state abscissae corresponding to given ordinates, rather than ordinates corresponding to given abscissae.

The "true rate" is also different for each machine and becomes a function of the variable life instead of a constant. If the book value formula of a single machine is so amended and then summed up with respect to the ordinate within the limits corresponding to successive positions on the horizontal time-scale, the book value curve of all original machines still in service at any time is found. The remainder of the work is as indicated in section I. Each small block of replacements must be treated in the same way as the original plant. A final summation leads to the composite book value curve. It will look very like those shown in the graphs, but will converge toward some other level depending upon the known functions of production and expenses. From it, both depreciation and annual plant rate curves can be derived as explained in the examples.

The "true rate," or price per unit of service as defined in this section, but averaged for the whole composite plant, is now obtainable by taking the "true rate" of the original plant at successive given times and adding to it those of each block of replacements as of the same times. In the case of static replacement costs, the "true rate" will not be a horizontal line, but will tend to be too high in the beginning, until stabilization occurs on a lower level. Prof. Mason's complaint that "a utility using much old property would have to charge different rates than one using much new property even though the service rendered by each was precisely the same"[22] can not be remedied in the general case. During the early years, that situation must arise, until the proportion of relatively inefficient machines, is reduced to the stable average.

III

The pure theory of depreciation can be readily developed in terms of mathematical symbols to a far greater extent than I

---

[22] *Op. cit.*, p. 58.

have here attempted. It must be realized, however, that the final step of substituting known functions for the symbols theoretically treated as known involves a lot of guesswork. Production and expenses can never be foretold accurately for a long time in advance. And if the guesses are wrong, the profit will differ from the fair return. The whole calculation is then upset, even if the promulgated "rate" had conformed exactly to the guesses.

If the fair return were both fixed and guaranteed, delayed adjustment by hindsight could be introduced. A consumers' surplus (deficit) account might in that case be opened, to which all differences between the fair return and the actual profit would be posted and the balance considered an asset or a liability, as the case might be. In addition, voluminous operating records would be necessary for individual machines. Upon discarding each, its real past book value curve could be computed and compared with the method used in keeping the books during the same period. The resultant entries to the consumers' surplus would cluster into frequency distributions and would indicate the direction in which the bookkeeping method has erred.

Except for the transition period of the early years, the composite book value is mainly a matter of levels. A flexible formula could therefore be used, in which only the value of a single symbol need be changed from time to time to create a trend toward any desired level per centum of the undepreciated cost. Now, theory requires that the formula of the composite book value under the straight line method be merely a special case of the annuity method's formula. The only difference between them is the discount rate, which is zero in the former and more than zero in the latter. This rate could be given any positive or negative magnitude and could serve as a "micrometer screw," to be turned slightly in one direction or another, until the adjustments calculated by hindsight become as small in aggregate as possible. That would make the regulation of depreciation policies a simple matter. As for the "rate," only the balance of the consumers' surplus and its trend of change would have to be watched to gain the necessary guidance for corrective measures. This balance would, of course, always lag in time behind the true, but unknown balance.

To avoid guaranteeing a fair return and to conform to court decisions holding that past depreciation errors can not affect future "rates," the consumers' surplus might be classified as part of the common equity, serving no other purpose than that of a gauge. That would be theoretically less acceptable, but practically more feasible.

Quite probably, complete value analysis would entail so much added expense as to suggest giving the utility the benefit of the doubt instead. At least tests ought to be made, however. By a scientific sampling process the significant errors could be caught. The point is that different life and service characteristics of different types of machines lead to different book value levels for any method except the retirement method. A level correct for one plant or industry might be grossly improper for another.

If all reforms be rejected, there remains only to speculate, which of the simple standard methods has the best chance of being closest to the truth in the majority of cases. Prof. Mason says in his "defense of the straight line method" that because repairs and maintenance almost always increase as the property becomes older, "the straight line method is not likely to result in an excessive return on the investment for any great length of time."[23] That sounds all right, until one realizes

---

[23] *Op. cit.*, p. 68.

that he is really defending the exorbitant rate described at the end of example A above.

The gradual increase of maintenance charges, etc., can not convert an otherwise excessive "rate" into a fair one, except during the first few years of the utility's exister ce. In the long run the effect is just the oposite, both under the static conditions to which Prof. Mason's attention is limited and under the moderately dynamic ones of examples B and C. What happens is that the tendency of services to decline in value with growing age calls for a lower ultimate book value level than would otherwise be proper. This boosts the "rate" for a few years, while the book value is dropping, because the slope of the big initial drop is steeper.[24] Thereafter, a lower level commands a lower "rate," unless conditions are relatively more extreme than in example D.

Similarly, the excessive "rate" granted to the straight line method can not be compared with the lower, but correctly calculated annuity "rate" for the purpose of concluding that "the compound interest methods are almost certain to give a deficient yield on the investment, when the plan is well under way."[25] All other things being equal and when the plan is well under way, the annuity method will lead to an excessive, not a deficient yield, when the straight line method leads to the correct one. The reverse can be true only in conditions which Prof. Mason did not examine, viz. when the expansion rate or the rate of increase in replacement costs or both are rather high. A careful study of the graphs submitted will go a long way toward clarifying these involved relationships.

In general, it can only be said that, apart from differences in depreciation

methods, the book value levels will be high when:

1. Mortality curves resemble closely the diagonal straight line 11 in Fig. 1.
2. Net rentals decrease only slowly with growing age. If they should increase instead, so much the better.
3. Scrap values are high.
4. Expansion rates are high.

The reverse will lead to low levels. In the case of mortality curves, the opposite extreme of shape is the vertical line 8 in Fig. 1. Steady changes in replacement costs will change levels only proportionately in the long run. Higher book value levels make higher rates and vice versa, until the combined critical rate of dynamic changes is exceeded. Thereafter the opposite is true.

In conclusion, it may be worth calling attention to the relationship between the average life of the plant and the annual plant rate. If the meaning of a unit on the horizontal time-scale is changed from one year to 7/6 of a year, Figs. 2 and 4 will tell, what rates must be paid per such unit of time for the use of a plant having an average life of $9\frac{1}{3}$ years, to yield 6% per annum on the rate-base, when: A. conditions are static; B. replacement costs increase at 1.714% p. a. C. the plant expands at 4.286% p. a.; and D. when both B and C are combined. Calculation of the *annual* plant rate for a 7% yield and for examples so changed is now a matter of simple arithmetic for all methods illustrated, except the annuity method.

The whole subject is so extremely complex and fascinating that it is difficult to know where to stop. All I set out to do was merely to show that purely literary efforts have very little chance of probing beneath the surface. That is by no means a reflection on Prof. Mason's achievement; he is in far too illustrious and numerous company for that.

[24] *Cf.* the technique of calculating depreciation in the examples.
[25] *Op. cit.*, p. 68.

"VALUATION AND DEPRECIATION"

Journal of Accountancy
(July 1938), pp. 46–48

VALUATION AND DEPRECIATION

Editor, THE JOURNAL OF ACCOUNTANCY:

DEAR SIR: May I submit some comments on Professor Saliers' recent review of the book, *The Science of Valuation and Depreciation*, by Professor Edwin B. Kurtz?

When an author speaks so highly of his work as Professor Kurtz does, not only in the preface and introduction, but throughout the text, I believe it is incumbent upon a reviewer to examine the sweeping claims made with more than ordinary care. I was quite surprised therefore to see Professor Saliers confine himself to a repetition of the author's statements either verbatim or in paraphrased form.

In particular, I object to the implications of the remark that "the shortcomings of the conventional straight-line method are discussed and scientific procedure explained" (THE JOURNAL OF ACCOUNTANCY, May, 1938, p. 452). The straight-line method appears at a disadvantage merely because Professor Kurtz is not immune to the temptation of comparing his own method at its best with the other method at its worst. Thus, he takes it for granted that accountants retain the cost of a discarded machine in the plant account after it has been scrapped—in short, that they depreciate a large number of machines in the same way as if the aggregate original cost had represented but a single machine. He ought to note that, if the origi-

nal cost of the plant were posted to one account and that of its replacements to another, the successive balances of the former account would outline the mortality curve, because the cost of discarded items is removed at once.

When the books are so kept and when, in addition, the entire cost of a scrapped machine (barring any scrap value) is always charged to the reserve, regardless of whether the same amount has had a chance to accumulate in it, the straight-line method is a distinct improvement upon Professor Kurtz' "scientific" method for the case without interest. Depreciation can be charged annually at a straight or constant rate corresponding to the reciprocal of the average life on the balance of the plant account, regardless of the more than average age of any machine in it. That is exactly what he does, except that he deliberately uses the wrong ordinates of the mortality curve and therefore gets too small a premium. He hastens to explain on page 112 that "this, of course, is not due to any inaccuracy . . . but rather to the difference in the number of installments to be paid. In the straight-line plan the number of payments is fixed by the average life, namely 1,000 . . . units. In the replacement-insurance plan the number of units in service at the beginning of each age interval fixes the number of premiums to be

46

collected to make possible paying the 100 benefits. These totals are 1,050. . . . Thus the total money collected is the same in each case." In other words, "the only scientific approach" (p. 6) consists of charging too little on more life units than there are in 100 machines, while the straight-line method is unscientific enough to charge simply the right premium on the right number!

The case against the sinking-fund method is no more substantial. When costs are deleted in the same way, the correct premium calculated by recourse to interest should equal the sinking-fund contribution. That, however, is not the entire depreciation charge; the interest must be added. In this respect, Professor Kurtz reminds me of the once famous Doctor Price who, around 1770, tried to lift England by its bootstraps through the magic of compound interest. Depreciation methods do not affect the cash position; sums put into the sinking fund would have had to be employed in some manner anyway. The label does not create any income that could not have been obtained otherwise.

As far as I can see, Professor Kurtz's undoubted contributions to theory have all been made in his first book: *Life Expectancy of Physical Property* (1930), which is a valuable reference work. There is one idea in the new book though, which should have been followed up. I refer to chapters IV and VI, dealing with what he misleadingly calls "remainder service life." In figure 16, he divides the area of the mortality curve into horizontal rectangular layers and bisects each into triangles by diagonal lines drawn from the upper left to the lower right corners. If the layers were thin enough, the height of a lower triangle at a given point of time would furnish the remainder life of the machines represented by the layer, per cent, of their total useful life. For instance, if one machine has a useful life of five years, the triangle shows at the three-year point that 40 per cent of its life is still ahead. Similarly, if another machine will live up to the age of 20 years, it has 85 per cent of its total life left. These two figures are added together and counted as 1.25 per cent of the total life units originally contained in the 100 machines. As a calculation of life units, the procedure is wrong because, if the average life is ten years, the total life-service units number 1,000, of

which the first machine has still to furnish 2 and the second 17. Therefore, the true proportion of remaining life units is 1.9 per cent of the total.

In his table VIII, Professor Kurtz performs the latter type of calculation, he multiplies each group of machines by its unexpired life and divides the sum of all products by all life units originally contained in all machines. That done, he proceeds to prove that table VIII and figure 16 are equivalent. The "proof" consists of inserting the results of table VIII into the chart, without bothering to see whether the rule of proportionality applied to the triangles would actually give the answers indicated at the point chosen. He never notices that table VIII considers all life units as equivalent, whereas figure 16 weights them by their variable cost on the ground that each machine was bought at the same price, regardless of the number of life units which it contains!

This basic misunderstanding is carried along to chapter VI entitled: "Composite Remainder Service Life," which pretends to furnish "convincing evidence of the soundness of the method . . . the logic . . . the accuracy . . . their correct joint use . . . a verification of the entire preceding analysis and a demonstration of the inherent unity of the whole body of principles presented" (pp. 5–6). Now, if "remainder service life" means remainder cost, it is clear enough from figure 16 that (since the area of a triangle is half that of a layer) the composite remainder cost must ultimately become 50 per cent for a plant currently maintained at a constant number of machines. On the other hand, if the actual life units remaining in a mature composite plant are compared with the units inherent in a new plant, the result must inevitably be more than 50 per cent.

How Professor Kurtz cuts this Gordian knot may be seen in table XX. To find the composite remainder service life, it is evidently necessary to average all products of the different age-groups of machines by their remainder service lives. The latter information is furnished by table VIII, per cent of the units originally contained in 100 machines; therefore, the original number of machines in each group and not only the survivors of each group are to be multiplied to get the correct composite. There is no warrant whatever in theory to multiply only the survivors (see p. 78), but Professor Kurtz must somehow get 50 per cent as his answer and therefore that is just what he does!

Proof is thus furnished, not of the "soundness," etc., of the method, but merely of the correctness of an irrelevant elementary rule of integration somewhat analogous to $2 \times 2 = 4$. The oscillations of the *remainder cost* corresponding to figure 16 will also come to rest on the ultimate level of $\frac{1}{2}$, but in the meantime the shapes of the true curves differ from those to which Professor Kurtz's empirical equations have been fitted in figures 24–30. Incidentally, these equations have no theoretical merit, even if fitted to the correct data, because the relationships are far more complex than he assumes (*Cf.* my article in *Econometrica*, July, 1938). A wave need not be a pure *sine* wave!

It is not clear why chapters IV and VI were written at all. Although it is stated on page 90 that the ultimate 50 per cent level "is further proof of the soundness of the per cent remainder service formula which is basic in this study," the formula (?) is abandoned then and there, no use being made of it for any purpose whatever. That is regrettable, because figure 16 really contains the germ of the true depreciation theory.

The utter lack of "inherent unity in the body of principles presented" (p. 6) becomes apparent in chapter VIII where the "normal" reserves calculated are found to be much smaller than the 50 per cent which was considered so basic. Table XXXII shows that for the case of zero interest the range is from 36.9 per cent to 46.7 per cent of original cost. These figures are of course affected by Professor Kurtz's way of apportioning the premium, but the discrepancies are not very great. Upon revising the apportionment so as to charge the right premium on the right number of units, the reserves obtained will be the exact complements of the book-value levels or true remainder-service life-levels which table XX and similar tables would have furnished, if the indefensible introduction of the mortality (survivor) curve into the multiplication had been omitted.

It is easy to demonstrate mathematically that, when interest is disregarded and when the plant always consists of the same number of machines, the absolute limits of ultimate book-value levels are $\frac{1}{2}$ and $\frac{2}{3}$ for the replacement-insurance method, i.e., for the straight-line method described. These levels refer only to the case without scrap value.

Should the latter be 10 per cent of cost, the limits will be $1\frac{1}{20}$ and $2\frac{1}{80}$ respectively. The important thing to remember is that the level is independent of the average life, but is influenced considerably by the shape of the mortality curve. Professor Kurtz should also have mentioned that plant expansion and increasing replacement cost raise the book value considerably per centum of the total cost of the machines in service at any given time. The true remainder-cost method of figure 16 is independent of the shape of the mortality curve, but also leads to a level higher than 50 per cent when the plant expands and replacement costs increase.

The foregoing comments will suffice to show that Professor Kurtz's new book does not measure up either to its sanguine preface and introduction, or to Professor Saliers' benevolently neutral review. Nor, for that matter, to its title, since the germ of the true depreciation theory is mentioned only inadvertently and the problems of value are not touched upon at all. To take up the latter subject would entail a presentation of the changing net rental or service in terms of changing selling prices, rates of production, operating expenses, replacement costs and rates of interest, profit, and expansion. The value theory of scrapping would also have to be mentioned. Finally, the relationship between the rate of production and the productive capacity, and the even greater stumbling block of obsolescence, i.e. gradual improvement in the type of replacements, are also unavoidable topics in any extended discussion of the science of valuation and depreciation. If there is any such science! Professor Kurtz himself hints that there may not be, when he says that "in conclusion the author wishes to point out that although this treatment is scientific and analytic in nature, actual valuation and depreciation estimating must always be accompanied by the judgment of a competent appraiser" (p.7).

I have gone to such lengths to review this book unasked, because I fully agree with Professor Saliers that the subject of composite depreciation is highly important to accountants who are notoriously prone to look at a single machine only. Those who are interested in a good introduction to the subject will find more as well as more accurate information in Professor Kurtz's first book. Yours truly, New York, N. Y.

GABRIEL A. D. PREINREICH

"The Practice of Depreciation"

Econometrica (July 1939), pp. 235–265

THE PRACTICE OF DEPRECIATION

By GABRIEL A. D. PREINREICH

IN A PREVIOUS article[1] I made a brief and incomplete survey of the theory of depreciation. In the present paper I discuss its practice. One obstacle to practical progress in this field is that mathematically trained minds are seldom well informed on what accountants actually do. The latter are therefore more often criticized for methods which they are not using than for those which they are. Even otherwise valuable contributions thus elicit opposition quite unnecessarily. The inappropriate antithesis tends to discredit the rest of the argument and prompts general retorts, for instance that "accounting is a tool of business . . . determined by the practices of business men.—Where accounting treatment diverges from economic theory, a similar divergence is likely to be found between economic theory and business practice."[2] Such an attitude, in turn, is not very helpful or progressive, even if the dangerous phrase "tool of business" is interpreted only in its best possible sense.

In the article cited, I probably added to the already existing confusion by calling sample methods by certain names without proper qualification, although the same names are commonly applied to substantially different methods. The truth is that the familiar "single-machine" formulae permit of different interpretations. To clarify the situation, the present paper identifies a greater number of methods unequivocally by developing their basic "many-machine" equations and comparing the results. References to practice and to individual writers' ideas are made wherever possible, before choosing a method which appears best suited to the practical needs of large enterprises and the investing public.

I

The task of translating the net effect of many debits and credits into a single mathematical formula requires some familiarity with certain elementary concepts used by statisticians. Although these were given in my survey of the theory, upon which this paper leans heavily, a restatement of the basic formulae seems desirable.

When a large number of similar machines is installed at the same time, the rate at which they will drop out of service forms a bell-shaped, but usually skew, *frequency distribution*. Let it be drawn in such a form

[1] "Annual Survey of Economic Theory: The Theory of Depreciation," ECONOMETRICA, Vol. 6, July, 1938, pp. 219–241.

[2] George Oliver May (Chairman, Committee on Accounting Procedure, American Institute of Accountants), "The Influence of Accounting on the Development of an Economy," *Journal of Accountancy*, January, 1936, pp. 11–12.

235

that its ordinates $f(0)$ at the time $t=0$ and $f(n)$ at the time $t=n$ be zero and that the total area enclosed by the curve and the axis of abscissae be equal to unity. For any other time between these limits the curve will be denoted by $f(t)$. Summation of $f(t)$ from t to n gives the *mortality curve* $M(t)$ per centum of the total number of machines installed at the time $t=0$:

$$(1) \qquad M(t) = \int_t^n f(\tau)d\tau; \qquad M(0) = 1; \qquad M(n) = 0.$$

It will sometimes be necessary to employ the mortality or survival function in the inverted form $M^{-1}(y)$, which expresses the abscissa corresponding to any given ordinate y. The usual form $M(t)$ states the ordinate corresponding to any given abscissa t.

The area enclosed by the mortality curve and the co-ordinate axes represents the total life units of service expected from the machines installed at the outset. Since the ordinates are expressed per centum, the area also equals the *average life* of the machines, i.e., their life expectancy at $t=0$. The *life expectancy* of the machines still in service at any other time t is the quotient of the remaining life units of service by the mortality curve:

$$(2) \qquad L(0) = a = \int_0^n M(\tau)d\tau; \qquad L(t) = \frac{1}{M(t)} \int_t^n M(\tau)d\tau.$$

In accord with this introduction, all formulae given hereafter take it for granted that the number of machines composing the plant is large enough to permit the use of continuous functions. Attention necessarily centers on the *undepreciated remainder per centum of the original wearing value* (i.e., cost less present worth of the scrap value) *of a large number of machines installed together*. This concept is denoted throughout the present paper by $r(t)$. It varies between $r(0) = 1$ and $r(n) = 0$ and will be defined in many different ways by as many different depreciation methods numbered consecutively. The *rate of depreciation* is $dr(t)/dt$ or $r'(t)$ for short. Scrap values are omitted, because it is simpler to consider them separately. Any remainder of wearing value $r(t)$ can be readily converted into the *book value or unexpired cost per centum* $c(t)$ by the operation:

$$(3) \qquad c(t) = \left[1 - s \int_0^n f(\tau)e^{-i\tau}d\tau \right] r(t) + s \int_t^n f(\tau)e^{i(t-\tau)}d\tau.$$

where $s = scrap\ value\ per\ centum$ of original cost. When the rate of interest is zero, this formula reduces to:

$$(4) \qquad c(t) = (1 - s)r(t) + sM(t).$$

The *depreciation rate on the book value* is $c'(t)+sf(t)$ in either event. In the survey of theory book values were used instead of wearing values. The notations are uniform in both papers, but a glossary of symbols is also submitted in the present Appendix B.

The presentation is entirely general, i.e., valid no matter what the shape of the mortality curve may be. Only for the sake of *graphic illustration* did I adopt the concrete sample:

$$(5) \qquad M(t) = \frac{12}{n^4} \int_t^n \tau(n - \tau)^2 d\tau; \qquad n = 20 \text{ years}.$$

My assumption of the maximal age n is purely arbitrary; in other respects, however, the function happens to reflect fairly closely the behavior of seventeen different types of equipment out of a total of fifty-two studied by Prof. Edwin B. Kurtz.[3]

Equation numbers appearing in heavy type in the text mean that those equations are plotted in the form of curves similarly numbered in one of the four figures submitted. For any formula containing either $M(t)$, or its derivative $-f(t)$, the figure is obviously valid only when these symbols refer to the sample (5) above.

To clarify the processes which lead to the continuous functions when the number of machines is very large, all four figures also show what would happen, if there were only ten machines. Each of the ten layers represents a machine, the horizontal dimension being its life graduated according to the sample (5) and the vertical dimension its original wearing value per centum of all such values. The area must then express the number of life-service units originally purchased. The method of depreciation is indicated by shading in such a manner that the shaded portions of any ordinate add up to that fraction of the original wearing value of ten machines, which remains unrecovered at any time t under the method illustrated.

The answers obtainable from the shading do not agree exactly with the continuous curves plotted, because a division of the plant into only ten machines is not sufficient. The discrepancies are surprisingly small, however. This shows that any reasonably large number of machines may be considered infinitely large for theoretical purposes. The use of continuous functions is therefore fully justified by the great saving in effort which they permit.

Nearly a score of different depreciation methods will now be analyzed in turn.

[3] *Life Expectancy of Physical Property*, Ronald Press Co., New York, 1930.

II

1. *The Economist's Straight-Line Method—Figure* 1

The vertical line of average life is drawn and the cost of each machine

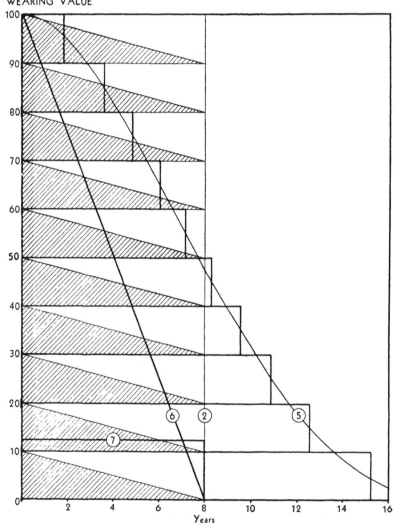

FIGURE 1.—THE ECONOMIST'S STRAIGHT-LINE METHOD

Shaded portions of any ordinate add up to undepreciated remainder wearing value per centum, when plant consists of ten machines of similar type, installed simultaneously. Life characteristics differ according to mortality curve (5).

When number of machines is very large, (6) = remainder wearing value per centum, (7) = rate of depreciation, and (2) = average life.

Maximal life $n = 20$ years. Numbering corresponds to equation numbers of text.

is distributed evenly over that period. The unexpired cost accordingly declines in a straight line, but the rate of depreciation is straight only with reference to the original number of machines, not per machine in service:

$$(6) \qquad\qquad r_1(t) = 1 - t/a, \qquad\qquad 0 \leqq t \leqq a,$$

$$(7) \qquad\qquad r_1'(t) = -1/a.$$

In terms of debit and credit the method implies the charging of all costs of acquisition to a "plant account." Periodic charges to operations at the rate $1/a$ per annum are credited to a "reserve for depreciation." Whether or not costs are canceled against the reserve a years after purchase is immaterial; the difference of the two accounts always gives the unrecovered cost.

Economists, statisticians, engineers, etc. should note that accountants do not use this method. Accounting textbooks or monographs written by accountants do not even mention it. Outside accounting literature it is nevertheless the standard antithesis which readily demonstrates the superiority of whatever other method a given writer may advocate.

2. *The Accountant's Straight-Line Method—Figure 2*

The plant account is charged with original cost and the reserve credited with depreciation charged to operations at the annual rate $1/a$, but only for a years or the actual life of the machine, *whichever be less*. Upon discarding, a bookkeeping entry is immediately made in the following form:

	Dr.	Cr.
Reserve for Depreciation	$\Delta y t/a$	
(8) Loss on Capital Assets	$\Delta y(1 - t/a)$	
Plant Account		Δy

In this entry Δy represents the original cost of a machine in the absence of a scrap value, as assumed.[4] If the machine outlives the average age a, there will be no loss and the entry made upon discarding is simply:

	Dr.	Cr.
Reserve for Depreciation	Δy	
(9) Plant Account		Δy

[4] When there is a scrap value, the credit remains Δy, but the debits shown will refer only to $(1-s)\Delta y$. An additional debit $s\Delta y$ is then necessary to an account which may be called "scrap inventory" for present purposes.

The important point to note is that if the cost of the originally installed machines had been charged to one account and that of their

PER CENTUM OF
WEARING VALUE

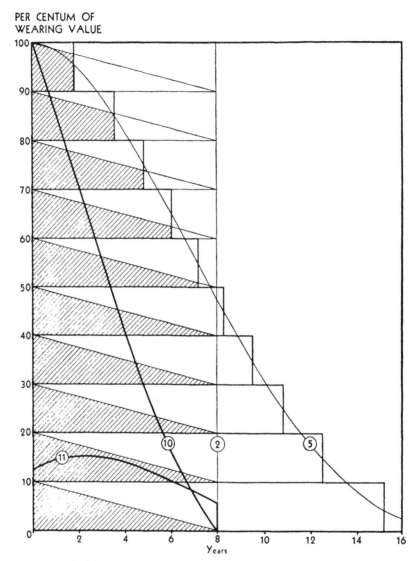

FIGURE 2.—THE ACCOUNTANT'S STRAIGHT-LINE METHOD

Shaded portions of any ordinate add up to undepreciated remainder wearing value per centum, when plant consists of ten machines of similar type, installed simultaneously. Life characteristics differ according to mortality curve (5).

When number of machines is very large, (10) =remainder wearing value per centum, (11) =rate of depreciation, and (2) =average life.

Maximal life $n = 20$ years. Numbering corresponds to equation numbers of text.

replacements to another, the successive balances of the former account would outline the mortality curve. Depreciation is charged at the rate $1/a$ only on the machines in service, but the early capital losses are in effect additional depreciation charges; the method is therefore not straight. Its formulae are:

$$(10) \qquad r_2(t) = \left(1 - \frac{t}{a}\right) M(t), \qquad\qquad 0 \leq t \leq a;$$

$$(11) \qquad r_2'(t) = -\frac{1}{a} M(t) - \left(1 - \frac{t}{a}\right) f(t).$$

3. *The True Straight-Line Method—Figure 3*

For practical reasons, method 2 distorts the general principle accepted by all accountants that "the capital sum to be recovered shall be charged off over the useful life of the property. The deduction . . . shall be limited to such ratable amount as may reasonably be considered necessary to recover during the remaining useful life of the property the unrecovered cost."[5] "If it develops that the useful life of the property will be longer or shorter than . . . originally estimated under all the then known facts the portion of the cost . . . not already provided for . . . should be spread over the remaining useful life . . . as re-estimated in the light of the subsequent facts."[6]

When the term "property" is interpreted to mean a large number of machines taken together, the rule evidently suggests that the rate of depreciation allowable is the quotient of the wearing value by the average life expectancy of the machines still in service:

$$(12) \qquad r_3'(t) = -\frac{r_3(t)}{\dfrac{1}{M(t)}\displaystyle\int_t^n M(\tau)d\tau} = -\frac{1}{a} M(t), \qquad 0 \leq t \leq n;$$

$$(13) \qquad r_3(t) = \frac{1}{a}\int_t^n M(\tau)d\tau = \int_0^{M(t)} \frac{M^{-1}(y) - t}{a} \, dy.$$

Application of the method consists of charging depreciation at the annual rate $1/a$ only on the machines in service, but throughout their entire life, whether that be more or less than a years. No early losses are recognized and the bookkeeping entry is always (9), regardless of when a machine is scrapped. Part of the cost of machines discarded before the age a is thus left, not in the plant account, but in the difference between it and the reserve, i.e., in the book value. This excess is

---

[5] *Revenue Act of 1936, Regulations 94*, Art. 23(1)–5.
[6] *Revenue Act of 1928, Regulations 74*, Art. 205.

PER CENTUM OF
WEARING VALUE

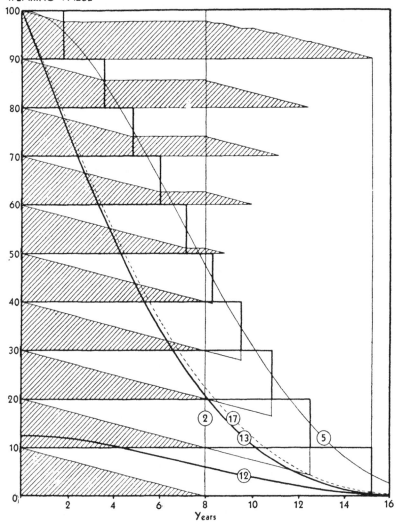

FIGURE 3.—THE TRUE STRAIGHT-LINE METHOD

Shaded portions of any ordinate add up to undepreciated remainder wearing value per centum, when plant consists of ten machines of similar type, installed simultaneously. Life characteristics differ according to mortality curve (5).

When number of machines is very large, (13) = remainder wearing value per centum, (12) = rate of depreciation, and (2) = average life. The broken line (17) = remainder wearing value per centum for Professor Kurtz' method.

Maximal life $n = 20$ years. Numbering corresponds to equation numbers of text.

gradually absorbed by continuing charges at the rate $1/a$ on the balance of the plant account even after machines recorded in it are past the average age. If a was correctly forecast, both the plant account and the reserve will be closed out after the last machine is discarded.

The depreciation rate is here a constant or "straight" rate per machine; the method considers a life unit equivalent to a cost unit, whether that unit be furnished by a short- or long-lived machine. This approach has the merits of *the averaging or insurance principle* so long as early "losses" are not recognized.[7] The principal difficulty is that of estimating the average life correctly. Errors have a cumulative effect on the book value of a composite plant; a separate statistical department is accordingly necessary. Only large enterprises, such as the Bell Telephone System, can afford to use this method.[8]

4. *The Method of Weighted Life Units—Figure* 4

The accounting principle quoted may also be applied to each machine separately. The purchase price of each having been the same, the cost of a life unit is inversely related to the number of units acquired. The weighting is done graphically by drawing a diagonal line across each rectangular layer, or mathematically by the formulae:

$$(14) \qquad r_4(t) = \int_0^{M(t)} \frac{M^{-1}(y) - t}{M^{-1}(y)} \, dy = \int_t^n (1 - t/\tau) f(\tau) d\tau,$$
$$0 \leqq t \leqq n;$$

$$(15) \qquad r_4'(t) = - \int_t^n \frac{f(\tau)}{\tau} \, d\tau.$$

The rate of depreciation being different for each machine, it is improper to refer to the unrecovered cost as the "remainder service life" per centum of the total useful lives of a large number of machines installed at the same time. That information can be obtained only by omitting the weighting process, i.e., in the manner shown in Figure 3.[9]

[7] The Revenue Act of 1938 again permits the deduction in full of losses as outlined in journal entry (8). In a few prior revenue acts the deduction is limited by the capital gain and loss provisions, but the new definition of capital assets "does not include . . . property used in the trade or business, of a character which is subject to the allowance for depreciation provided in section 23(1)" [Cf. Section 117(a)(1)].

[8] Cf. Allan B. Crunden and Donald R. Belcher, "The Straight-Line Accounting Practice of Telephone Companies in the U. S.," *Proceedings of the International Congress of Accounting*, New York, 1929, pp. 351–386.

[9] The value of Professor Edwin B. Kurtz's book, *The Science of Valuation and Depreciation*, Ronald Press Co., New York, 1937, is seriously impaired by his belief that methods 3 and 4 are equivalent. His Table VIII calculates the cor-

PER CENTUM OF
WEARING VALUE

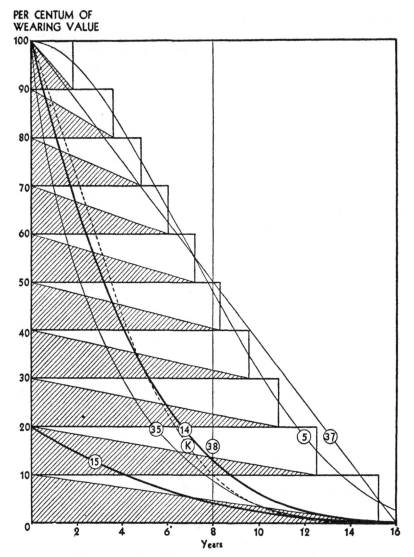

FIGURE 4.—THE METHOD OF WEIGHTED LIFE UNITS

Shaded portions of any ordinate add up to undepreciated remainder wearing value per centum, when plant consists of ten machines of similar type, installed simultaneously. Life characteristics differ according to mortality curve (5).

When number of machines is very large, (14) = remainder wearing value per centum and (15) = rate of depreciation. The broken line (K) = remainder wearing value obtained by Professor Kurtz (see note 36); (35) = example of remainder wearing value for the theoretical public-utility method, when mortality curve is not (5), but coincides with the limit of shape (37). Other limit of shape of all possible mortality curves normalized to same area is (38) = (2) = average life.

Maximal life $n = 20$ years. Numbering corresponds to equation numbers of text.

It may be seen now that method 2 really attempts to follow method 4. Errors in past depreciation rates can be definitely ascertained only upon scrapping. The correction is then made by entry (8), if the machine drops out sooner than expected. In the opposite event the cost has already been written off so that, broadly speaking, it is recovered within the life of the machine in either case. That is about all that can be done at present in general practice. The Bureau of Internal Revenue does not ordinarily disallow the use of standardized rates on the basis of method 2, even though tax blanks demand that new life estimates be made from year to year. Voluntary revisions are made occasionally.

5. *The Kurtz Method of Replacement Insurance*

According to Professor Edwin B. Kurtz this method is "the only scientific approach to the problem"[10] of depreciation. It consists of applying the fundamental insurance formula,[11] which prescribes that the discounted sum of all premiums must equal the discounted sum of all benefits paid. In order to obtain an algebraic approximation, the number of premiums due is measured by the survivors at the beginning of each year and the benefits due by the sudden drop at the end of the year.

In terms of continuous functions the correct premium is evidently:

$$(16) \qquad P = \frac{\int_0^n f(\tau)e^{-i\tau}d\tau}{\int_0^n M(\tau)e^{-i\tau}d\tau} \cdot$$

When the discount rate is zero, it follows from this formula that the premium is $1/a$ per machine, i.e., just what it is in method 3. Instead of that, however, Professor Kurtz gets $P = 1/(a+\frac{1}{2})$ from his approximation. He explains that "this of course, is not due to any inaccuracy . . . but rather to the difference between the number of installments to be paid. In the straight-line plan the number of units is fixed by the average life, namely 1000, 2000, 3000, or 4000 for the 100 units. In the replacement-insurance plan the number of units in service at the beginning of each age fixes the number of premiums to be collected to make possible paying the 100 benefits. These totals

rect remainder service life by arithmetical processes corresponding to formula 13, but his Figure 16 is similar to the present Figure 4. The equivalence of the two is then "proved" by forcing a sample of Table VIII into Figure 16, without bothering to verify whether the rule of proportionality applied to the triangles would give the results indicated thereon. Cf. pp. 42–47. For the consequences see note 36 below.

[10] *Ibid.*, p. 6.

[11] *Ibid.*, pp. 96–97.

are 1050, 2050, 3050 and 4050 for the 10, 20, 30 and 40 year groups respectively. The total money collected is the same in each case."[12]

We thus learn from Professor Kurtz himself that the only scientific approach consists of charging too little on more life units than there are in 100 machines, whereas the straight line method is unscientific enough to calculate the premium by reference to the right number! As his chart shows,[13] he has method 1 in mind, when concluding that his procedure is more scientific than the straight-line plan. The proper antithesis is method 3, which promptly demonstrates the pointless distortion. For the sake of comparison, Professor Kurtz's method may be expressed in the form:

$$(17) \qquad r_5(t) = 1 - \frac{t}{a + \frac{1}{2}}, \qquad\qquad 0 \leqq t \leqq \tfrac{1}{2};$$

$$= \frac{1}{a + \frac{1}{2}} \int_t^{n+1/2} M(\tau - \tfrac{1}{2}) d\tau, \quad \tfrac{1}{2} \leqq t \leqq n + \tfrac{1}{2}.$$

This curve is plotted as a broken line in Figure 3 to show its divergence from the true method of replacement insurance for the case without interest.

6. *The Sinking-Fund and Annuity Methods*

Variations may be devised to correspond to any of the first four methods. For the counterpart of method 1 the premium is $P = i/(e^{ia} - 1)$, which leads to the formula:

$$(18) \qquad r_{6.1}(t) = \frac{e^{ia} - e^{it}}{e^{ia} - 1}, \qquad\qquad 0 \leqq t \leqq a.$$

This form also serves as a favorite antithesis. In practice the counterpart of method 2 is usually employed:

$$(19) \qquad r_{6.2}(t) = \frac{e^{ia} - e^{it}}{e^{ia} - 1} M(t), \qquad\qquad 0 \leqq t \leqq a.$$

The true replacement-insurance method for $i > 0$ would be:

$$(20) \quad r_{6.3}(t) = M(t) - P \int_0^t M(\tau) e^{i(t-\tau)} d\tau + \int_0^t f(\tau) e^{i(t-\tau)} d\tau,$$
$$0 \leqq t \leqq n;$$

where P is taken from formula (16). The book value equals the difference between the cost of the machines still in service and the reserve,

[12] *Ibid.*, p. 112.
[13] *Ibid.*, p. 113, Figure 43.

to which premiums and interest are credited and benefits charged. The annuity formula is simpler and equivalent:

$$(21) \qquad r_{6.3}(t) = \phi \int_t^n M(\tau)e^{i(t-\tau)}d\tau; \qquad \frac{1}{\phi} = \int_0^n M(\tau)e^{-i\tau}d\tau.$$

The transformation of (20) into (21) is readily accomplished upon observing that $P = \phi - i$.[14] For equations (18) and (19) the equivalence of the sinking-fund and annuity methods is immediately apparent.

The discounting process can be applied to method 4 in the same way:

$$(22) \qquad r_{6.4}(t) = \int_0^{M(t)} \frac{e^{iM^{-1}(y)} - e^{it}}{e^{iM^{-1}(y)} - 1} \, dy = \int_t^n \frac{e^{i\tau} - e^{it}}{e^{i\tau} - 1} f(\tau)d\tau.$$

When i is the fair rate of return, this would be the equitable method of public-utility depreciation, if both the output and the operating expenses were constant.[15] No one ever uses it, of course. The device of dual rates is commonly employed to enhance the "rate" or unit price chargeable to consumers beyond a fair figure. According to the *trust-fund theory*, the sinking fund must be safely invested in behalf of the consumer, who is thus obliged not only to pay the "fair" or legal rate of return on the capital actually rendering a public service, but also to make good the deficiency in the earning power of the capital which he has already repaid.

It is unnecessary to present the formulae for the dual-rate methods, because the trust-fund theory is generally applied directly to the calculation of the "rate," without affecting the bookkeeping entries. The regulations usually endorse the "principle" that "the fund is a necessary part of the property of the utility and should not be excluded from the rate base; it may be considered as part of the working capital. A larger income must be permitted on the main operating property, in order to compensate for the deficiency of the earnings of this part of the invested capital."[16]

This conclusion is directly contradicted by the composite-book-value curve,[17] which shows that a very substantial part of the originally necessary capital is liquidated in the normal course of business and

---

[14] That the sinking-fund contribution is less than the depreciation, is overlooked by many writers. Despite the memorable failure of Dr. Richard Price—who, around 1770, insisted that John Bull could lift himself by his bootstraps through the magic of compound interest—the claim is still being advanced that the sinking-fund method is cheaper than any other.

[15] Cf. method 11 below.

[16] Perry Mason, *The Principles of Public Utility Depreciation*, American Accounting Association, Chicago, 1937, p. 81.

[17] Cf. *op. cit.* in note 1, Figure 1, p. 228.

ceases to render any public service thereafter. Even in the case of expansion and increasing replacement costs, large sums remain idle for a long time, until used for the purchase of necessary equipment.[18] In the meantime, these sums have no claim against the consumer.

Since the Bell Telephone System uses the straight-line method 3, it does not even credit the actual earnings of the sinking fund toward the "fair rate" calculated on the original(?) cost of the equipment in service. Federal Communications Commissioner Paul A. Walker's endorsement of the trust-fund theory[19] amounts merely to a demand that that be done. He does not question the validity of the theory itself. If capital can spill over from the original plant investment into a liquid fund, is that not conclusive evidence of its inability to render any public service?[20]

7. *The Diminishing-Balance Methods*

Four different approaches corresponding to methods 1 to 4 are again possible. A scrap value $s > 0$ is essential. The book value of a single machine is for the first two cases:

$$(23) \qquad B(t) = s^{t/a} = e^{-kt}; \qquad k = -\frac{1}{a} \log_e s.$$

Omitting the first case, we obtain for the second:

$$(24) \qquad r_{7.2}(t) = \frac{1}{b}(s^{t/a} - s)M(t), \quad b = 1 - s, \quad 0 \leqq r \leqq a.$$

The third possibility is:

$$(25) \quad r_{7.3}(t) = \frac{1}{b}\left[e^{-kt} - s\int_0^t f(\tau)e^{k(\tau - t)}d\tau - sM(t)\right]; \quad 0 \leqq t \leqq n.$$

If k, as determined from (23) is again applied, the essential condition $r_{7.3}(n) = 0$ will not be fulfilled. Such a method is therefore quite crude.

---

[18] *Ibid.*, Figure 3, p. 230.

[19] *New York Times*, April 2, 1938, p. 2, Summary of Telephone Report: "The accumulated reserves, as well as future additions thereto, should be administered by the company for the benefit of subscribers present and future."

[20] For a discussion in greater detail, cf. my paper, "The Principles of Public Utility Depreciation," *Accounting Review*, June, 1938, pp. 149–165.

As the present paper goes to press, I must acknowledge Prof. Ragnar Frisch's courtesy in lending me a copy of Prof. P. O. Pedersen's contribution "On the Depreciation of Public Utilities" (*Ingeniørvidenskabelige Skrifter*, B Nr. 12, pp. 69–99, Dansk Ingeniørforening, Copenhagen, 1934). Lack of time and space prevents me from doing justice to certain new and interesting aspects presented therein, e.g., effect of errors in life estimates, simultaneous scrapping of a whole plant, varying degrees of utilization, etc.

The defect can be remedied, however, by using a rate k given by that condition. The result is the insurance premium (for $i=0$), which must, be charged on the basis of *composite* book values, instead of on cost as in method 3. The form of (25) re...ains unchanged; its new meaning may be denoted by $r_{7.30}(t)$.

For the fourth variety of the diminishing-balance method, $B(t) = s^{t/M^{-1}(y)}$, which leads to the formula:

$$(26) \qquad r_{7.4}(t) = \frac{1}{b} \int_0^{M(t)} (s^{t/M^{-1}(y)} - s)dy, \qquad 0 \leq t \leq n.$$

Of these methods, the only one occasionally employed in practice is 7.2. American accounting writers usually mention that it is used more extensively in Great Britain. The comment is also generally made that the method counteracts the increase in maintenance charges, as a machine grows older.

8. *The Sum-of-the-Year-Digits Method*

The depreciation charge is apportioned in accordance with a declining arithmetic series. For instance, if $a=8$, the first year's charge would be 8/36, the next year's 7/36 and that of the last year 1/36. The procedure amounts to calculating the remaining area, at the time t, of the shaded triangles of Figure 1. Thus for the counterpart of method 2, there is obtained:

$$(27) \qquad r_{8.2}(t) = \left(1 - \frac{t}{a}\right)^2 M(t), \qquad 0 \leq t \leq a.$$

That is no doubt the only form in which the method might possibly occur. I have never seen it applied, but many accounting textbooks mention it. Presumably, it also means to counteract the declining efficiency of a machine.

9. *The Retirement Method*

Depreciation is disregarded altogether, so that no reserve for depreciation appears on the books. The balance of the plant account is also the book value of the machines in service. The cost of scrapped machines is deleted promptly by direct charge to operations:

$$(28) \qquad r_9(t) = M(t), \qquad 0 \leq t \leq n.$$

So-called retirement reserves are created merely to smooth out the fluctuations between theoretical and actual rates of replacement. Such reserves seldom exceed one per cent, of the plant account, and are the best evidence that a large replacement fund is unnecessary.

The retirement method is used extensively in the public-utility field, where it combines the advantages of an undepreciated rate base with freedom from both legal and financial restrictions on dividend payments. Superfluous capital can be paid out without hindrance, because it is legally classified as surplus or undivided profit, and because the rate base will not be reduced by the distribution. When another method is used, the same sums are classified as a necessary replacement fund, the distribution of which is contrary to law, because such action would impair the corporate capital! This legal inconsistency is no doubt responsible for the trust-fund theory. The correct principle appears to be the one which I have elsewhere called "the principle of good management,"[21] according to which the company shall neither hoard idle funds, nor part with or fail to raise any, which can be productively reinvested. For public utilities, this principle must of course be applied from the consumer's viewpoint of what constitutes idleness.

10. *The Canning Method*

The method of Professor John B. Canning[22] consists of the simpler and therefore more practical features of the Taylor-Hotelling method,[23] which was already examined.[24] Whereas methods 1 to 9 are concerned only with the distribution of original cost over the life of a machine, Professor Canning also considers "outlays . . . that will most probably have to be incurred as a direct . . . consequence of . . . ownership and operation, if the machine's service is to be had most economically."[25] There is reason to believe that this means chiefly repairs and maintenance, i.e., current physical upkeep. Professor Hotelling's operating expenses are probably all-inclusive, although he does not define them. Both methods look alike when the rate of interest and the scrap value are considered constant:

$$(29) \qquad B(t) = \int_t^T \left[wQ(\tau) - E(\tau) \right] e^{i(t-\tau)} d\tau + s e^{i(t-T)}.$$

[21] See *The Nature of Dividends*, New York, 1935, p. 9, pp. 175 *et seq.* Not to distribute reinvestable funds may mean in practice either no distribution at all, or stock dividends, or an offsetting combination of cash dividends and subscription rights.

[22] *The Economics of Accountancy*, Ronald Press Co., New York, 1929.

[23] J. S. Taylor, "A Statistical Theory of Depreciation," *Journal of the American Statistical Association*, December, 1923, pp. 1010–1023; Harold Hotelling, "A General Mathematical Theory of Depreciation," *ibid.*, September, 1925, pp. 340–353.

[24] See *op. cit.* in note 1, pp. 234–239.

[25] Canning, p. 291.

In this notation, $B(t) =$ book value of a single machine, $w =$ unit cost including time cost, $Q(t) =$ rate of production, $E(t) =$ expenses, $s =$ scrap value, and $T =$ date of scrapping. Professor Canning considers only $B(t)$ and w as unknown so that a second equation expressing the original cost $B(0)$ is sufficient. In the Hotelling theory T is to be determined simultaneously from the additional relation $dB(t)/dT = 0$.

Professor Canning holds that "no formula . . . will show exactly when an asset is worn out, but the good ones [i.e., his own with or without interest] will . . . show that a wrong estimate of T has been made before any substantial real loss has been incurred."[26] They "serve notice . . . by finding negative valuations long before the end of the Tth period."[27] These remarks refer to his example G,[28] where a sharply declining rate of production coupled with sharply increasing outlays soon leads to negative book values.

That the emergence of negative values need not give timely warning, may be inferred from example D,[29] where the rate of production is constant. An outlay of \$25 is there made during the tenth and last year of life on a \$100 machine having a book value of \$7.47 at $t = 9$. Unless the profit (after all other expenses including depreciation, but before the outlay) is more than 334.7 per cent, of the investment, it would also have been better to scrap the machine. As in Professor Hotelling's theory, the real market price of the product is omitted from the problem.

Methods similar to Professor Canning's are sometimes employed, especially in the simplified form $i = 0$, which he really prefers. For many machines the formula becomes in practice a variation of method 2:

$$(30) \qquad r_{10.2}(t) = \frac{M(t)}{b} \int_t^a [wQ(\tau) - E_C(\tau)]d\tau, \qquad 0 \leq t \leq a.$$

Under this procedure the cost of repairs, etc., is charged to the reserve and not to operations. The periodic debit to operations and credit to the reserve is $wQ(t)\Delta y$ per machine, but journal entries analogous to (8) or (9) are also made when scrapping takes place before or after the average age a. A difference arises in each case between the actual repair charges and the amounts previously credited to the reserve to provide for repairs. Unless such balances are promptly traced and closed out to operations, an error in average repair estimates will have a cumulative effect upon the book value of a composite plant. When

[26] *Ibid.*, p. 264.
[27] *Ibid.*
[28] *Ibid.*, p. 349.
[29] *Ibid*, p. 346.

this danger is overlooked, as it sometimes is, the official description of the depreciation method may become misleading.

11. *The Theoretical Public-Utility Method*

Although no depreciation theory may be described as the general[30] one, that of Professor Hotelling appears to be the correct solution of the specific problem presented by regulated monopolies. The only change necessary is to substitute the legal rate of return p for the rate of interest i, which he would employ in every instance. If his three equations are so revised, the simultaneous solution yields the correct date of scrapping and the correct unit cost plus profit, i.e., the fair "rate" chargeable for the services of a single machine. In terms of many machines installed at the same time, the method will then amount to:

$$(31) \qquad c(t) = \int_0^{M(t)} B_p(y, t)dy, \qquad 0 \leqq t \leqq n,$$

where B_p means formula (29) with p substituted for i. The inclusion of y indicates that the functions T, w, Q, and E differ from machine to machine. The last two vary of course also with time. The equation $dB(y, t)/dT = 0$ now furnishes the mortality curve $T = M^{-1}(y)$, which must be employed if the service of all machines "is to be had most economically."[31] We therefore obtain an elaboration of method 4:

$$(32) \quad r_{11.4}(t) = \frac{1}{\beta} \int_0^{M(t)} \int_t^{M^{-1}(y)} [w(y)Q(y, \tau) - E_H(y, \tau)]e^{p(t-\tau)}d\tau dy,$$

where β is the factor of $r(t)$ in equation (3), when p is read for i. If Q and E_H are independent of time, $w(y)Q(y) - E_H(y) = \beta p/(1 - e^{-pM^{-1}(y)})$ and formula (32) reduces to (22). In that case mortality must be a physical rather than a value phenomenon.

That the theory of public-utility depreciation can be definitely stated in mathematical terms does not mean that it is readily applicable in practice. Some of the legal and financial obstacles have already been mentioned.[32] Practical difficulties are the lack of foresight, the clerical expense of keeping the voluminous records required to make deferred adjustments by hindsight and the complexity of the calculations which arise. To give an indication of the latter, I shall cite the simplest example I was able to construct. Bearing in mind the three simultaneous equations, let:

[30] Cf. note 23.

[31] Cf. note 25.

[32] Cf. also my *op. cit.* in note 20 and my earlier paper, "The Law of Goodwill," *Accounting Review*, December, 1936, pp. 317–329.

(33) $w(y)Q(y, t) = [ps + E_H(y, T)]e^{q(T-t)}$

and

(34) $E_H(y, t) = \dfrac{q + p - s(qe^{-pT} + pe^{qT})}{e^{(k+q)T} - \dfrac{k+q}{k-p}e^{(k-p)T} + \dfrac{q+p}{k-p}} e^{kt}.$

Now, if $k = 3p$, $q = p$, and $T = 2a(1-y)$, the solution of (32) is:

(35)
$$r_{11.4}(t) = \frac{1}{4ap\alpha\beta}\left[\frac{s(\alpha^2 + \alpha^4)}{z} + 2\alpha^4 \log z - (\alpha^2 - 1)^2 \frac{1 - sz}{z^2 - 1}\right.$$
$$\left. - (\alpha^4 - 1) \log \frac{(z + 1)^{s+1}}{(z - 1)^{s-1}}\right]_\alpha^\epsilon.$$

In this notation, z is the variable of integration $e^{2ap(1-y)}$, for which the limits $\epsilon = e^{2ap}$ and $\alpha = e^{pt}$ have not yet been substituted. For the special case $a = 8$, $p = .07$ and $s = .1$, the graph is shown in Figure 4, although it has no connection with the mortality curve (5), but refers to $M(t) = 1 - t/16$. For the curve (5), $M^{-1}(y)$ is the second root of a quartic equation, which is already too involved for an example. An actual case is far worse.[33] A less simple relationship of k, q, and p also increases the difficulties.

III

One general measure of the differences in depreciation methods is the ultimate composite-book-value level determined in the absence of scrap value, expansion, or change in replacement costs. The general formula of the level is:[34]

(36) $$R(\infty) = \frac{1}{a} \int_0^n r(t)dt.$$

It is of interest to see how differences in the shape of mortality curves affect the ultimate levels. All observed mortality curves[35] normalized to the same area a lie within the extremes:

(37) $M(t) = 1 - t/2a,$ $M^{-1}(y) = 2a(1 - y),$

and

(38) $M(t) = 1,$ $M^{-1}(y) = a.$

[33] See the frequency distributions fitted to actual data by Professor Kurtz, *op. cit.*, in note 3, pp. 103–106.

[34] By *ibid.* in note 1, formula (17), when $x = 0$, $q = 0$, $s = 0$ and $t = \infty$.

[35] Cf. seven mortality curves calculated by Professor Kurtz, *ibid.*, in note 3, p. 74.

177

Upon inserting (6) into (36) we obtain:

$$(39) \qquad R_1(\infty) = \frac{1}{a} \int_0^a (1 - t/a)dt = \frac{1}{2} \cdot$$

The method itself requires the use of (38), so that (37) cannot be applied. The levels of the next three methods may be written in their general form, placed between the extremes (37) and (38) in that order:

$$(40) \qquad \frac{5}{12} < R_2(\infty) = \frac{1}{a} \int_0^a (1 - t/a)M(t)dt \qquad < \frac{1}{2},$$

$$(41) \qquad \frac{2}{3} > R_3(\infty) = \frac{1}{a^2} \int_0^n \int_t^n M(\tau)d\tau dt \qquad > \frac{1}{2},$$

$$(42)^{36} \qquad \frac{1}{2} = R_4(\infty) = \frac{1}{a} \int_0^n \int_t^n (1 - t/\tau)f(\tau)d\tau dt = \frac{1}{2} \cdot$$

[36] The mistake of considering methods 3 and 4 as equivalent frustrates Professor Kurtz's efforts to obtain the result (42) by valid mathematical processes, because the proper use of his Table VIII (cf. note 9) leads to (41). He must get a stable level of $\frac{1}{2}$ however. A shaded triangle having half the area of a layer in Figure 4 above, it is evident enough that the ultimate static composite level is 50 per cent for that method, no matter what the shape of the mortality curve may be. Professor Kurtz cuts this Gordian knot by saying that "each group of survivors is multiplied by the per cent remainder service life" (p. 78) taken from Table VIII, which is equivalent to formula (13) above, except for the difference between discrete and continuous functions. In his Table XX he thus gets arithmetically the results:

$$(K) \qquad r_K(t) = \frac{1}{a} M(t) \int_t^n M(\tau)d\tau;$$

$$(42K) \qquad \frac{1}{2} = R_K(\infty) = \frac{1}{a^2} \int_0^n M(t) \int_t^n M(\tau)d\tau dt = \frac{1}{2}.$$

This is considered as "convincing evidence of the soundness of the method . . . the logic . . . the accuracy . . . their correct joint use . . . a verification of the entire preceding analysis and a demonstration of the inherent unity of the body of principles presented" (pp. 5–6). Actually, he proves nothing but the elementary rule $\int v dv = v^2/2$, which is not applicable, because there is no warrant in theory to multiply only the survivors of successive renewal groups by the corresponding percentages of Table VIII. To do so would have been proper only if that table had been calculated per centum of the number of life units originally contained only in the machines surviving at any time t. In fact the percentages are based upon all life units contained in all machines at $t = 0$.

It follows that before the renewal rate $u(t)$ is stabilized at $1/a$, the true damped waves of composite remainder cost for method 4 differ from those to which Professor Kurtz's empirical equations have been fitted in his Figures 24–30. That is to say, $r_4(t) \neq r_K(t)$ as shown in my Figure 4 and therefore $R_4(t) \neq R_K(t)$, even

The formulae for the remaining methods will be omitted. Results for simple concrete assumptions are given in Table 1.

TABLE 1

Method	Level for Mortality Curve		Other Assumptions
	(37)	(38)	
5	0.688	0.531	$a = 8$
6.1	—	0.546	
6.2	0.451	0.546	$a = 8,\ i = 0.07$
6.3	0.724	0.546	
6.4	0.564	0.546	
7.2	0.281	0.323	
7.3	0.329	0.323	$s = 0.1$
7.30	0.442	0.323	
7.4	0.323	0.323	
8.2	0.292	0.333	none
9	1.000	1.000	
10.2	0.301	0.343	See formulae (33) and (34) for $T = 8$. $$wQ(t) = w(\tfrac{1}{2})Q(\tfrac{1}{2},\ 0)e^{-.07t}$$ $$E_C(t) = E_H(\tfrac{1}{2},\ 0)(e^{.21t} - 1)$$
10.3	0.702	0.417	Anticipated from part IV. $$E_C(y,\ t) = E_H(y,\ 0)(e^{.21t} - 1),\ \text{or}$$ $$E_C(t) = E_H(\tfrac{1}{2},\ 0)(e^{.21t} - 1),$$ corresponding to $T = 16(1 - y)$ or $T = 8$.
11.4	0.387	0.377	Formulae (33) and (34) with $T = 16(1 - y)$ or $T = 8$.

(For methods 10.2 and 10.3: $a = 8$, $s = .1$)

The levels corresponding to (38) do not really exist, but are mere averages, because no damping can take place. All composite-book-value curves remain forever similar to the edge of a saw, dropping gradually from unity to zero and jumping back suddenly every a years. Damping is intensified as the shape of a mortality curve approaches the opposite extreme (37).

---

though $R_4(\infty) = R_K(\infty)$. In addition, simple damped sine functions do not fit the oscillations of either the right or the wrong data.

Why the stable level (42K) was calculated at all is not apparent. Professor Kurtz abandons it immediately after declaring that it is "basic in this study" (p. 90). His "normal" insurance reserves for $i = 0$ are not $\tfrac{1}{2}$, but differ only slightly from $1 - R_3(\infty)$, because (17) is fairly close to (13), as seen in Figure 3 above. The enormous volume of arithmetical calculation performed to determine these levels by "causing the property to pass through its early history or by a 'reverse liquidation process'" (p. 125) is also wholly unnecessary. See formula (36) above.

The table is valid only in the absence of expansion and only for static replacement costs. Steady increases in the purchase price of new machines and in the number of machines in service lead to higher levels per centum of the rising original cost. Irregular changes perpetuate the fluctuations.

IV

Another significant test of differences in depreciation methods is the degree of fluctuation which they introduce into the net profit. For brevity, I shall omit an adequate presentation and merely call attention to the samples of composite depreciation curves shown in Figures 2 and 4 of my survey of the basic theory.[37] The methods there numbered from 1 to 4 are identified by the subscripts 9, 3, 6.3, and 7.3 respectively in the present paper.

A study of the question, what method is most suitable for competitive enterprise, must start from the principle already established that the depreciation problem is fundamentally indeterminate. The theory of economic life can furnish only the average life-span. Within that period, the wearing value may be written down in innumerable different ways, some of which look more reasonable than others. In such circumstances, the choice remains in part a matter of opinion; some progress can be made, however, toward accomplishing practical objectives. The principal one is that of facilitating forecasting, i.e., appraisal by the stock market. Related to it is the task of developing a method of cost accounting, which will be most informative to the management. For both purposes, a method is required, which distributes all predictable costs as evenly or proportionately as possible.

From this strictly practical viewpoint, it is necessary, first of all, to give up the idea that the figure at which capital assets are stated in the balance sheet means anything in particular, except *at best* "actual expenditure not hitherto charged against profits."[38] Similarly, *lasciate*

---

[37] *Op. cit.* in note 1, pp. 229, 231.

[38] That is the best theoretical, i.e., wishful, definition available (Anonymous: "Goodwill and Advertising," *Accountant*, London, February 18, 1914, pp. 287 *et seq.*). Mr. May concludes merely that a balance sheet "is a highly technical production, the significance of which is severely limited and has in the past often been greatly overrated" (*op. cit.* in note 2, p. 20).

A Statement of Accounting Principles, published under the auspices of the American Institute of Accountants (New York, 1938) still contains the hoary platitude that "a balance sheet is a statement which purports to exhibit the financial condition of the business" (p. 55). To understand how little this means, it is necessary to note that "practice has in the course of time hardened into a set of general conventions" (p. 56) expounded in 110 pages. The gist of these is that, subject to legal limitations and after careful consideration, an accountant should do what he thinks best, at least "unless and until sound

ogni speranza[39] that the theory of economic life[40] can soon be applied in practice. When to scrap a machine will have to remain for the present a matter of technical judgment, aided perhaps by records of output and expenditure kept for isolated samples. If these major aims of theory are abandoned, it immediately follows that there is no point in calculating interest. By eliminating that refinement also, a great practical advantage is gained; it becomes possible to measure exhaustion of service-capacity in terms of production units instead of time.[41]

Once this stage is reached, the choice falls automatically on the true straight-line method 3, because it will charge a constant insurance premium per unit. That charge will not be affected by either the age of the plant or a variable rate of expansion $x(t)$. When replacement costs increase at the rate $q(t)$, the premium increases only in proportion to the average change in the total cost of the plant arising from that source:

$$(43) \qquad P(x, q, f, t) = \frac{1}{a} R_9(x, q, t) e^{-\int_0^t x(\tau) d\tau}; \quad P(x, 0, f, t) = \frac{1}{a}.$$

If desired, most of the fluctuation due to replacement costs can be

---

business judgment dictates" (p. 39 and to the same effect elsewhere) that he do something else for reasons not divulged. For details of "such abnegation, such subservience," see W. A. Paton, "Comments on 'A Statement of Accounting Principles'," *Journal of Accountancy*, March, 1938, pp. 196 *et seq.* Also Howard C. Greer, "What Are Accepted Principles of Accounting?" *Accounting Review*, March, 1938, pp. 24–31.

[39] Inscription above the portal to Dante's *Inferno*.

[40] Several months' intensive study of this problem convinces me that it is far more complicated than Professors Taylor and Hotelling conceived it to be fifteen years ago, or myself for that matter, as late as last year. The disconnected comments made in my "Theory" are in order, as far as they go, but they fail to tell the whole story.

Depreciation is merely a distorted shadow cast upon the books by replacement policies. The theory of the latter appears to be essentially a theory of scarcity. As many different rules of replacement can be had as there are ingredients of production or possible combinations of such scarce ingredients. Since the relative weights of different ingredients vary even within a single field of endeavor, each individual enterprise will have its own rule. The sole exception is the case where the market price is fixed by law or otherwise. This rigid limitation overrules the influence of all elastic scarcities.

At the moment when the galleys of the present article are before me (May 25), my MS on economic life is in the hands of Professor Hotelling, to whom I submitted it in recognition of his priority in this field. It is hoped to publish this in the near future.

[41] It is the omission of interest which makes it possible to avoid guessing the future course of production. Otherwise the difficulty is simply shifted to the discount factor. Accounting writers realize this well enough, but a few others, including Professor Kurtz, give no indication of doing so.

eliminated by adopting "Stabilized Accounting,"[42] i.e., keeping books not in dollars, but in terms of an index of general purchasing power. Some variation will remain, because the individual indexes of many different types of equipment always show dispersion.

The distribution of costs of acquisition can thus be made fairly even. Next, let us extend the insurance principle to expenses which can be predicted with a reasonable degree of accuracy. Repairs and maintenance are a good illustration. For a large number of machines installed at the same time, such expenditures form the frequency distribution:

$$(44) \qquad \eta(t) = \int_0^{M(t)} E_C(y, t)dy,$$

which may be treated in the same way as that of replacement. The premium covering both risks will be:

$$(45) \qquad P(x, 0, f + \eta, t) = \frac{1}{a}\left[1 + \int_0^n \eta(\tau)d\tau\right].$$

The search for the method most suitable for practical purposes thus leads to a second application of Professor Canning's single-machine theory:

$$(46) \qquad r_{10.3}(t) = \int_t^n \left[PM(\tau) - \eta(\tau)\right] d\tau.$$

To what extent expenses are to be included, depends upon the accuracy attainable in forecasting them. The aim is to even out the fluctuations, but it is also essential that the differences between the premiums credited to the reserve and the actual expenses charged thereto be adjusted by hindsight from time to time for suitable groups. If foresight is too poor, the adjusting entries may cause greater fluctuation in the time shape of expenses, than if the least predictable items had been excluded from the averaging process and charged currently instead. For a large and *mature* enterprise a substantial degree of equalization will occur even without any special effort. For this reason the Bell System is apparently content to use only the simple method 3. Its special problems call for apportionment on the basis of time, despite cyclical changes in the volume of production. Where wear and tear from use is the principal cause of capital consumption, a distribution of cost over production units seems preferable. This changes only the meaning of t and the form of all functions dependent on it, but not the symbolic formulae.

[42] Title of a book by Henry W. Sweeney, Harper & Bros., New York, 1936.

As already stated, no variety of method 3 should be applied in practice, unless a company maintains a competent statistical department. Others had best adhere to the old stand-bys, methods 2 and 7.2, or perhaps 10.2. Most American companies do indeed use method 2, generally in terms of time, but occasionally on a production basis. Some concession to method 3 is frequently made by disregarding the "loss on capital assets" (8) for purposes of cost accounting. This item then appears in the financial, instead of the operating section of the profit-and-loss account.

It is perhaps ironical that the one enterprise generally known to use method 3 on the proper actuarial basis is a public utility. Still, an unbiased appraisal of the enormous difficulties connected with the theoretically true special method 11.4 may well lead to the conclusion that the straight-line method is most suitable for that field also. If it be found easier to adjust the nominal rate of fair return than the depreciation method, that is the obvious alternative. The essential consideration remains the actual rate of return.

When the expansion rate $x(t)$ is fairly steady, the simple straight-line method 3 can be made more flexible by varying the premium P, which would ordinarily be $1/a$, within the limits:

$$(47) \qquad \chi - x \leqq P \leqq \chi,$$

where χ is the asymptote $u(x, \infty)e^{-zx}$ of the renewal rate. Any such premium will be linearly but inversely related to the ultimate composite-wearing-value level per centum:[43]

$$(48) \qquad R(\infty) = \frac{\chi - P}{x}.$$

The straight-line method could thus be used by a mature and steadily expanding company in such a way as to duplicate closely the true book-value level determined by a process of testing or sampling based on the theory of method 11.4. Regardless of this suggestion, a periodic test of the book-value level should be recognized as an essential element of regulatory policy. The profit-and-loss account of a public utility may be written in the simplified and purely symbolic form:

$$(49) \qquad Z = A + P + iB + p(C + W - B),$$

wherein Z = gross revenue claimed to be fair, A = expenses not provided for in the premium, B = borrowed capital (including preferred

---

[43] By *op. cit.* in note 1, formula (34). Replace $b = 1 - s$ by unity and delete sx. See also formula (32) and Figures 1 and 3, *ibid.*

stock), iB = its hire, p = fair rate of return, and W = rate-base assets other than the plant, e.g., working capital. By substituting the results of the test for the actual premium P and the actual book value C, it can be readily ascertained to what extent Z is too large or too small. The development and application of such a test should have been among the principal aims of the recent investigation of telephone companies by the Federal Communications Commission.

On the whole, then, accountants are not greatly to blame for their depreciation methods, as far as competitive business is concerned. In the public-utility field, on the other hand, they are distinctly reluctant to face the facts and inclined to continue passing them off as matters of opinion. To call attention to what remains undone in practice, it seems appropriate to close this paper by quoting a few "accounting principles" on public-utility depreciation:

> The question of the adequacy of so-called retirement and similar provisions for depreciation can be answered only from an examination of the total amounts actually provided for depreciation and maintenance over a considerable period. It is the sum of the two which is to be regarded as adequate or inadequate. . . . In the opinion of many competent observers, retirement methods do in fact result in inadequate charges for depreciation, especially when considered with respect to the maintenance of the original investment.[44]

> The provision for depreciation . . . is probably the most controversial subject related to the accounts of public utilities . . . on which professional accountants are expected to have definite opinions. . . . Within the committee there are definite differences of thought. . . . Those who favor the straight-line method . . . point critical fingers at a utility company which shows in its income-tax return a deduction for depreciation computed by the straight-line method and . . . in its published financial statements . . . a smaller amount as the provision for retirements. . . . They are distrustful because the . . . officials of the utility use their independent judgment . . . without being bound by any fixed formula of estimated service life . . . The retirement advocate does not see any need for . . . reserves such as would measure . . . lack of newness . . . He is not impressed by the argument that the officials of a utility must be compelled to provide for depreciation in amounts other than those dictated by their own judgment, merely because some other person has estimated a list of service lives for *pieces* of the very system which the officials view as a unit . . . He reasons that taxable income is a statutory concept, not a determination based on economic principles. . . . One may dissent very strongly about the wisdom of a statute and . . . be completely obedient to it. . . . The presentation of the arguments on both sides of the controversy does not provide a solution to the problem. . . . The committee has taken no action within the current year, on this subject.[45]

> It has been said that we owe our great railroad facilities . . . in a large measure to unsound finance; but if it be held that depreciation provisions are an essential element of sound railroad accounting, then unsound accounting must share in the responsibility for the tremendous economic development that has taken

[44] *A Statement of Accounting Principles*, pp. 31–32. Cited in note 38.

[45] "Report of the Special Committee on Public-Utility Accounting," *Midyear Review*, American Institute of Accountants, 1938, pp. 66–69.

place since railroad enterprises were first begun. . . . It is no doubt true that, as a result of the accounting methods followed, large amounts of capital have been lost by investors . . . This, however, merely emphasizes the truth too often ignored . . . that, in the aggregate, the community pays only a relatively small return to capital for the amount invested, and that it is the community that is the one sure gainer therefrom. . . . The community can well afford to allow the few who meet with unusual success to receive and retain substantial rewards as a part of the price which it pays for all the capital invested.[46]

These views do indeed sound as if accounting were only what Mr. May says it is.[47]

New York, N. Y.

Professor John B. Canning, who refereed this paper, was good enough to propound a number of questions, which he thought many readers might wish to ask. Professor Frisch decided to have these questions and my answers appended to the paper. They follow:

1. Anent the "true" straight-line method:—Is this "true" in any sense except that: (1) it is free of certain objections to which 1 and 2 are open; and (2) it conforms to certain (not exclusive) provisions of *Income Tax Regulations?* On page 243 the author himself notes an objectionable feature of the "true" method. To refer to the method in question as a "third" method (or by some other noncommittal term) and then set forth its formulae and their properties would in no way weaken the high substantive merit of the section and would be more likely to keep his critics on the rails (see his first paragraph).——*Answer:* The description "true straight-line method" was not intended to imply that this is the "true" method, but merely that it is the only "truly straight" one. In other words, method 3 makes a charge corresponding to the asymptote of the renewal rate, which is a horizontal line in the static case. The charge per machine per unit of time (or per unit of output, if preferred) is constant even when the plant grows at a variable rate. It is similarly independent of the age of the machines. See Section IV.

2. The elementary single-machine book-value formula of which his composite functions are constructed is of the form $v = a_0 + a_1 t$. One may suggest another, namely, $V = A_0 + A_1 t + A_2 t^2$. If the constants in both are to be fitted, by whatever criteria, then, in no case, can his formulae give results superior to those of the alternative, for his formula becomes merely the limiting case (in fitting) in which A_2 approaches the limit 0.——*Answer:* The only curve to be fitted is the frequency distribution $f(t)$, the nature of which I left unspecified, in order that all

[46] May, *op. cit.* in note 2, part III, March, 1936, p. 175.
[47] Cf. statement identified in note 2.

$r(t)$ formulae be entirely general. The example (5) serves only the purpose of graphic illustration. No occasion arises for fitting the curves suggested and certainly they are not the elements of *my* composite functions. In so far as any similar expression occurs in the text, it simply defines a depreciation method, which I did in no sense originate. I am merely the translator of debits and credits. Accordingly *my* formulae are not supposed to be superior, but merely correct in reflecting a certain method, which may be open to many objections.

3. Can $r(t) =$ "undepreciated remainder per *centum* . . ."? By (6), we have $r_1(t) = 1 - t/a$, in which $0 \leq t \leq a$. Hence $r_1(t)$ has unity as a maximum at $t = 0$. Isn't $r_1(t)$ rather an "undepreciated remainder per *unit* . . ."?——*Answer:* Stand corrected. It should be clearly understood, however, that the *unit* is the whole plant and not a single machine. To cite the classic illustration, 248,707 new telephone poles would be represented by unity. Single-machine formulae would be for instance the integrands in the second form of equation (13) or the first form of (14).

4. In connection with the accountant's method it might be well—say by footnote—to distinguish between formal charges (adjusting entries) to (manufacturing) operations and definitive charges against the income of the year in which the operations occur. In algebraic effect, an increment of the formal depreciation debit is reversed by a credit to income (*via* the goods-in-process and finished-goods inventories). This is not well understood by statisticians. It derives its importance from changes in inventory carryovers—especially in the case of concerns that, in effect, speculate in their own products (see ECONO-METRICA, Vol. 1, pp. 54–55, notes 3 and 5).——*Answer:* That is true enough, but has no bearing upon the book value or wearing value of the plant, with which I am alone concerned. Manipulation of inventories is an interesting subject, but it has no connection with depreciation, even if depreciation figures are used for the purpose in preference to others.

5. Method 6.4. Wouldn't the remark that "this would be the equitable method of public-utility depreciation, if both the output and the operating expenses were constant," be more apropos of the "theoretical public-utility method" here referred to for comparison?——*Answer:* I don't think so. Formula (22) is a special case of (32) and the latter in turn is the special case where output and expenses vary with the age of the machine, but economic conditions are otherwise static. General dynamic conditions upset the theory of economic life inherent in the Hotelling approach. The life spans of successive replacements can then be calculated only backward, step by step, i.e., in the reverse order of chronology, beginning with the last machine, which will never be re-

placed (and probably has not even been invented as yet). This being absurd, economic life must be guessed within a reasonable margin, as Professor Canning holds in substance. The public-utility problem would still be definite, however, if errors of foresight (apart from those inherent in any decision to scrap) were corrected by hindsight, i.e., by charging or crediting a "consumers' surplus." The analysis of single and composite chains of replacement is among the topics of my latest study. See note 40.

6. Methods 7 and 8. Do the comments that these methods counteract the increase in maintenance charges or decrease in efficiency have enough merit to warrant inclusion? The same could be said of an unlimited number of other formulae, e.g., of other members of the same family of curves. Any particular declining series of charges can be appropriate (given the criteria) only by accident. Cf. Hatfield, *Accounting*, pp. 153–154.——*Answer:* These are merely historical comments not intended to imply that either method can possibly be correct, except in case of a highly improbable accident, capable of verification only in the public-utility field.

7. Sentence after quotation identified by note 25. Properly inferred for many items, for the reasons suggested on pp. 273 and 298 of the book referred to. But for the inclusion of others (e.g., annual license fees) see p. 201.——*Answer:* Stand corrected.

8. Page 251, 3rd paragraph. Point well made. Moreover, an asset may have a positive value at or immediately before salvage sale and have, earlier, a quite proper negative book value. This would be the case, for example, if demolition and removal charges are expected numerically to exceed the receipt from salvage sales.——*Answer:* True enough from a practical viewpoint. In theory, the continuous time-shape of depreciation is indeterminate, as shown by the fact that depreciation does not enter into the theory of capital value at all. It is therefore difficult to say what would or would not be "quite proper," except by reference to such practical criteria as suggested in Part IV.

9. Isn't the "real market price" of the product a "will o' the wisp" save in the instance of a few commodities and services at a few of their stages between extraction and consumption? When numerous types of assets are jointly employed in the concurrent production of a varied "line" of products and when each concern's "line" changes in ways impossible of prediction n years hence, is it possible in any useful realistic sense to speak of *the price* of the *product?* (See *Economics of Accountancy*, p. 232 and p. 299, note, and the references there cited.) ——*Answer:* The theory of economic life could never be developed without recognizing that the omission of the market price from the problem is incorrect. In practice I agree whole-heartedly, as seen in

Section IV. But it is better to keep theory a step ahead of common sense than to let it trail behind, as I am afraid it does, in some respects, in the accounting field.

10. To be sure, we have not yet developed a theory of economic life that omits the market price of the product from the problem—but that is hardly conclusive evidence that it cannot be done. If economic life, in fact, proceeds despite such an omission, may not a theory consonant with the omission be devised? In any event, when theory deviates from practice, one needs to know whether the direction is "ahead" or just "off" before one can be sure that theory is leading practice or merely deserting it.——*Answer:* That, of course, is *the* question! It will be easier to discuss it, after my tentative theory of economic life is published (see note 40). The late President Wilson's advice that any theorist should have a sign on his desk reading "Don't be a damned fool!" is valuable indeed, but not everyone can hope to match Professor Canning's skill in devising a "realistic theory" in one fell swoop. I find it easier to begin by turning the sign to the wall and investigating, first of all, what we ought to do, if we could. Then, turning the sign front again, the excess of theory can be readily whittled down by an application of realism. In the present instance, the results happen to be almost identical. The seemingly useless trip into the realm of theory nevertheless gives an added feeling of security, which I would be loath to miss.

APPENDIX B

Symbols employed frequently, or far from the spot where they were introduced, are redefined in the following glossary:

$t =$ a variable representing time, or a more suitable measure of the exhaustion of service capacity. Alternatives practicable only when interest is omitted.

$\tau =$ a variable of integration corresponding to t.

$y =$ a variable of integration denoting divergence in individual behavior-characteristics of machines of similar type.

$n =$ maximal life span, i.e., limit of longevity, measured in the same unit as t.

$a =$ average life-expectancy of any new machine in same unit as t.

$s =$ scrap value, divided by original cost.

$b =$ original cost, less scrap value, divided by original cost.

$\beta =$ original cost, less present worth of all scrap values of a large number of machines installed together, divided by original cost.

$f(t) =$ frequency distribution (of disappearance or scrapping) of a large number of machines installed together.

$M(t) =$ mortality or survival curve, i.e., cumulative frequency distribution.

$r(t) =$ undepreciated remainder of wearing value of a large number of machines installed together, divided by their original wearing value.

$r'(t) =$ rate of change, i.e., rate of depreciation of $r(t)$.

$c(t) =$ undepreciated cost of many machines installed together, divided by their original cost.

$M^{-1}(y) =$ inverted mortality formula, expressing life of the yth machine out of a very large total number, when their lives are extended horizontally and arrayed from top to bottom, from the shortest to the longest.

$T = a =$ economic life of any machine, when all behave alike.

$T = M^{-1}(y) =$ ditto, when individual characteristics differ.

$B(t) =$ book value of any single machine, when all behave alike.

$B(y, t) =$ ditto, when individual characteristics differ.

$\left.\begin{array}{c} w \\ w(y) \end{array}\right\} =$ unit cost of product, including time cost. Same distinction.

$\left.\begin{array}{c} Q(\tau) \\ Q(y, \tau) \end{array}\right\} =$ rate of production of any single machine at age τ.

$\left.\begin{array}{c} E(\tau) \\ E(y, \tau) \end{array}\right\} =$ rate of operating expenses of any single machine at age τ. Indexes C and H identify Canning and Hotelling concepts respectively.

$P =$ insurance premium per machine per unit of time or some alternative unit.

$R(\infty) =$ ultimate level of composite wearing value, when a plant has been maintained at a constant number of machines for a theoretically infinite, but practically moderate, multiple of n years.

"NOTE ON THE THEORY OF DEPRECIATION"

Econometrica (January 1941), pp. 80–88

NOTE ON THE THEORY OF DEPRECIATION

By Gabriel A. D. Preinreich

K.-G. Hagstroem closes his "Remarks on the Theory of Depreciation"[1] by saying that

> ... according to Preinreich, the search for the true depreciation method has apparently ended in a failure. It seems to me that the reason for this statement must be found in the principles which I have tried to apply.[2]

This remark suggests that, had I been aware of his principles, I would not have said what I did.[3] Accordingly, I studied the remainder of his paper with care, hoping to discover, what principles I had overlooked. Having failed to find any, it occurred to me that a further discussion of this important point might be of interest.

Hagstroem's argument may be summarized and commented upon as follows:

> ... I have frequently come back to the question of depreciation and of real or hypothetical insurance against the risk of destruction of mortal property. I have always suspected that in this range of ideas there should be hidden some fundamental connection between prices of consumption commodities and prices of capital goods, ... In 1925, H. Hotelling published a general theory of depreciation which tried to find the connection I have had in view.[4]

It appears from this introduction, the title of the paper, and the comment on my conclusion, that Hagstroem had intended to establish the connection between the capital value $V(t)$ and the unexpired cost $B(t)$ of a capital good, i.e., to find the "true" method of depreciation.

> The valuation principles may be exemplified by the following treatment ... of a piece of real estate. Denote by:
> a the value of the ground,
> b the cost of a building, if constructed at the present moment,
> s the total life of a building of this kind,
> t the present age of the building to be valued,
> h the net yield of the estate after deducting expenses and costs of maintenance, but no amortization (depreciation).
> Letting i denote an arbitrary rate of interest and $\delta = \log_e(1+i)$, $v = 1/(1+i)$, $a_{\overline{n}|} = (1-v^n)/\delta$, we have the following identity:

$$[1] \qquad a + b\frac{a_{\overline{s-t}|}}{a_{\overline{s}|}} + \int_0^{s-t}\left[h - a\delta - \frac{b}{a_{\overline{s}|}}\right]e^{-\delta w}dw = av^{s-t} + h\,a_{\overline{s-t}|}.[5]$$

[1] Econometrica, Vol. 7, October, 1939, pp. 289–303. All subsequent references to this work are identified only by pagination.

[2] P. 303.

[3] Cf. "Annual Survey of Economic Theory: The Theory of Depreciation," Econometrica, Vol 6, July, 1938, p. 239.

[4] P. 289.

[5] P. 290.

80

On the left side of this formula, the unexpired cost, book value, or investment,

$$(2) \qquad B(t) = b\,\frac{a_{\overline{s-t}|}}{a_{\overline{s}|}} = \int_0^{s-t} \frac{b}{a_{\overline{s}|}}\, e^{-\delta w}dw = b\,\frac{1 - e^{-\delta(s-t)}}{1 - e^{-\delta s}},$$

occurs twice, preceded by opposite signs. Hence [1] consists simply of:

$$(3) \qquad V(t) + B(t) - B(t) = \text{capital value}.$$

Hagstroem continues:

... we see accordingly that this value may be interpreted as the present value of the estate according to the depreciation scheme,

$$a + b\,\frac{a_{\overline{s-t}|}}{a_{\overline{s}|}} \quad \begin{bmatrix} = \text{the ground value plus the present worth} \\ \text{of an appropriate annuity for future de-} \\ \text{preciation} \end{bmatrix},$$

increased by the value of the future net output after deduction of [the present worth of] an appropriate annuity for future depreciation . . . and of the interest on the ground value.[6]

Upon deleting the duplication, we obtain the simple capital-value formula

$$(4) \qquad V(t) = av^{s-t} + ha_{\overline{s-t}|}$$

given by Hagstroem himself. The "fundamental identity" [1] is obviously incapable of establishing any connection betweeen capital value and unexpired cost; it can "interpret" only the former and not the latter. No matter what we choose to add to capital value, if we promptly deduct it again, we still have only capital value. The "principle" which prompted Hagstroem to express unexpired cost in the particular form (2), i.e., to adopt the well-known annuity method of depreciation, amounts simply to the assumption that the capital value and the unexpired cost of the building are linearly related to each other. That is indeed the approach which first comes to mind and therefore the oldest one.[7] It implies, however, that, as the original cost $B(0) < V(0)$ dwindles away, the remnant $B(t)$ becomes more and more profitable until, in the absence of a scrap value, we wind up with an infinitely high rate of return on nothing. Such behavior hardly conforms to the conventional notions of investment and its productivity.

To overcome this defect, it has long been customary to increase the discount rate, i.e., to hold that, whereas the net rental stream dis-

[6] P. 291.

[7] Cf. testimony on depreciation methods, *Third Report, Select Committee on Audit of Railway Accounts*, House of Lords, X Parliamentary Papers, London, 1849.

counted at the rate of interest gives capital value, the same stream discounted at the rate of profit gives investment. Hagstroem denotes this higher discount rate by i_0+j on page 291 and by $\delta+\mu$ on page 292, interpreting μ alternatively as the "constant force of mortality." His second "scheme" would thus appear to be fully presented. Nevertheless, he goes on to say:

> We start again from our fundamental identity, interpreted now according to the new scheme of depreciation, and we obtain the following identity:[8]

The formula which follows at the top of page 294 is the same as [1]; only the symbols have been rearranged in the process of substituting $\mu+\delta$ for δ. What the significance of this restatement may be, I cannot imagine. Quite apart from the futility of adding and deducting the same thing in the same breath, the suggestion made was that the difference between capital value and unexpired cost lay in the discount rates used; nevertheless, he again applies one rate to both, as in [1]. Further description of the mechanism follows, in the course of which the notation $V(t)$ represents the book value $B(t)$ instead of the capital value, as in the beginning.

Finally

> ... we shall give a new modification of our scheme of depreciation ... [which] starts from the fact that premium payments should preferably be payable in proportion to the remaining value ... of the property, its economic productivity being to a certain extent decreasing, as the depreciation proceeds.[9]

The steps taken lead to the same annuity formula as twice before, except that the discount rate is now $\mu+\delta-k<0$, where k is defined in accordance with the preference expressed. The "fundamental identity" so modified duly turns up a third time at the bottom of page 299.

Hagstroem's contribution to the theory of depreciation thus appears to be limited to the restatement and elaboration of a method or "scheme," which has been known for at least a century, and to which I thought it sufficient to devote the first four lines of point 6 in my paper: "The Practice of Depreciation."[10] That the rate, at which an appropriate annuity for future depreciation is discounted, may be considered merely a "micrometer screw" to be turned in one direction or another, I have also pointed out upon a previous occasion.[11] This makes it possible to obtain in the long run any composite-book-value level per centum of the original cost of all "machines" in service. Since, for public utilities, a "true" depreciation method and hence also a true composite-

---

[8] P. 293.

[9] P. 295.

[10] ECONOMETRICA, Vol. 7, July, 1939, p. 246.

[11] Cf. "The Principles of Public Utility Depreciation," *Accounting Review*, June 1938, p. 164.

book-value level can be determined,[12] it follows that the annuity method so generalized might serve as a practical substitute. Such considerations, however, are beyond the scope of Hagstroem's "Remarks . . . ."

We shall now try to obtain an identity corresponding to the fundamental equation, which we have employed above for interpreting the actuarial valuation. Putting $a = 0$ and $b = 1$ we can write this identity

$$[5] \qquad h a_{\overline{s-t}|}(\mu) = V + \int_0^{s-t} \left[h - \frac{1}{a_{\overline{s}|}(\mu)} \right] e^{-(\mu+\delta)w} dw$$

$$= \text{depreciated value} + \text{supervalue}.[13]$$

Before discussing this aspect of the double identity (3), it will be best to generalize the notation. The symbol V here represents the unexpired cost

$$(6) \qquad B(t) = \int_0^{s-t} \frac{1}{a_{\overline{s}|}(\mu)} e^{-(\mu+\delta)w} dw$$

corresponding to Hagstroem's second scheme, viz., the annuity method at a discount rate $\mu + \delta$. But, since the right side of the identity (6) is deducted from its own left side within formula [5], the latter will hold no matter what our concept of unexpired cost may be. Accordingly it is admissible to substitute the pure tautology

$$(7) \quad B(t) = \int_t^s \left[iB(\tau) - B'(\tau) \right] e^{i(t-\tau)} d\tau + B(s)e^{i(t-s)},$$

$$w = \tau - t, \, i = \mu + \delta.$$

The rate of profit on investment is evidently $p(t) = [h + B'(t)]/B(t)$. Noting further that the left side of [5] is the capital value $V(t)$, we obtain

$$(8) \qquad V(t) = B(t) + \int_t^s \left[p(\tau) - i \right] B(\tau) e^{i(t-\tau)} d\tau.$$

This is the famous capital-value formula based exclusively on the books, the verbal equivalent of which may be found in any accounting textbook.[14] Though derived for brevity only for a single capital good, $B(t)$ therein may also be considered the book value of a composite plant continuously renewed.[15] For this purpose, it seems simplest to

[12] Cf. *op. cit.* in note 10, p. 252.

[13] P. 296.

[14] I gave this formula on p. 240 of *op. cit.* in note 3. How old the idea is, may be inferred from the fact that an adequate explanation occurs in a student's prize essay by J. H. Bourne, *Accountant*, London, Sept. 22, 1888, pp. 605–606.

[15] In that case, of course, the rate of depreciation will no longer be $B'(t)$. Instead, $D(x, q, t)$ as defined in *op. cit.* in note 3, formula (18), should be substituted in the formula of the rate of profit.

place $s = H + t$, where $H =$ horizon of foresight. Various alternatives have been suggested from time to time by hundreds of writers, mostly in the form of elementary numerical examples.

If the books of an enterprise are kept on the basis of *any* reasonable and consistent accounting method for a number of years, the trends of the resultant book-value and rate-of-profit curves may be roughly extrapolated into the future (subject to expected changes in conditions) and will thus be of material aid in appraising present capital value by means of (8). This is true especially for mature enterprises supplying essential commodities or services. The trustworthiness of such forecasts is greatly enhanced, when most enterprises in the same field adhere to the same method. Comparative data made available by trade associations bring about a standardization of the outlook, which need be modified only in the light of individual variations from the average. For the many assumptions, qualifications, etc., to which this inadequate statement is subject, I must refer the reader to my previous publications.[16] At the moment, I merely wish to emphasize that, in formula (8), $V(t)$ is still independent of $B(t)$, despite appearances and a widespread belief to the contrary. By hindsight, therefore, the capital value calculated in this manner must always be the same, no matter how $B(t)$ was manipulated during the past H years. On the other hand, when we are concerned with a future period H, undisclosed past changes in method will be mistaken for changing prospects, thereby distorting the forecasts and misinforming those who believe that there is anything fundamental about the double identity (8). The Securities and Exchange Commission is largely concerned with this danger to the investing public.

Is it not characteristic of the application of the classical theory in this field that the main thing obtained by it seems to be some conclusion about the scrap value?[17]

I can't say I understand this question. The writers whose opinions I had occasion to discuss in the past were unanimous in considering the scrap value as known; so did I for that matter. No need could thus arise for drawing conclusions about what was simply taken for granted. The term "scrap value" obviously means the selling price of the capital good, i.e., its final capital value, when usefulness to the present owner ends. Certain types of capital goods pass through the hands of several owners, before they are actually scrapped. What is scrap value to one becomes original cost to the next. In other words, a sale by the jth owner at the date T_j establishes the equality $V_j(T_j) = B_{j+1}(T_j)$. No writer on

---

[16] Cf. *loc. cit.* in note 14. Also "The Law of Goodwill," *Accounting Review*, December, 1936 and "Goodwill in Accountancy," *Journal of Accountancy*, July, 1937, where court decisions and the views of about 150 recent authors are compared.

[17] P. 303.

depreciation has ever questioned this principle, as far as I know. It does not deserve special emphasis, however, because the depreciation problem really consists of measuring the supposedly gradual loss in investment, while the property is in the hands of the same owner.

To overcome the uncertainty concerning $B_j(t)$ within any period $T_{j-1} \leqq t \leqq T_j$, appraisals are often resorted to. Such appraisals are ordinarily based on so-called "depreciated reproduction cost" and therefore involve partly circuitous reasoning. The records of public-utility litigations are full of argument on this point. The alternative of watching the market price of similar capital goods in a similar condition has also been debated pro and contra for many years, but is now commonly rejected on the ground that the state of the market has no bearing upon the value of goods not intended for sale. Indeed, the market price is what it is, precisely because these goods have not been offered. Disputes on this point were gradually stopped by the Federal income-tax laws.

Hagstroem's example is too simple to permit adequate consideration of the typical depreciation problem. The starting point must be his admission that the economic productivity of the property is "to a certain extent decreasing, as the depreciation proceeds."[18] Accountants, among others, began making this vague remark about sixty years ago,[19] but it apparently remained for J. S. Taylor[20] to express the idea in concrete terms. In the notation hitherto employed by me, the net rental or income stream was written $zQ(t) - E(t)$, where $z =$ selling price of a unit of product, $Q(t) =$ rate of output, and $E(t) =$ rate (growing with age) of operating expenses, excluding depreciation and interest. Hotelling's familiar capital-value formula accordingly reads:

$$(9) \qquad V(t) = \int_t^T [zQ(\tau) - E(\tau)] e^{-\int_t^\tau i(\nu) d\nu} d\tau + S(T) e^{-\int_t^T i(\nu) d\nu}.$$

By way of analogy, the unexpired remainder of the known original cost $B(0)$ can be expressed either as

$$(10) \qquad B(t) = \int_t^T [zQ(\tau) - E(\tau)] e^{-\int_t^\tau p(\nu) d\nu} d\tau + S(T) e^{-\int_t^T p(\nu) d\nu}$$

or in the form

$$(11) \qquad B(t) = \int_t^T [w(\tau)Q(\tau) - E(\tau)] e^{-\int_t^\tau k(\nu) d\nu} d\tau + S(T) e^{-\int_t^T k(\nu) d\nu}.$$

[18] P. 295.

[19] The counterpart, in accountancy, of Hagstroem's third scheme is the diminishing-balance method, which varies, not the premium, but the rate of depreciation in proportion to the book value of the property. Cf. *op. cit.* in note 10, p. 248. Interest is thus omitted on the ground that, since the method amounts merely to a rough guess, such refinements are pointless.

[20] "A Statistical Theory of Depreciation," *Journal of the American Statistical Association*, December, 1923, pp. 1010–1023.

The new symbols appearing in these three equations are $T=$ economic life,[21] $S(T)=$ scrap value, $w(t)=$ "cost" of a unit of product, $i(t)=$ rate of interest, $p(t)=$ rate of profit on investment, and $k(t)=$ any arbitrarily chosen function, usually either the rate of interest or zero.

Equations (10) and (11) contain two unknown functions each, or three altogether, namely $B(t)$, $p(t)$, and $w(t)$; hence no unique solution can be had without a further condition. Any depreciation method ever devised amounts merely to an arbitrary assumption of this missing condition, sometimes made unwittingly. Hagstroem chooses the simplest course by assuming at once the answer $B(t)$ without further analysis. Hotelling, at least at one stage of his argument,[22] holds that, when z is constant and $k=i$, then $w(t)$ ought to be constant also. On this basis, equation (11) and its special form $B(0)$ can be readily solved for w and $B(t)$. By inserting the latter result in (10) I have shown that, when $z>w$, this assumption leads to a contradiction similar to the one inherent in Hagstroem's first scheme. The books will report the property to be most profitable at the moment when it is discarded for the reason that it is no longer profitable enough.[23] The corresponding remedy would be to use (10) instead, choosing $p(t)$ subject to the insufficient terminal condition $p(T)=[zQ(T)-E(T)]/S(T)$.

More elaborate presentations recognize that, within limits, the rate of output may be varied at the owner's discretion,[24] thereby affecting not only the selling price $z(t)$ defined by the demand function, but also the expenses $E(t)$. C. F. Roos[25] accordingly uses concepts which, in my present notation, become $zQ(z, z', t)$ and $E(z, z', Q, Q', t)$ respectively. The problem now enters the realm of the calculus of variations. This awe-inspiring branch of mathematics, however, merely happens to be the appropriate tool of solution; the basic reasoning need not be overshadowed by it. In terms better suited for general discussion, we need only observe that Roos' capital-value concept is:

$$(12) \quad V_R(t) = \int_t^T [zQ(\tau) - E(\tau) - P(\tau)]e^{-\int_t^\tau i(v)\,dv}d\tau + B(0)e^{-\int_t^T i(v)\,dv},$$

[21] How to determine T in various circumstances is the subject of my paper "The Economic Life of Industrial Equipment," ECONOMETRICA, Vol. 8, January, 1940, pp. 12–44. For present purposes, it suffices to consider T as known.

[22] Cf. "A General Mathematical Theory of Depreciation," *Journal of the American Statistical Association*, September, 1925, pp. 340–353.

[23] Cf. *op. cit.* in note 3, pp. 237–238.

[24] Hotelling made this suggestion, *loc. cit.*, and again in the appendix of my paper cited in note 21. See also his article, "The Economics of Exhaustible Resources," *Journal of Political Economy*, April, 1931, pp. 137–175.

[25] "The Problem of Depreciation in the Calculus of Variations," *Bulletin of the American Mathematical Society*, 1928, pp. 218–228. Also "A Mathematical Theory of Depreciation and Replacement," *American Journal of Mathematics*, 1928, pp. 147–157.

wherein he defines $P(t)$ as the rate of depreciation, although it appears from his connecting relation

$$(13) \qquad S(T) = B(0) - \int_0^T P(\tau) e^{-\int_T^\tau i(\nu)\,d\nu} d\tau$$

that $P(t)$ is really the premium or sinking-fund contribution.[26]

Comparison of (9) and (12) shows that $V(t) = V_R(t)$ only when $t = 0$. At any subsequent time (12) expresses, not the capital value of the property, but that of the property plus the sinking fund.[27] Though Roos may make $V_R(t)$ a maximum, the result would lead us into the error which made the Rev. Richard Price famous around 1770, namely the assumption that the sinking fund creates income which could not have been had otherwise. If an enterprise is more profitable than a bond, the accumulated premiums can be put to better use than the earning of interest in a sinking fund earmarked for the eventual replacement of a specific unit of equipment. To attack the problem properly, we must therefore eliminate the sinking fund from the right side of (12). This leads to a duplication of type (3) and reduces readily to the correct Hotelling formula (9). Since the latter does not contain the depreciation concept, it is thus demonstrated that even the calculus of variations cannot establish any connection between capital value and unexpired cost. Equation (13), however, may be regarded as a depreciation scheme in itself, if $S(t) \equiv B(t)$, $0 \leq t \leq T$. This proposal of carrying property on the books at a figure at which it could be sold, if a sale were intended, was already mentioned earlier in this paper. Hotelling avoided it deliberately by specifying only $S(T) = B(T)$.[28]

These samples will suffice to illustrate the range of ideas on the subject. An unlimited number of methods can also be had by considering my rules of economic life[29] as schemes of depreciation, provided it be clearly understood that the economic significance of these rules is limited to the determination of T. How to distribute the costs incurred within that period remains purely a matter of pen and ink.

[26] *Loc. cit.*, p. 221. On p. 225 of the same paper, he says that the rate of depreciation is $V'(t)$. To avoid misunderstanding, I should perhaps mention that the subject of depreciation studies is the rate $B'(t)$.

[27] Note that $V(T) = S(T)$, whereas $V_R(T) = B(0)$. What happened is that Roos substitutes $S(T)$, as defined by (13), in the initial form $V(0)$ of (9) and combines the two integrals into one to get $V_R(0)$, i.e., the initial form of (12). Then he substitutes t for zero without noticing that he has thereby violated (13) and, in effect, changed the meaning of $S(T)$ from salvage value to salvage value plus sinking fund. Cf. first *op. cit.* in note 25, p. 225. The error is carried forward to the second paper, which starts with the assumption that formula $V_R(t)$ is correct.

[28] Cf. Roos' comparison of his theory with that of Hotelling. *Loc. cit.* in note 25, p. 225.

[29] *Op. cit.* in note 21.

Before one depreciation method can be proclaimed superior to any other, it is necessary to answer the question, what purpose such apparently irrelevant figures can possibly serve. The principal one may well be that of facilitating the appraisal of an enterprise by its past record. Although individual book figures $B(t)$ and $p(t)$ are meaningless, their orderly sequence supports the assumption that developments consistent with past behavior may be expected in the future. Acceptance of this premise furnishes a definite criterion by which the merits of depreciation methods may be judged. I have been trying for some time to break a path in this general direction, but realize that most of the work still remains undone. For this reason I should like to suggest the following curriculum to earnest students of the depreciation problem:

1. Critical history of methods, leading to avoidance of antiquated, well-scoured, and now dry channels of thought based exclusively on "single-machine ideology," i.e., failure to see the wood for the trees;

2. Theory of economic life;

3. Renewal theory properly correlated to 2;[30]

4. Laboratory work in applying some "accepted," some unaccepted, and even some wholly capricious methods to a large plant which is continuously being renewed in accordance with natural variations in the behavior of similar machines;

5. Laboratory work, using the results of 4 to forecast future trends and deriving therefrom estimates of capital value by formula (8) above.

The first-hand experience gained from these tedious and intricate exercises is bound to lead to conclusions which narrow the choice considerably. There will remain, at least in my humble opinion, only a few rather simple practical principles.

New York, N. Y.

[30] For an attempt to clarify the basic concepts, see my, *The Present Status of Renewal Theory*, Waverly Press, Inc., Baltimore, 1940.

BOOK REVIEW OF ROBLEY WINFREY, DEPRECIATION OF GROUP PROPERTIES

The Accounting Review (April 1944),
pp. 207–209

BOOK REVIEWS

Sidney G. Winter

Depreciation of Group Properties. Robley Winfrey. (Ames: Iowa State College Bulletin, 1942. Pp. 131.)

Mr. Winfrey's work may be fairly described as a revised edition of Prof. Edwin B. Kurtz's book: *The Science of Valuation and Depreciation.* (New York: The Ronald Press Co., 1937.) At the Iowa Engineering Experiment Station, both authors have collaborated extensively in the compilation of observational data concerning the life expectancy of homogeneous groups of physical property, classifying the latter according to their survival characteristics.

The raw material for both books is thus identical. The same may be said for the general mental attitude adopted toward the problem of depreciation, as well as for its presentation and treatment. On the principal conclusion, full agreement is also in evidence, in the sense that each author "proves," and by the same means too, that he alone is right. That creates an interesting situation, because it so happens that Kurtz's "only scientific approach" differs materially from Winfrey's "only mathematically correct method."

Both methods have long been known and are hereinafter referred to as the Kurtz and Winfrey methods merely for convenience of language. This reviewer has compared them mathematically and graphically in "The Practice of Depreciation," *Econometrica*, July 1939. To state the difference in the simplest terms, let us suppose that 100 similar machines are acquired for $10,000. In the light of past experience it seems certain that such machines have an average life of 10 years, even though each one will actually be retired at a different date between zero and 20 years.

Now, what did we actually buy, 100 machines at $100 each, as stated in the bill of sale, or 1,000 life units of service at $10 each? Winfrey endorses the former and Kurtz the latter interpretation, except that Kurtz, though admitting the existence of only 1,000 life units, thinks it more scientific to pretend that there are 1,050. This pointless distortion may be disregarded for present purposes.

Whether we charge off $100 per machine or $10 per life unit of service, the $10,000 will be recovered at the end of 20 years. In the meantime, however, the periodic credits to the reserve are not the same. For instance, with respect to an unidentifiable single machine which will drop out at the end of 5 years, Winfrey would credit $20 and Kurtz only $10 per annum to the reserve. Conversely, in the case of another machine which remains in service for 20 years, Winfrey's credit to the reserve would be $5 per year and Kurtz's still $10. Similar computations made for all surviving machines should be summed up to get the total annual additions to the reserves. It will then be found that Winfrey's reserve always exceeds Kurtz's, except at the two end-points.

Winfrey's concept of the "condition percent" of this property group is the sum of all individual ratios of un-expired life to total life, divided by the original number of machines and expressed per centum. Thus, at the end of the third year, the five-year machine is said to be in a 40% and the twenty-year machine in an 85% "condition," their combined contribution toward the condition of the group being counted as 1.25%. Kurtz's "remainder service life" concept is identical, but becomes irrelevant when he fails to make use of it in the end.

The computation of the "condition per cent," which Winfrey specifically defines as "100 times the ratio of present depreciable value to depreciable value, when new" (p. 12), is clearly inconsistent with the statement that "the analysis is based solely upon the service given up by the property" (p. 50), because his basic assumption is that each machine renders an equal measure of service per unit of time. His "condition per cent" is determined, not by the service, but by the allocated cost "given up" by each machine, under a literal interpretation of the bill of sale, the terms of which, viz. 100 @ $100 = $10,000, are meaningless by the testimony of his own survival curves. If he wanted to know how much service still remains in the property group, he would have to count the remaining life units and divide them by the original number. Returning to the previous random illustrations, the five-year machine has 2 and the twenty-year machine 17 such units left. Accordingly, they contribute not 1.25%, but 1.9% to the total remaining service.

Kurtz eventually shifts to the latter type of calculation, whereas the failure to distinguish between equal units of service and the unequal costs allocated to them pervades Winfrey's whole work. Another good instance is the following passage: "Wholly independent of any method of estimating depreciation is the fact that *the service remaining in the group of units comprising a stable property is exactly 50% of the service available in the same units when new*" (p. 81, italics his). An accurate statement would be: Wholly independent of the shape of the survival curve and the average life is the fact that the cost allocated by this particular method of depreciation to the services remaining in a group of units comprising a stable property is exactly 50% of the cost of the services available in the same units, when new.

It follows from the general shape of all observed survival curves that a stable or mature plant, i.e., one that has been continuously maintained at 100 machines, must contain more than one-half of the life units of service inherent in a plant composed of the same number of new machines. The theoretical extremes are 2/3 when the survival curve is a diagonal straight line (as in Fig. 3, p. 39), and ½ when it is a vertical line coinciding with the average life. In the latter event the level does not really exist but remains a mere average, since no damping takes place.

How a mature plant which retains more than 50% of its service-capacity can be said to be in a 50% condition is not apparent, until one realizes that Winfrey's concept of "condition" flouts his avowed aim expressed thus: *"Obviously, any acceptable method must distribute the depreciation over the full life of the property and result in depreciated values at all ages which are in harmony with the service remaining in the survivors"* (p. 75, italics his). It is the Kurtz method which, upon being purged of its minor blemishes, will achieve such harmony. When the rate of interest is zero and there is no scrap value, Kurtz's ratio of unexpired cost to original cost is the same as the ratio of remaining service-capacity to original capacity. The Bell Telephone System has been using this method for more than two decades.

It is now in order to turn to the much emphasized "proof of the correctness of the present-worth principle" (p. 50) which convinces Winfrey that he can not be wrong. It consists simply of a demonstration that—in the absence of scrap value, interest and growth—his choice of a depreciation method leads ultimately to a reserve balance of 50% for any type of survival curve and any average life. The mathematics department, called in for the purpose, rises to the occasion in nine pages of calculus which boil down to a formula given by this reviewer four years ago, viz.:

$$\frac{1}{a} \int_0^n \int_t^n (1 - t/\tau) f(\tau) d\tau dt = \tfrac{1}{2}$$

wherein a = average life, n = maximal life, t = age, τ = life and $f(\tau)$ = a normalized frequency distribution of any shape or form whatsoever. (N.B. The term "normalized" signifies merely that the area below the curve shall be unity.)

The obvious is thus explained in terms of the abstruse, in the best tradition of mathematicians. What it all means is that, if a rectangle be divided into two triangles by a diagonal line $1 - t/\tau$ connecting opposite corners, then the area of each triangle is just half that of the rectangle. More completely, that the same theorem remains true for the sum of an infinite number of rectangles of equal infinitesimal heights and random bases. Upon deleting t/τ from the formula, the rectangles will be summed up and the answer is unity.

From this result, only two legitimate conclusions can be drawn. The first is that the Winfrey method amounts to splitting rectangles of equal height diagonally. That fact leaps to the eye in the reviewer's graph mentioned above. Second, it also follows that the arithmetic of Winfrey's corresponding tables is in order. In short, we know now that he did correctly what he *thought* he had to do. But how do the integrals prove that it was a good idea to do it? How do they justify the following final claims repeated incessantly?

"The unit-summation procedure of the present-worth method is shown to be the only mathematically correct method. It is not admitted that more than one correct method exists for applying an age-life ratio to property groups, when estimating depreciation" (p. 6, italics his).

"It is proved that group properties in normalized condition have a ratio of remaining *units of service* to available *units of service* when new of 0.50, regardless of the average life of the group and of the characteristics of the retirement curve. Consequently, the condition

percent of the depreciable *value* of the group at a zero interest rate is 50 percent" (p. 6, italics the reviewer's).

To hold that proper performance of a routine task proves the worth of the underlying idea is indefensible. In addition, the result does not even conform to the original idea of *"harmony"* and thus stands convicted by Winfrey's own definition of an *"acceptable method"* (p. 75, quoted in full above). This obviates any present need to ask whether there is such a thing as an "only correct method."

An interesting *curiosum* is that Kurtz was similarly fascinated by the magic of 50% which, in his modest opinion, constitutes "convincing evidence of the soundness of the method . . . the logic . . . the accuracy . . . a verification of the entire preceding analysis and a demonstration of the inherent unity of the body of principles presented" (*loc. cit.* pp. 5–6). That places him in an even less enviable position, for his method can not lead to a fixed 50% level, as already stated. His faith that it must was so great, however, that it led him into just the right mathematical error at the right time (see "The Practice of Depreciation," cited above). The practical merit of the method which achieves the "harmony" sought by Winfrey is in no way impaired by its failure to behave as expected.

When the rate of interest is introduced, Winfrey admits that the correct maturity level of his method rises above 50%. The reason is that he no longer splits his rectangles by straight lines, but by annuity curves which increase the area of the triangles he must sum up. Kurtz's level will of course also rise from wherever between 2/3 and $\tfrac{1}{2}$ it would otherwise be.

In the case of growth or expansion, Winfrey also recognizes a rise in the maturity level, but states that "additional studies are needed to show the limits of the range of such influence for various retirement distributions, average lives and rates of growth of property units in service" (p. 66). This is an instance where calculus could save him a lot of trouble. The correct level of his method for any constant rate of expansion is simply

$$\frac{a}{\int_{\frac{1}{2}}^n M(t)e^{-xt}dt},$$

by the formula given above, when the average life a, which also expresses the entire area of the survival curve $M(t)$, is replaced by the same area discounted at the expansion rate x. Since $\tfrac{1}{2}$ is thus multiplied by a greater number than it is divided by, the level rises again. It is no longer independent of the shape of the survival curve, however, because the discounting process affects different shapes to different extents. Translated into the obvious, the formula means that an expanding plant contains a greater proportion of relatively new machines, in which more service and therefore also more allocated cost must remain.

Winfrey's graphs showing the oscillations of the "condition percent" of continuously renewed property depreciated by his particular method look all right to the naked eye and, if he computed them by arithmetic are probably accurate enough. They could not possibly be, had he emulated Kurtz in acting on their joint belief that "the dampened sine wave /is/ characteristic of the theoretical behavior of the renewals in continuous property composed of similar individual units" (p. 46). There is a superficial resemblance, but that is all. Renewal theory is far too complex to be touched upon here, but its literature is readily available.

Speaking of literature, perusal of the *Bulletin* gives a strong impression that Winfrey is aware only of those contributions to his chosen subject which the former or present faculty and students of Iowa State College happened to make. Neither in the footnotes nor in the text can any outsider's name or idea be spotted. Such isolationism is bound to cause much waste of effort, especially when conclusions have to be reached by arithmetic. The information he seeks so diligently and laboriously has been waiting for him in libraries for years. A good example is the second formula above. The additional studies he is planning on the subject of growth may take a year or more, but he can check the formula in a couple of days. It answers all questions now raised by him in this connection.

In conclusion, one statement may be quoted, with which no disagreement is possible. "Depreciation should not be destined to be a subject of everlasting controversy among those concerned with engineering valuation, utility rate-making and taxation" (p. 8). Unfortunately, such a millennium can not arrive, until writers on depreciation develop more reticence in their claims and more rigor in their proofs.

GABRIEL A. D. PREINREICH
New York

Internal Auditing—A New Management Technique. John B. Thurston, Editor. (Stamford: Brock and Wallston, 1943. Pp. xi, 450. $3.50.)

This book is described as a symposium of addresses, discussions and other material developed under the direction of the Institute of Internal Auditors. The addresses were presented to the members and guests of the Institute at meetings held from the date of its organization to its first annual conference in New York November 10, 11, 12, 1942. The discussions are those that followed the addresses. The material in the book was edited by John B. Thurston, first president of the Institute of Internal Auditors.

The timeliness of this review is slightly dulled by the advent of the second annual conference of the Institute held in New York October 10, 11, 12, 1943.

The addresses range in subject from an exploration of the functions of the internal auditor, his education and training, and his relation to the public accountant, to such widely separated subject matter as an address on the economic future of American business in South America.

The most provocative part of the book lies in that part as mentioned in the title, an exploration into the functions of internal auditing as a new management technique. The concept of the internal auditor in performing a new management technique, as expressed by several of the founders of the Institute, is his service as an appraiser of the results of all departments of a business and of the business itself. As an appraiser, the internal auditor must be responsible to the board of directors only, or to the board through the top executive officers. Mr. Thurston has enumerated the three major functions which the internal auditor can or should perform as follows:

(1) He directly participates in the verification of financial statements.

(2) He rounds out and perfects the system of internal control.

(3) Finally, but most important of all, the internal auditor acts as an arm of management. In this role, he is one of the principal means by which modern management achieves effective control over administrative activities.

The concept of the internal auditor as the arm of management, which is one of the principal means by which modern management achieves effective control, probably represents the goal toward which internal auditors individually and as an organization will strive. Although there are internal auditors who at present perform all the functions enumerated above, it is apparent both from some addresses and from discussions following the addresses that many members of the Institute do not fully comprehend the role which is contemplated for the internal auditor in the corporate organization.

This reviewer found the addresses relating to the development of manuals and reports for the internal auditor to be interesting and factual, and an aid to internal auditors in a phase of their work which is often enervated through devotion to other more pressing duties.

The organization of the Institute of Internal Auditors focuses attention to the ever increasing phase of the internal auditor in the corporation, and it is believed that the material, publication of which is sponsored by the Institute, is aimed more at directing attention to the field, than to exploring procedures to be followed in the performance of the functions outlined.

R. H. HASSLER
Connersville

For Product Safety Concerns and Information please contact our EU
representative GPSR@taylorandfrancis.com Taylor & Francis Verlag GmbH,
Kaufingerstraße 24, 80331 München, Germany

Printed and bound by CPI Group (UK) Ltd, Croydon, CR0 4YY
01/05/2025
01858347-0001